IMAGES
of America

GROVEPORT AND MADISON TOWNSHIP

OHIO

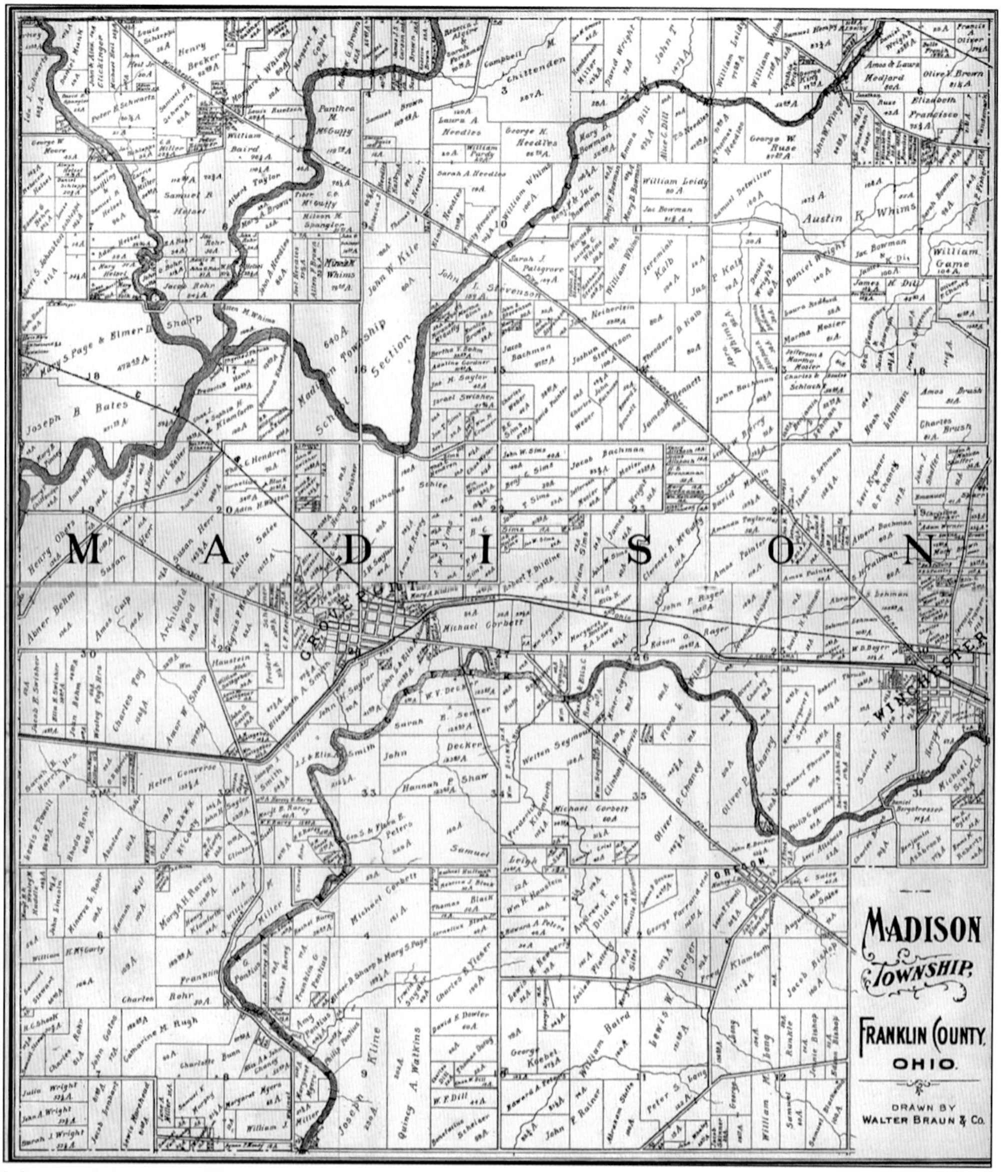

MAP OF MADISON TOWNSHIP, 1900.

IMAGES
of America

GROVEPORT AND MADISON TOWNSHIP OHIO

Richard Lee Palsgrove

ARCADIA
PUBLISHING

ISBN 978-0-7385-1977-7

Published by Arcadia Publishing
Charleston, South Carolina

Printed in the United States of America

Library of Congress Catalog Card Number: 2002104757

For all general information contact Arcadia Publishing at:
Telephone 843-853-2070
Fax 843-853-0044
E-mail sales@arcadiapublishing.com
For customer service and orders:
Toll-Free 1-888-313-2665

Visit us on the Internet at www.arcadiapublishing.com

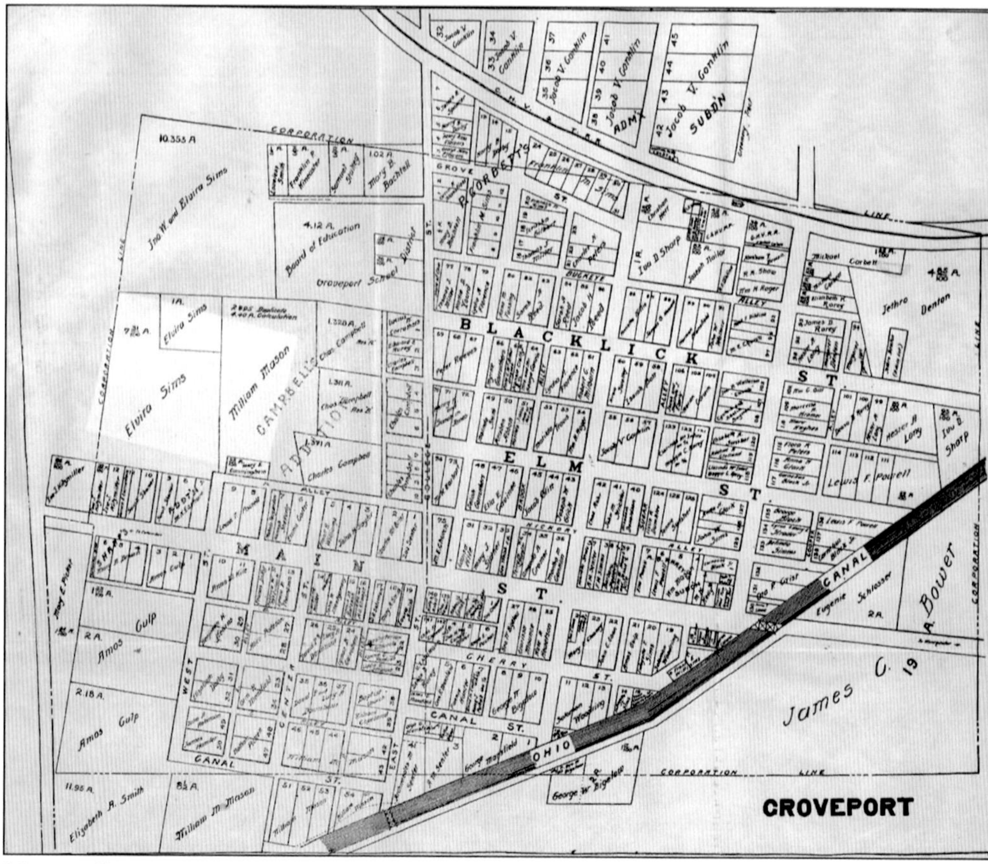

MAP OF GROVEPORT, 1900.

Contents

ACKNOWLEDGMENTS

Preserving local history is not just the work of a lone historian. The efforts of many individuals are vital in illuminating the shadows of history and giving the past meaning in our modern lives.

I wish to thank the Groveport Heritage and Preservation Society for the use of its Groveport Heritage Museum archives in collecting material for this book. Significant donations to the museum include items from the collections of Kenneth Ackerman, Nora Carruthers, Lana Hollinger, the Rarey family, the Watkins family, and countless others too numerous to mention but all greatly appreciated.

The author wishes to thank historian Richard Barrett for access to his extensive and well researched collection of historical postcards. My thanks also extend to historian David Meyer. His book, *Life Along the Ohio Canal: Licking Reservoir to Lockbourne and the Columbus Feeder*, is the most comprehensive book on the canal history of the area that I have read. Early twentieth century canal historian Lewis Cook's work also proved invaluable.

I am also indebted to historian Nancy Bowker for her work on John S. Rarey and Cruiser, as well as historian Mary Leidy for her writings on the history of local churches. Historians Frances Steube and Lillian Carroll and their research of Canal-Winchester proved most helpful, as well as the collection of information gathered by Charles Coon and Warren Rarey as part of Groveport's 1947 centennial. Also appreciated is the work of photographer Mary Circelli.

The author is grateful for the information made available from the Village of Groveport, Madison Township, Groveport Madison Local Schools, the Canal Winchester Historical Society, the Ohio Historical Society, and the *Southeast Messenger* newspaper.

Most importantly, I am forever appreciative of the work of historian George Bareis. His book, *History of Madison Township: Including Canal Winchester and Groveport, Ohio*, published in 1902, is an excellent resource and inspiration for any historian studying the history of the area.

I wish to thank my parents, Jim and Jeannette Palsgrove, for nurturing a sense of history within me as a youth.

This book is a reflection of the efforts of all those mentioned. If I have missed anyone I offer my most sincere apologies.

INTRODUCTION

The Ohio frontier of the early 1790s was the scene of conflicts between a confederation of Native Americans and the United States military. The Native Americans scored a significant victory over General Arthur St. Clair's troops in 1791. However, an intensified and more organized effort by General Anthony Wayne eventually subdued the Native American confederation at the Battle of Fallen Timbers in 1794, which resulted in the 1795 Treaty of Greenville.

The Greenville treaty made settlement in Central Ohio a promising option for settlers wishing to find rich farm land and business opportunities, while at the same time avoiding dangerous conflicts with Native Americans. Many headed for southeastern Franklin County and what would become Madison Township.

Nature shaped and enriched the land of Madison Township over thousands of years. Located in the glacial till plains, the lands of Madison Township are considered some of the most fertile in Ohio. The area is well watered with four major creeks—Big Walnut, Blacklick, Alum, and Little Walnut—as well as several smaller streams. Spring rains gorged these waterways, causing them to spill over their banks and replenish the fertility of the bottom lands. The waterways not only encouraged farming, but also agricultural related enterprises.

Madison Township formed on March 4, 1810, and is named for the nation's fourth president, James Madison. Ebenezer Richards and George Hays served as its first justices of the peace. Madison Township measures eight miles north and south and seven miles east and west, and it was originally the largest township geographically in Franklin County.

Around the same time Madison Township formed, pioneers began settling near the central portion of the township of what would become Groveport. In 1812, Adam Rarey opened a tavern, on what is now Groveport's east Main Street, to serve travelers moving back and forth between Columbus and southeastern Ohio.

By 1831, two small settlements—Wert's Grove and Rarey's Port—began to form side by side along the banks of the Ohio and Erie Canal. The canal's opening in the area on September 25, 1831, proved to be a boon to the two settlements as warehouses, tanneries, mills, a canal boatyard, and other enterprises sprang up as part of the canal and agricultural economy of Madison Township.

A rivalry developed between Jacob Wert and William Rarey, the settlements' founders. Wert, acting as postmaster, would change the address from "Rarey's Port" from any mail he received to "Wert's Grove." Rarey encouraged businessmen and residents to list "Rarey's Port" as their home. A prosperous businessman and landowner, he laid out the plat for the town of Rarey's Port along the western banks of the canal. At the same time, Wert, who also proved to be a successful businessman and landowner, laid out Wert's Grove just to the west of Rarey's Port. The two men did not officially file their village plats until years later: Rarey in 1844 and Wert in 1845. Confusion emerged as to which was the principle settlement in the area. Wert's Grove had the post office and the stagecoach stop for the area. Rarey's Port was listed as the landing point on canal passenger packet timetables. Citizens found the two towns located side by side cumbersome and decided to merge into one town in 1847. Dr. Abel Clark suggested the name "Groveport," combining the two suffixes of the formerly competing villages.

Rarey continued as a community leader and lived until 1877. Wert moved west to Obetz, after the towns merged, and died in 1850.

Groveport proved to be an adaptable community growing and changing along with new forms of transportation. When the canal began to wane as a principal form of transportation, the village secured a railroad right of way in 1868. Groveport also took advantage of the new electric traction line railway when it opened in 1904. Likewise, when automobiles, trucks, and buses became the norm, Groveport embraced these modes of transportation to enhance its business opportunities and public welfare. Twenty-first century Groveport has turned its attention to the skies to develop warehouses and businesses in response to air freight cargo landing at the Rickenbacker Port Authority just southwest of town. Where Groveport was once a canal and railroad town with warehouses bursting with farm produce, it is now a modern business community with warehouses brimming with high tech equipment, clothing, and a variety of other products.

Though Groveport embraces new ideas and technology, it retains its small town flavor and sense of identity.

The past two centuries have seen Madison Township change from primarily a land of farms to a more urbanized environment with housing developments and businesses rising from the fields. Geographically the township has shrunk as the growing state capital, nearby Columbus, annexes more and more land.

Throughout history, the common link between Groveport and Madison Township has been the public school system. School is often the one shared experience for everyone in a community. The first public school to educate Groveport and Madison Township children opened on Groveport's Walnut Street in 1848. The Groveport Madison Local School District has been educating area students ever since.

This book will try to capture the sense of community and shared history of Groveport and Madison Township through representative illustrations from the early pioneer days until the twenty-first century.

One

Early History

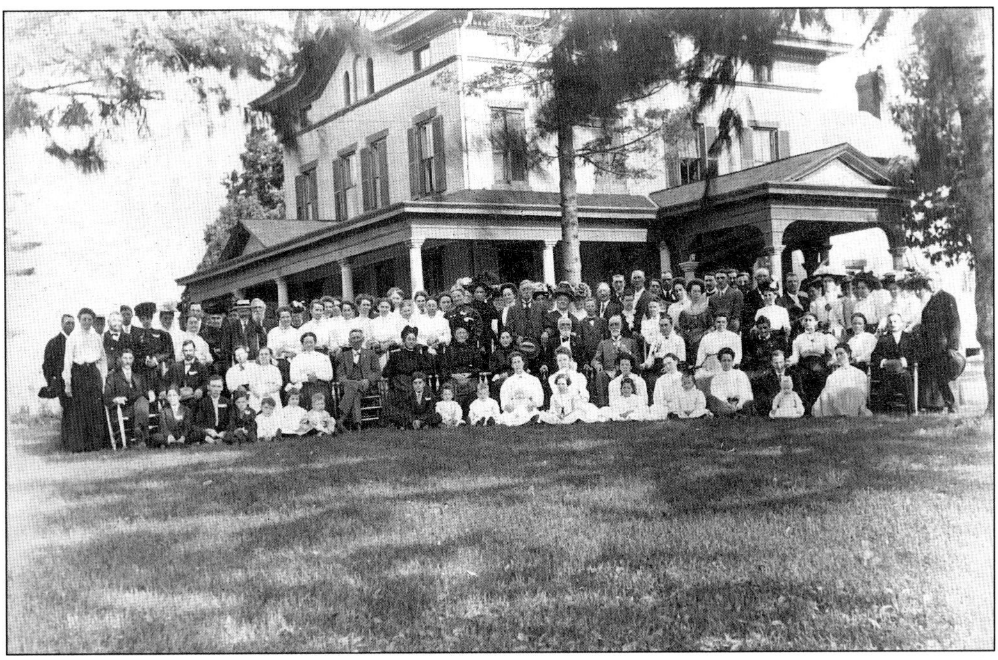

Rarey Reunion at the Elmont, 1907. The Rareys were one of the original families to settle in Groveport. Adam Rarey founded a tavern in 1812 along what is now Main Street where the Freshman School now stands. This 1907 reunion was held at the Elmont Hotel, on the site of the original tavern homestead. Members of the family continue to live in the area and Rarey reunions are still held regularly in Groveport.

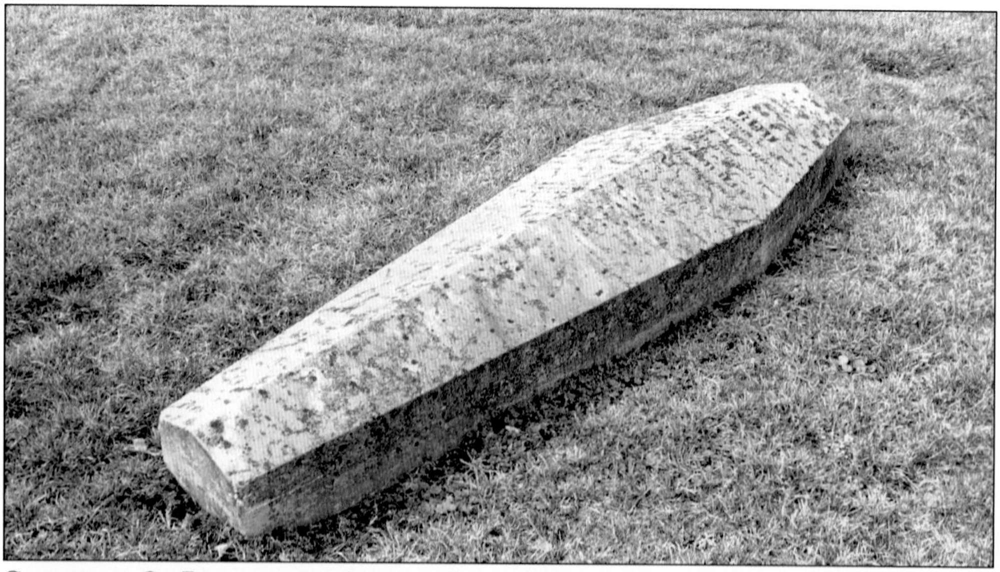

CATHERINE G. RICHARDSON GRAVE. This coffin shaped tombstone marks the grave of Catherine G. Richardson and is the first grave in the Groveport Cemetery. The inscription on the marker reads: "Sacred to the memory of Catherine G., consort of John C. Richardson, M. D. and daughter of Capt. Isaac Bowman, all natives of Shenandoah County, Virginia. Born December 23, 1787, departed this life January 19, 1809, aged 22 years."

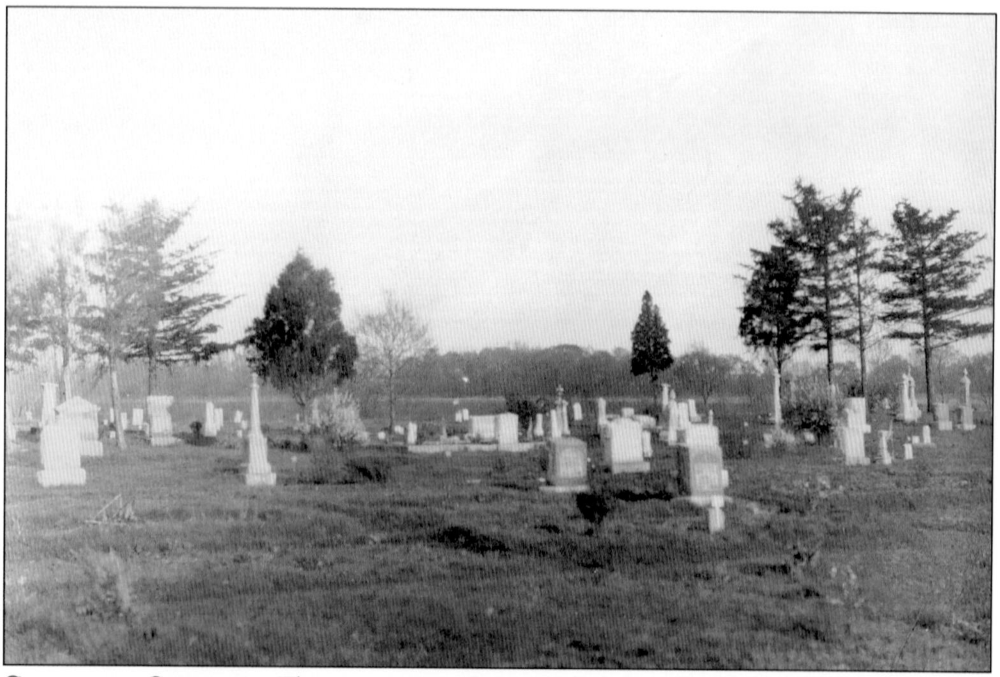

GROVEPORT CEMETERY. This is a view of the Groveport Cemetery, located along Wirt Road, around 1900. The graves of internationally famous nineteenth-century horse tamer John S. Rarey and Groveport co-founder William Rarey are located here. In recent years, the cemetery has been expanded and has undergone renovations including the erection of a wrought-iron fence and gate.

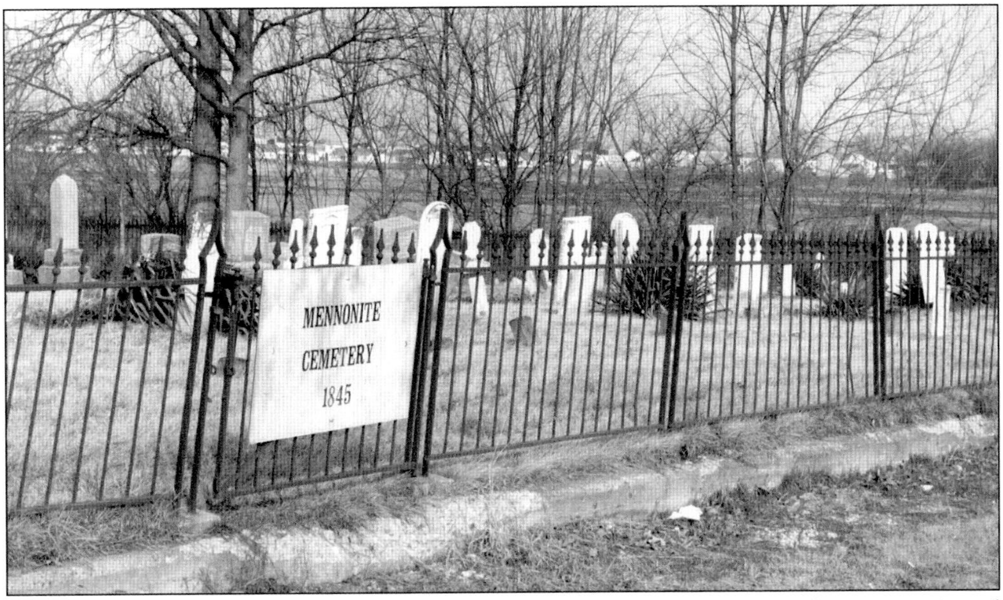

MENNONITE CEMETERY. Mennonites began meeting in Madison Township in 1843 and established this cemetery in 1845. In 1850, a frame meeting house was built east of Hibernia Road and north of the Columbus-Winchester Pike. The group met there until 1898, when another structure was built to the east in Violet Township, Fairfield County.

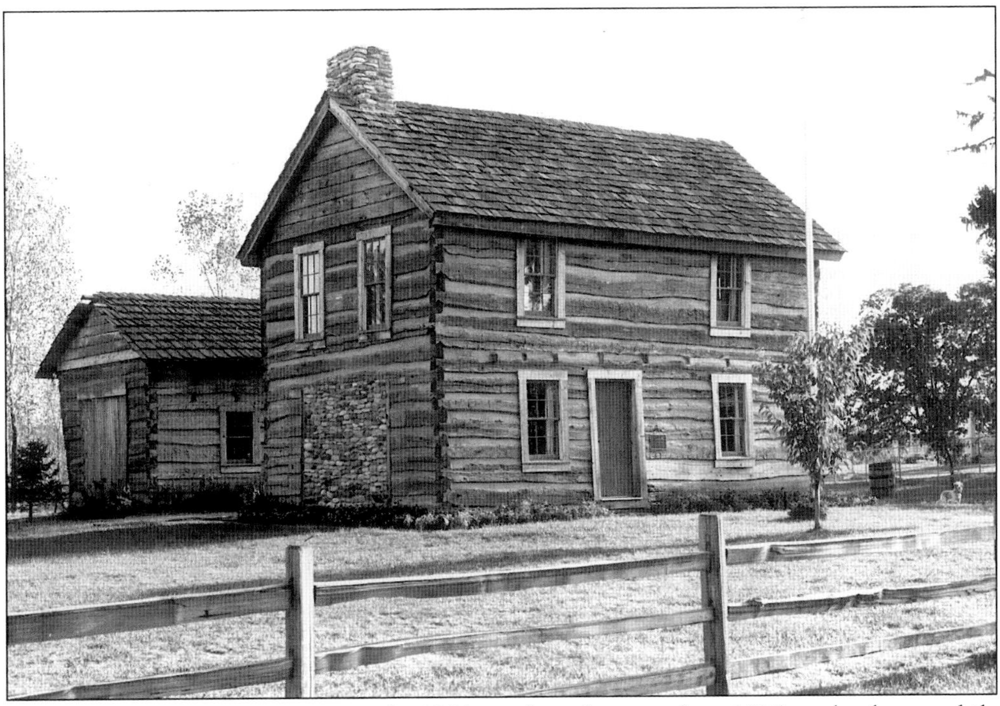

GROVEPORT LOG HOUSE, C.1978. In 1974, workers discovered an 1815-era log house while dismantling a home on the southwest corner of Main and Madison streets to make way for the construction of a new post office. The Groveport Heritage and Preservation Society was told it could take possession of the log house if it could move it to another location.

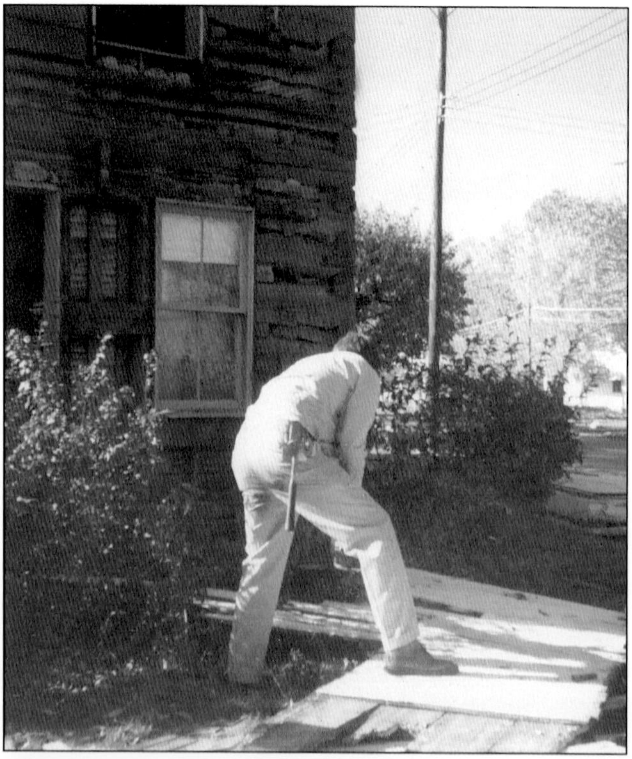

Log House Readied for Move, 1974. Volunteer Steve Blum is shown here preparing the log house for its move to its new location on a lot east of the Groveport Cemetery. Many community volunteers pitched in to preserve this piece of early Groveport history. The house was separated into two pieces (main structure and kitchen) to help ease the transport.

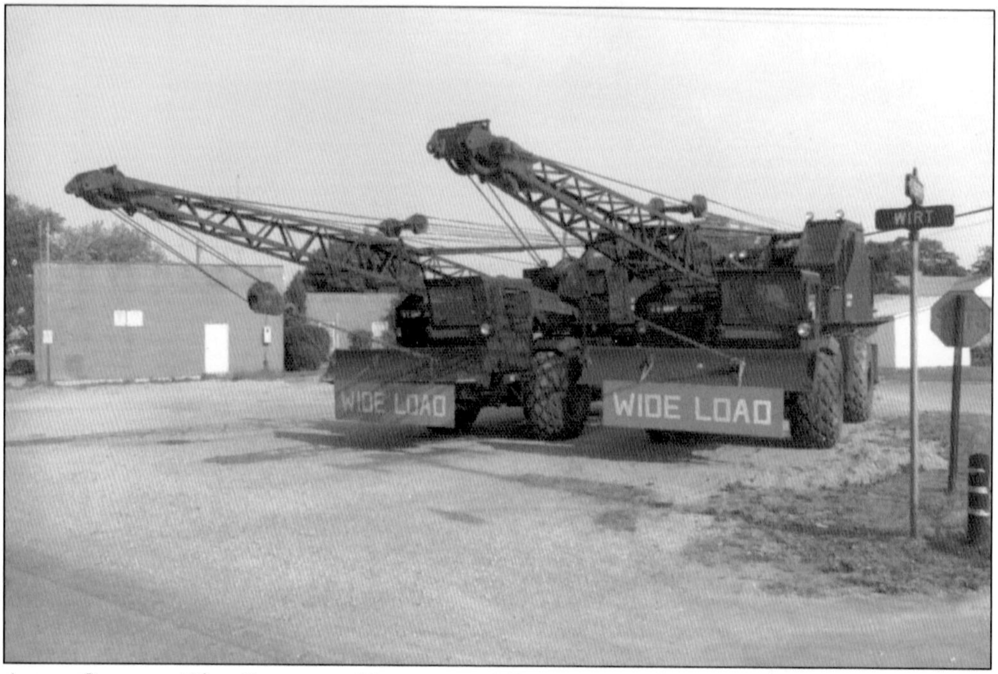

Army Cranes. The Groveport Heritage and Preservation Society enlisted the aid of the United States Army Corps of Engineers to help move the log house. These large cranes were just some of the heavy equipment used to lift and move the pioneer structure. Once in place at its new site the house was restored to reflect its original condition.

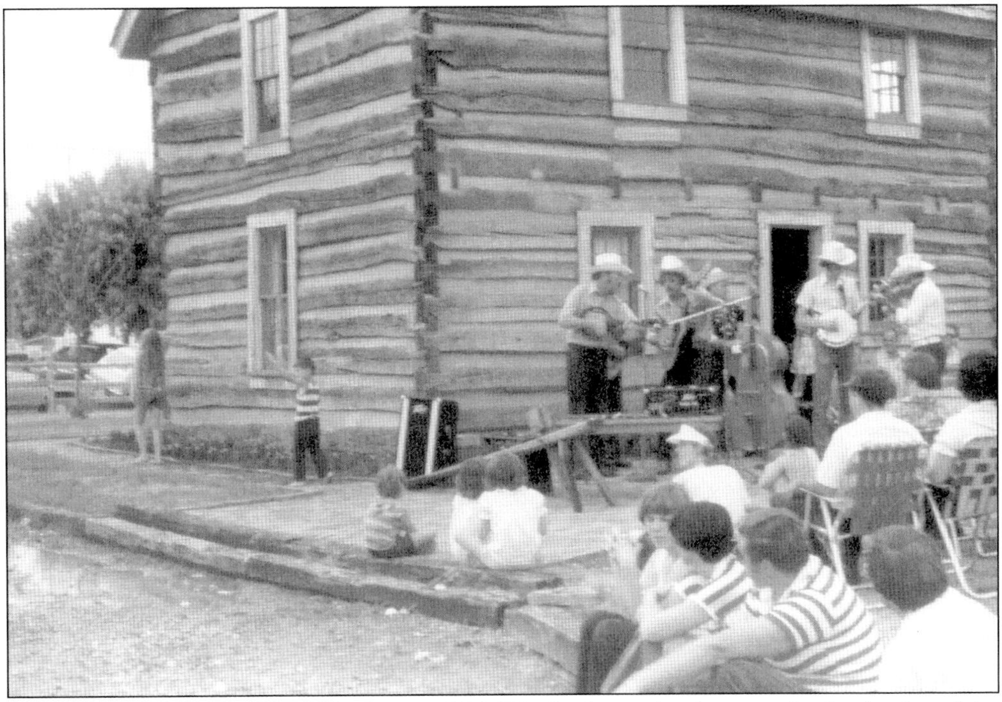

APPLE BUTTER DAY AT LOG HOUSE, C. 1976. The log house has become the focal point of the Groveport Heritage and Preservation Society's Apple Butter Day celebration, held annually on the second Saturday in October. The historically themed festival hearkens back to the village's pioneer roots and serves as a homecoming for friends and relatives who have moved away.

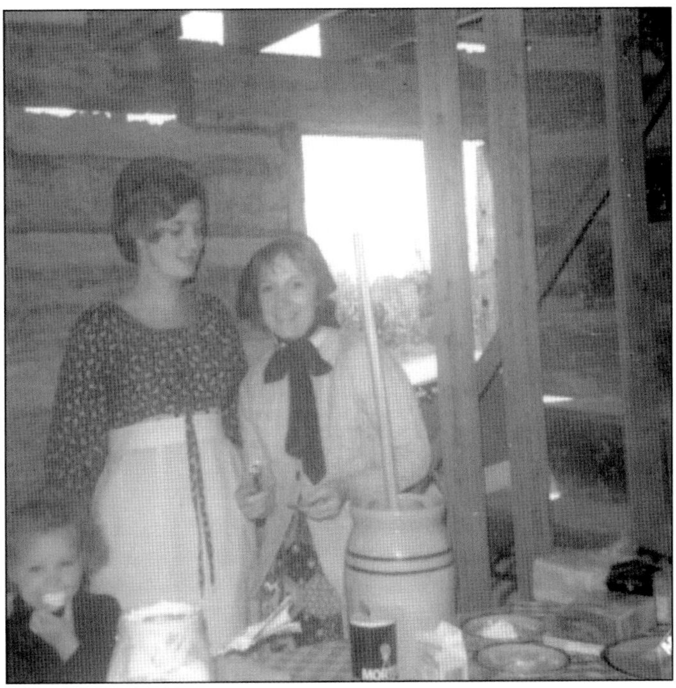

LOG HOUSE INTERIOR, 1976. Apple Butter Day is fueled by the efforts of volunteers. Here, dressed in period costume are, from left to right, Mindy Montgomery, Kristi Blum, and Joan Montgomery as they prepare to serve homemade apple butter to hungry festival visitors. From this photo we can see the interior renovations to the log house were not yet completed.

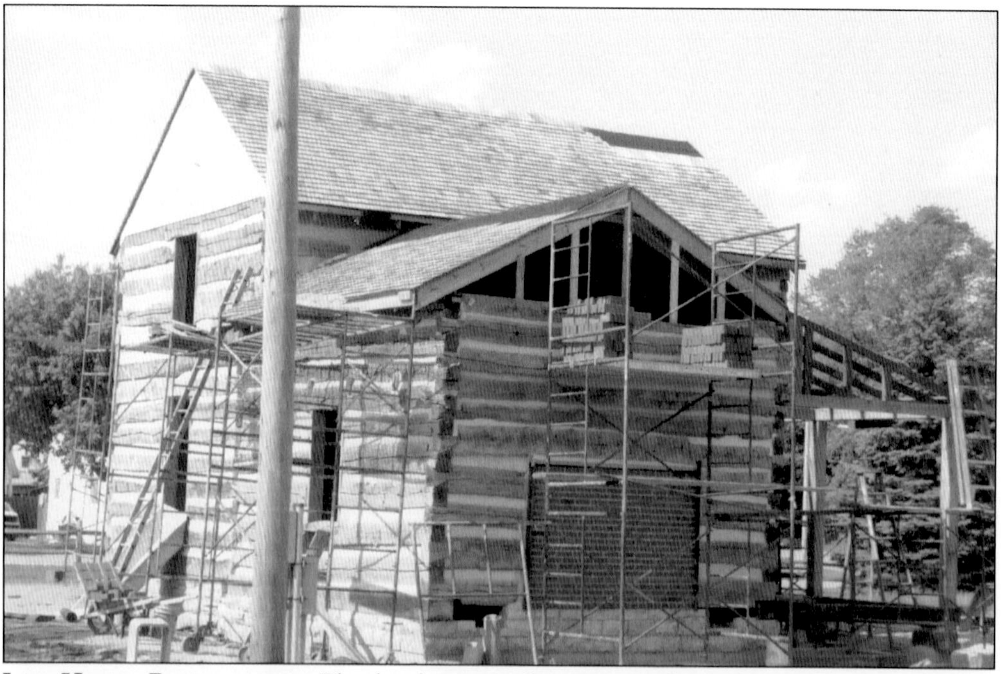

Log House Renovations. The log house underwent significant historical restoration in 1995–96. The kitchen section that was detached during the 1975 move was put back in place. Workers also disassembled the house and rebuilt it to strengthen it structurally. Modern plumbing was installed to enable the building to be used for a wider variety of community activities.

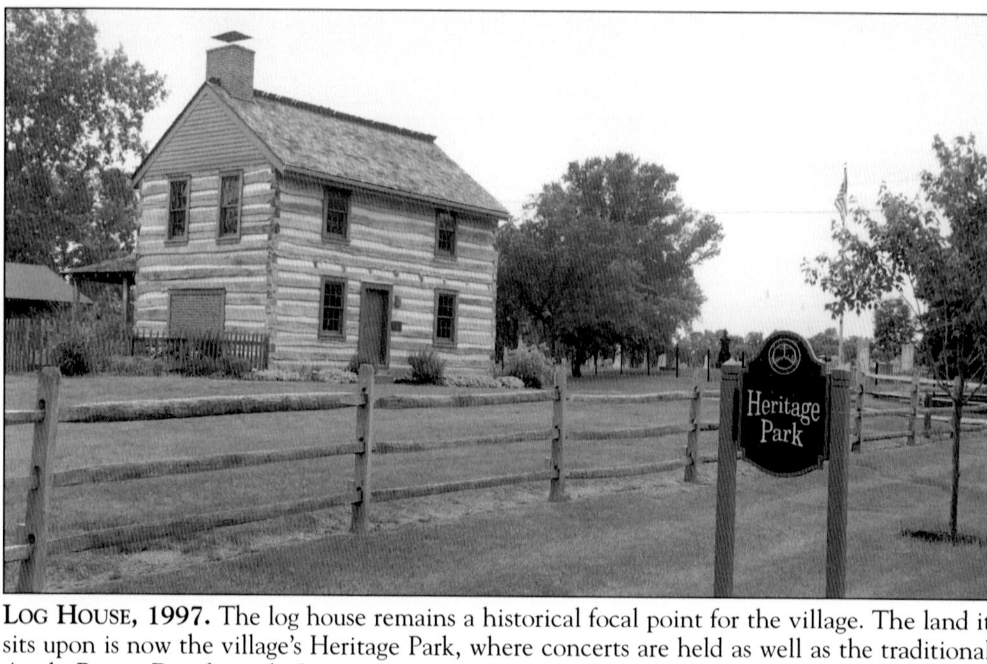

Log House, 1997. The log house remains a historical focal point for the village. The land it sits upon is now the village's Heritage Park, where concerts are held as well as the traditional Apple Butter Day festival. Community groups and private gatherings also use the house for festivities throughout the year.

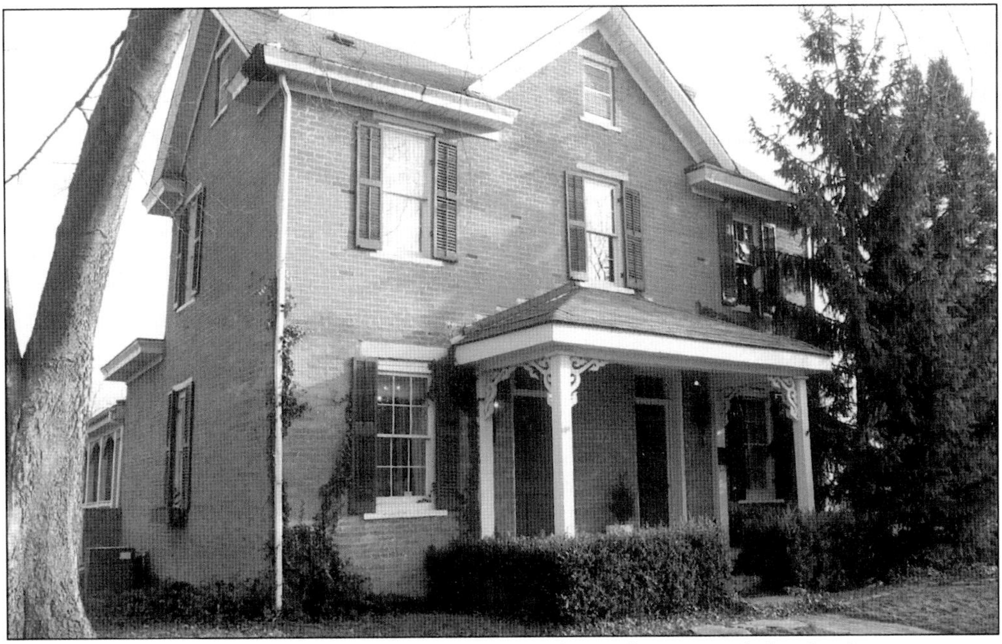

HOME OF FIRST GROVEPORT MAYOR. Abraham Shoemaker erected this brick structure on Cherry Street around 1840. Shoemaker was elected Groveport's first mayor on April 17, 1847, after the citizens merged the two towns of Wert's Grove and Rarey's Port into Groveport. Sixty-two men voted in the election, which also elected Dr. Abel Clark recorder and Samuel Sharp, E.M. Dutton, J.P. Bywaters, C.J. Stevenson, and William Mitchell as trustees (council). This home is now the private residence of the Akers family.

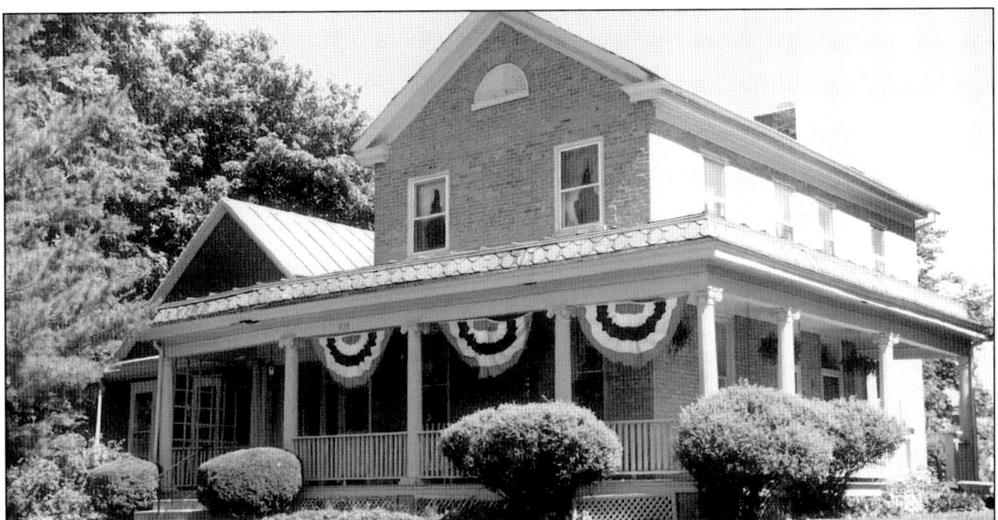

WILLIAM RAREY HOME. William Rarey, born February 16, 1812, was the eldest of early settler Adam Rarey's 11 children. Exhibiting a good head for business, he successfully operated grain warehouses and other enterprises. He also accumulated land and built this Federal-style home on Main Street west of Front Street in 1840. It was Rarey, along with rival Jacob Wert, who formed the two towns of Rarey's Port and Wert's Grove that would become Groveport. This home is now the private residence of the Cox family.

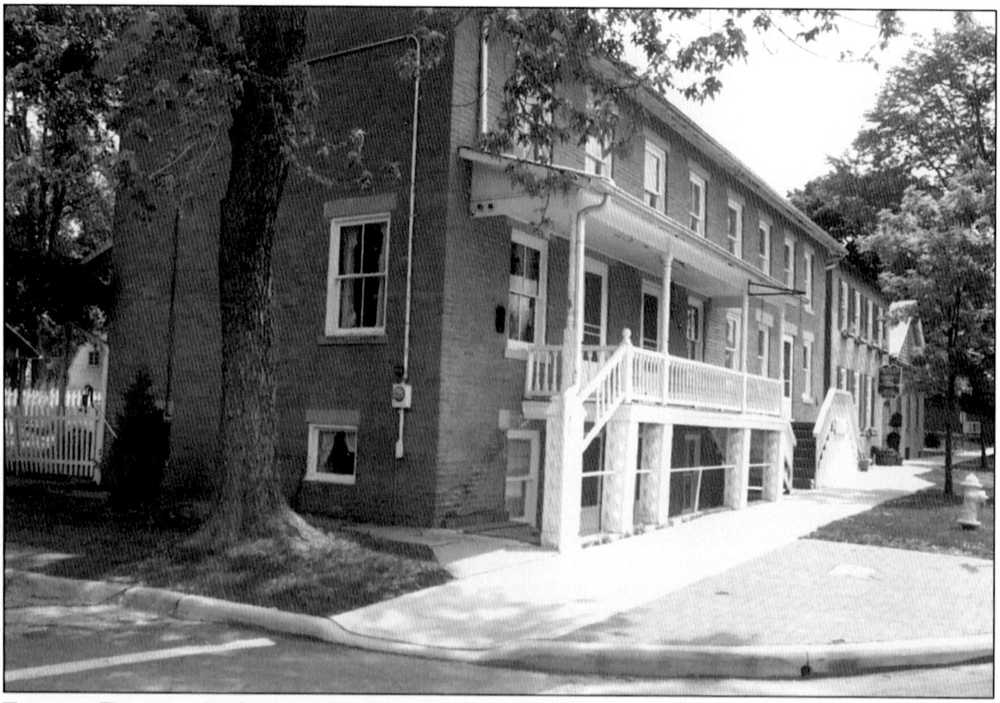

FORMER TAVERN. Built around 1830, this Federal-style residence and former tavern, located on the northeast corner of Main and Walnut streets, was one of the first brick buildings constructed in Groveport. The porch was added much later. This is now the private residence of the Froehlich family.

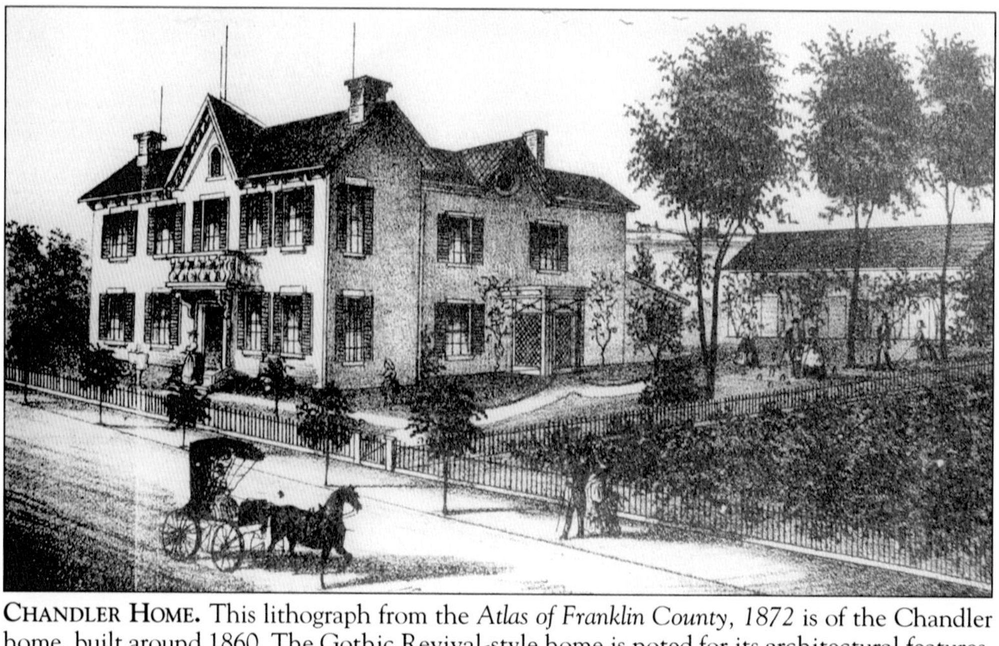

CHANDLER HOME. This lithograph from the *Atlas of Franklin County, 1872* is of the Chandler home, built around 1860. The Gothic Revival-style home is noted for its architectural features, which include a central gable, pointed arch opening, two dimensional scroll work, accentuated gables, and bracketed cornice. This is now the private residence of the Hollingshead family.

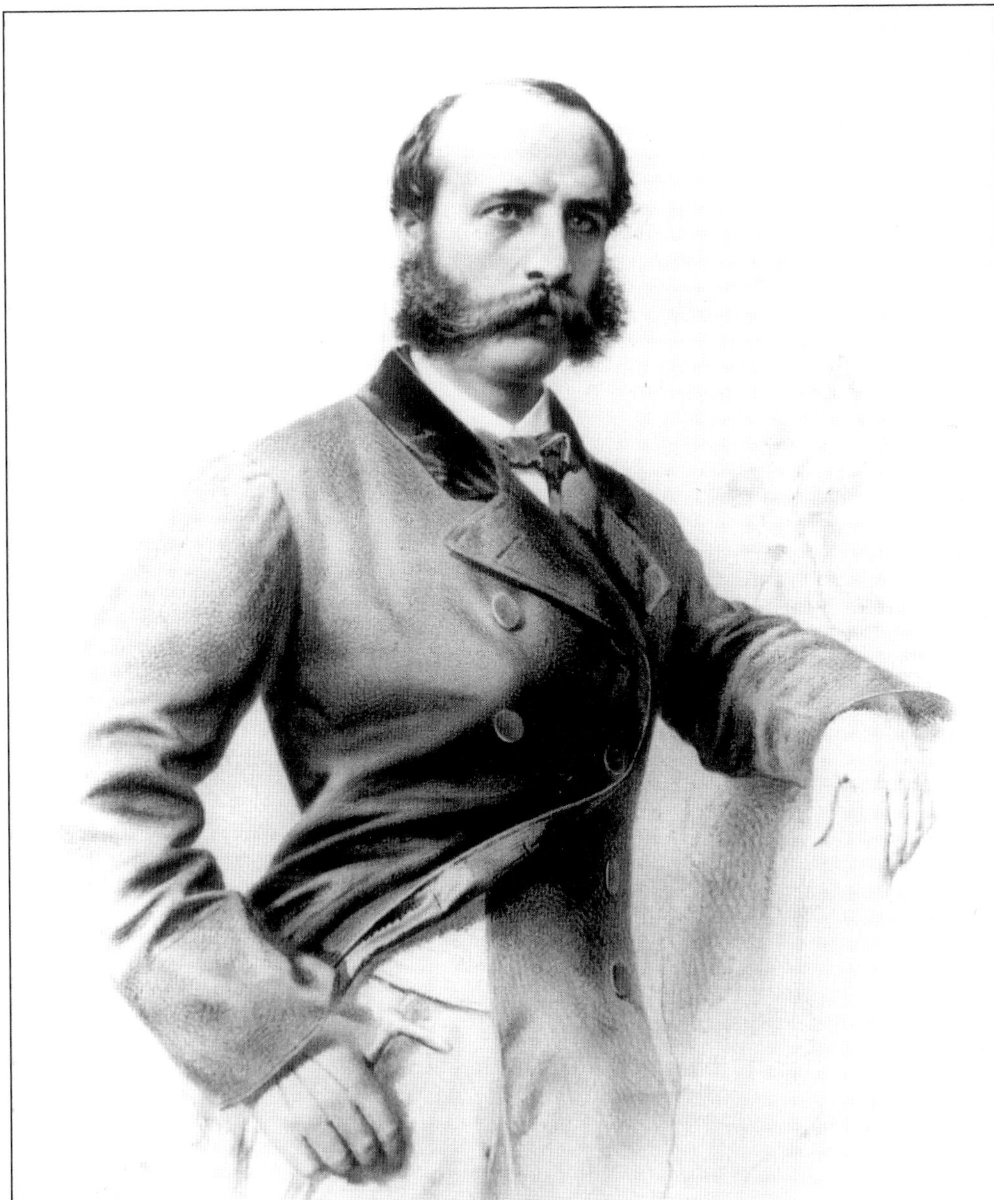

JOHN S. RAREY. Rarey was born Dec. 6, 1827, in his father Adam's tavern in what would become Groveport. At a young age John exhibited a talent for horsemanship and people from throughout the area brought their unruly horses to him to be trained. As he grew into adulthood, John refined his humane "Rarey Method" of training horses and built a strong reputation nationally as a horse trainer. It was in England in 1858, where he had traveled to work with the British military and its horses, that Rarey impressed the military men as well as Queen Victoria with his unusual methods of using kindness, firmness, and patience to train horses. This led to a challenge from the Earl of Dorchester. Dorchester owned the stallion, Cruiser, who was considered the fastest horse in England, yet was too vicious to race and considered untrainable. Rarey stunned Dorchester and other onlookers when he went into Cruiser's stall and amazingly emerged riding the horse in three hours.

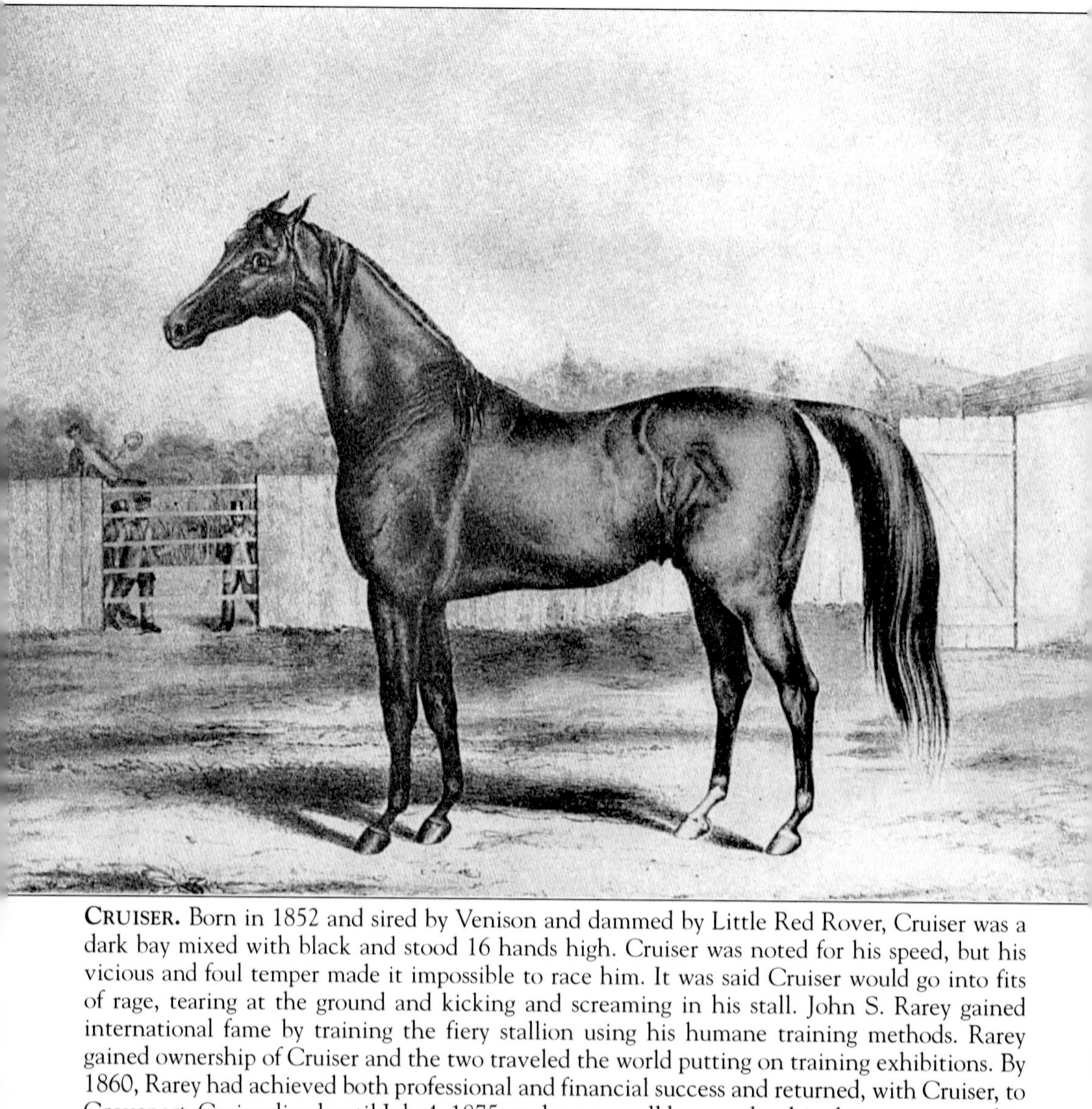

CRUISER. Born in 1852 and sired by Venison and dammed by Little Red Rover, Cruiser was a dark bay mixed with black and stood 16 hands high. Cruiser was noted for his speed, but his vicious and foul temper made it impossible to race him. It was said Cruiser would go into fits of rage, tearing at the ground and kicking and screaming in his stall. John S. Rarey gained international fame by training the fiery stallion using his humane training methods. Rarey gained ownership of Cruiser and the two traveled the world putting on training exhibitions. By 1860, Rarey had achieved both professional and financial success and returned, with Cruiser, to Groveport. Cruiser lived until July 4, 1875, and was so well known that his obituary appeared in the *New York Times*. In honor of his spirit, Cruiser serves as the mascot for Groveport Madison High School's athletic teams because the of horse's example that power and discipline bring success. The school's colors of red and black reflect Cruiser's dark coat and fiery disposition.

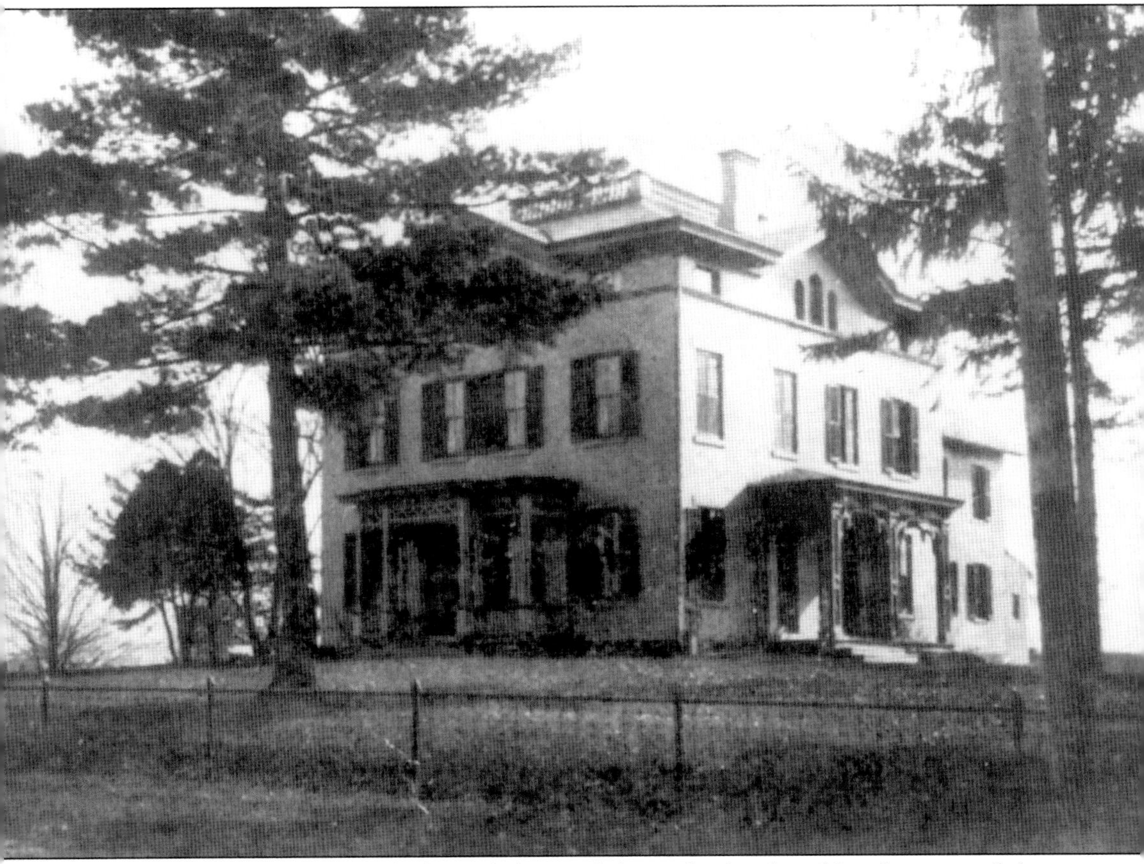

CEDARLAWN. John S. Rarey built Cedarlawn while at the height of his fortune and fame in 1862, at a cost of $23,000. The 24-room Renaissance Revival mansion incorporated the existing brick home built as a tavern on east Main Street in 1812 by his father Adam Rarey. The home featured a landscaped lawn of cedar trees, shrubs, and gardens. The house was surrounded by 90 to 100 acres of land used for pastures and farming. A stable was built for Cruiser on the northeast section of the lawn where it remained until being moved to the rear of the property after the stallion died. Directly across from the mansion Rarey laid out a pasture for his Shetland ponies. Rarey often received visitors from around the world to his lavish home. Townspeople knew when a foreign guest was staying at Cedarlawn as Rarey would fly the flag of the visitor's home land from atop the mansion.

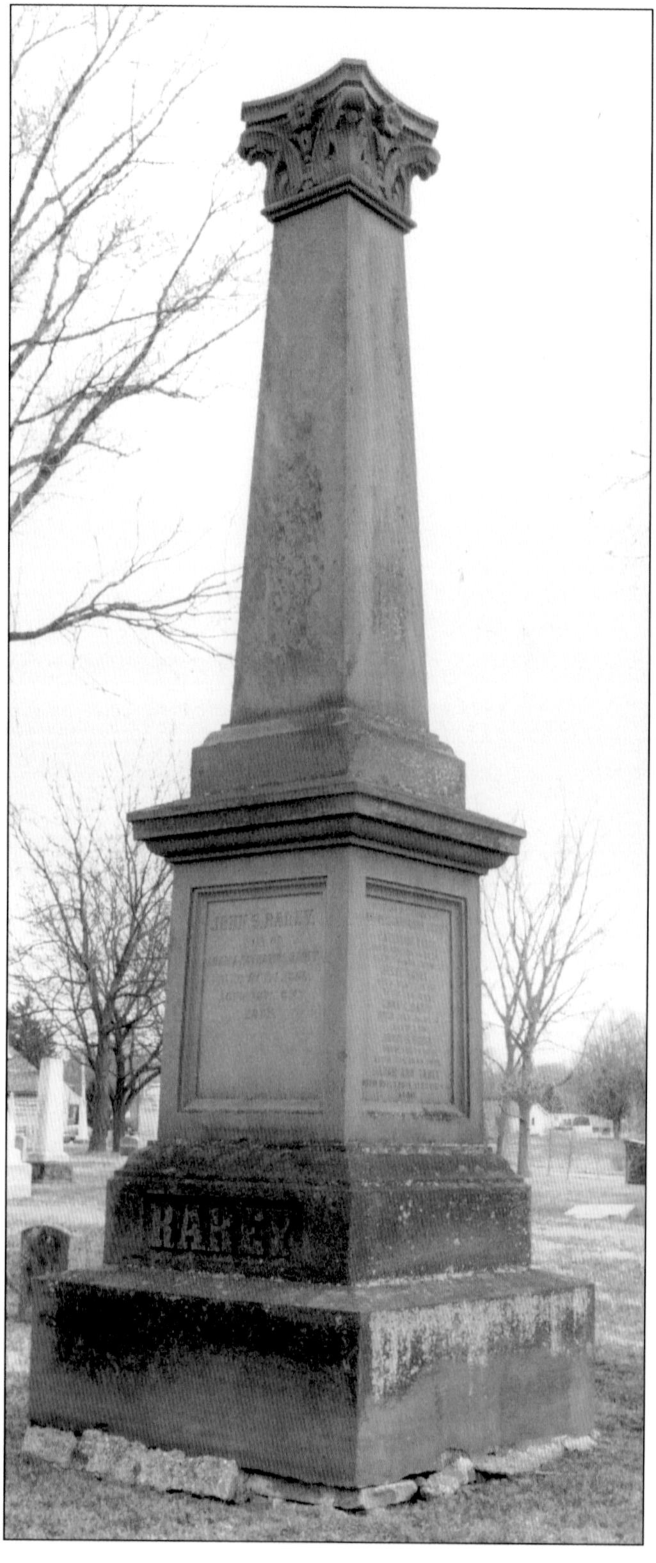

JOHN S. RAREY GRAVE SITE, GROVEPORT CEMETERY. Rarey died in Cleveland, Ohio, on October 4, 1866, at age 38 after suffering a stroke. Some of his last words were of his horse, Cruiser. "If I could only get back once more to the old farm and put my arms round my dear horse's neck I believe I should get well," he said. Rarey made certain Cruiser would be well cared for in his will. He instructed that Cruiser was not to be exhibited and was to remain properly cared for at Cedarlawn. Rarey specifically noted Cruiser was never to be sold. Cruiser reverted to his vicious ways following Rarey's death and it is said no one dared get close to the stallion. While Rarey's grave site is well known, there are many local legends as to where Cruiser is buried. For many years it was believed the great horse was buried in a pasture that became the football field behind what is now the Freshman School. However a nineteenth-century letter has surfaced indicating Cruiser is buried on "Fred Rarey's horse farm." Old maps indicate Fred Rarey had two horse farms in Groveport and Madison Township, so the mystery remains of exactly where Cruiser rests in peace.

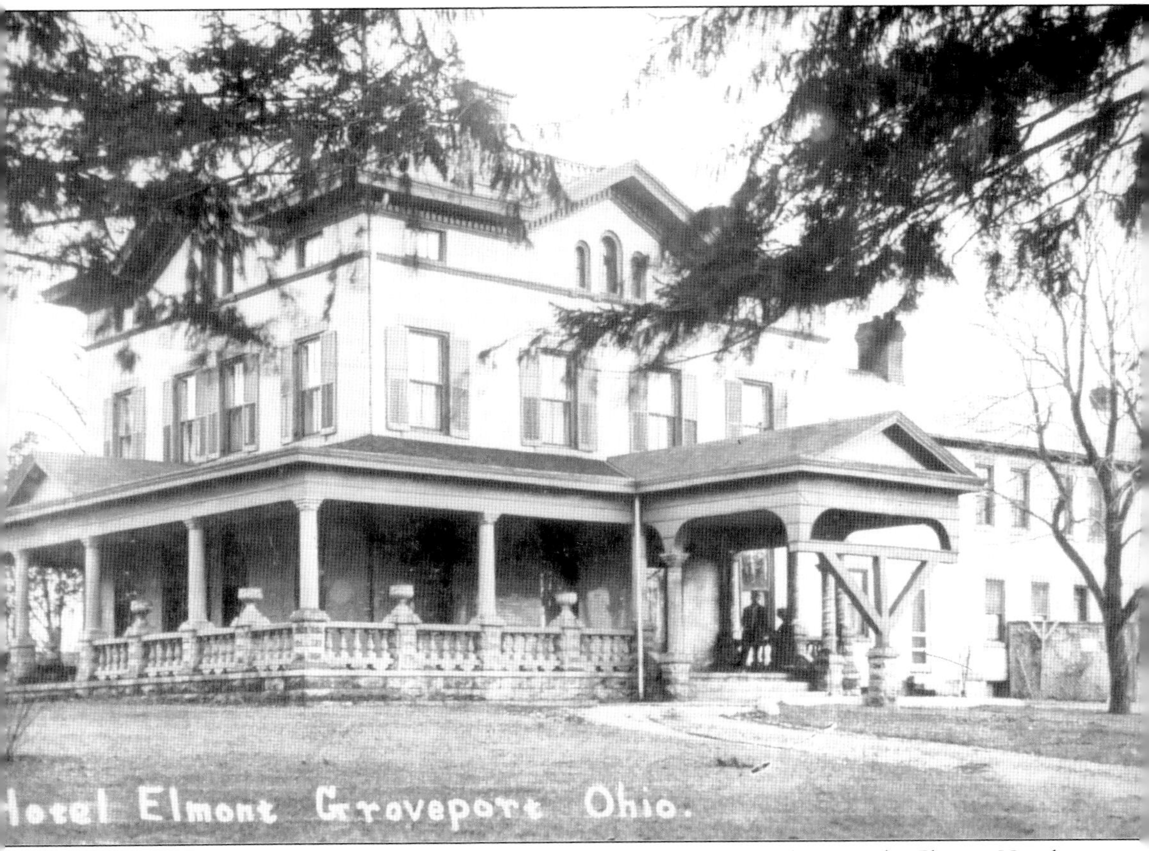

Elmont Hotel. In the twentieth century, Rarey's home Cedarlawn became the Elmont Hotel, a Groveport showplace through the first half of the century. A grand wrap around porch was added to the Renaissance Revival mansion and an extra room to bring the total to 25. The magnificent structure featured black marble mantel pieces and a large ballroom. The Elmont hosted weddings, special dinners, and other social events of all occasions. Fraternities and sororities from Ohio State University and Capital University held dances there, arriving in Groveport on special traction line charters. Situated on the hotel grounds were several cottages that visitors from Columbus rented in the hot Ohio summers to escape the heat of the city.

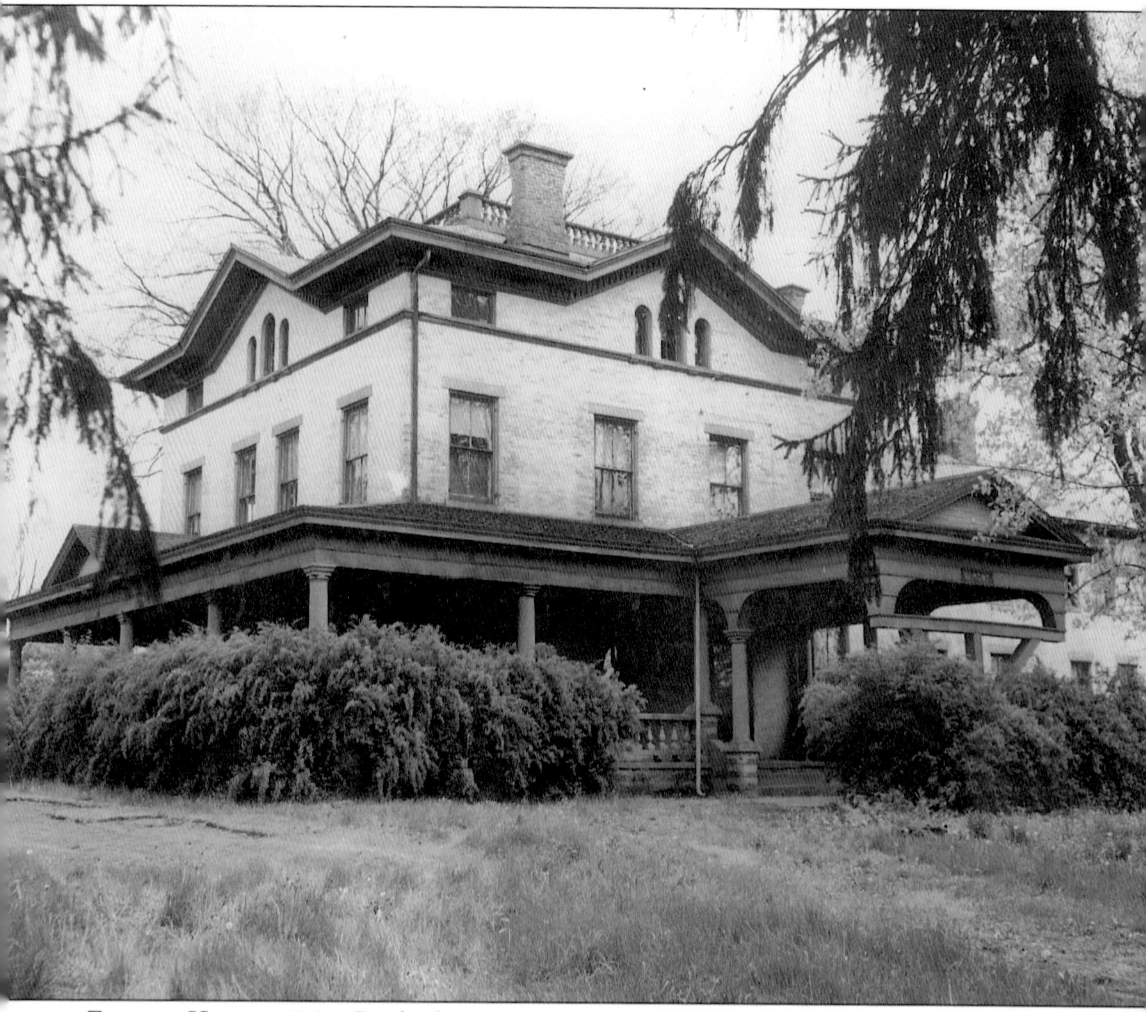

ELMONT HOTEL, 1950. By the late 1940s, the grand old Elmont had begun to deteriorate. Then owner J.C. Yaekle found it more and more costly to maintain. Around that time, the Groveport Madison Board of Education was searching for a site to build a new high school to accommodate the post World War II population boom. The Elmont sat beside the existing Groveport School and was considered a convenient site for the new school. In March, 1950, the board bought the then 8.33-acre property for $21,000, with Yaekle retaining the rights to the four cottages, which he later moved and sold as private residences. In this photo to the lower left one can see where the board was having sod removed which it later resold. No organized public effort arose to save the Elmont and it was razed in the fall of 1950. Before its demolition, Groveport students were given a tour of the historic building to get a last look at what once was Rarey's Cedarlawn.

Two

Transportation

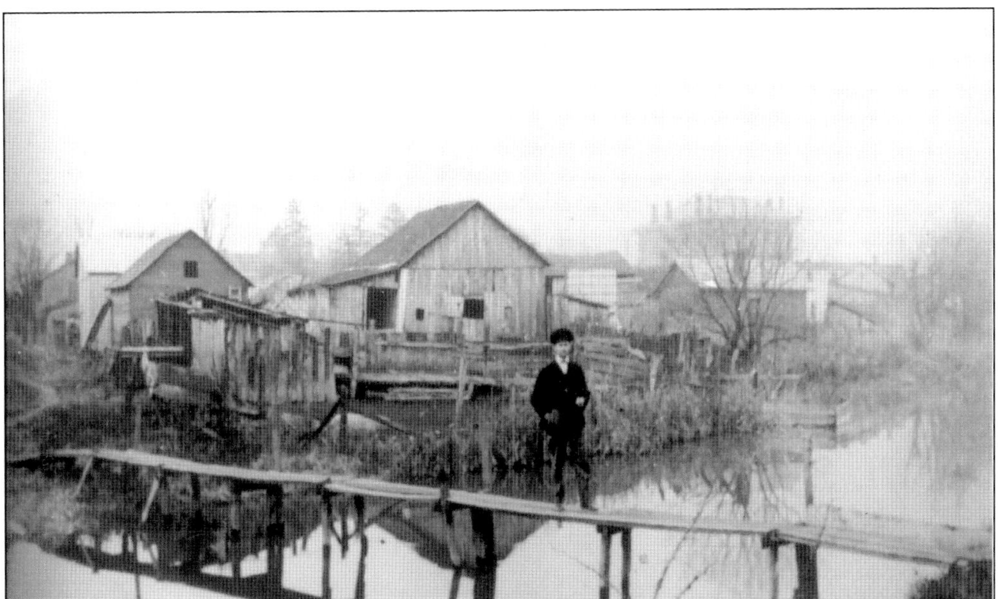

Ohio and Erie Canal in Groveport. Byron Seymour stands on the Walnut Street footbridge over the Ohio and Erie Canal in 1908, near what is now the intersection of Wirt Road and Walnut Street. Canal traffic had virtually ceased on the canal by this time. Notable in this photo is the Groveport Town Hall looming in the upper right background. Walnut Street is a mere footpath to the left.

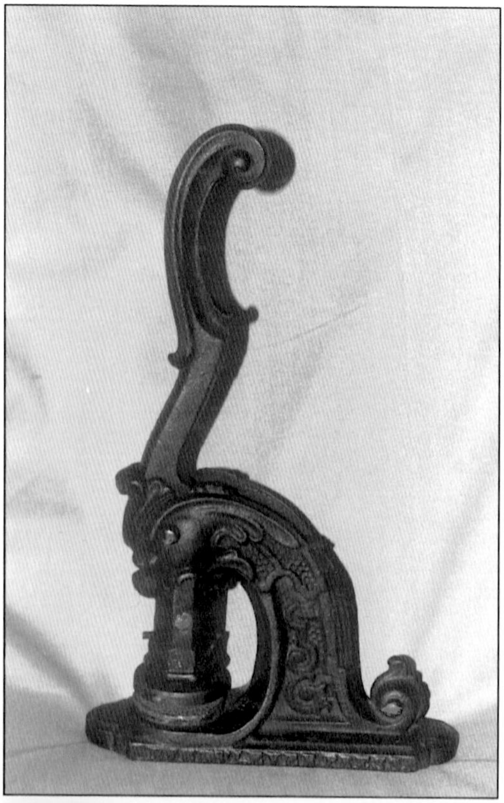

EMBOSSER. Groveport's Main Street originally was a toll road known as the Columbus-Lancaster Pike. The Groveport toll house stood on the eastern edge of the village and is still in use today as a private residence. Toll house workers used this embosser to stamp travelers papers to show they had paid the toll. The stamp made by the embosser reads, "Lancaster, Lithopolis, & Groveport...Turnpike Road Company."

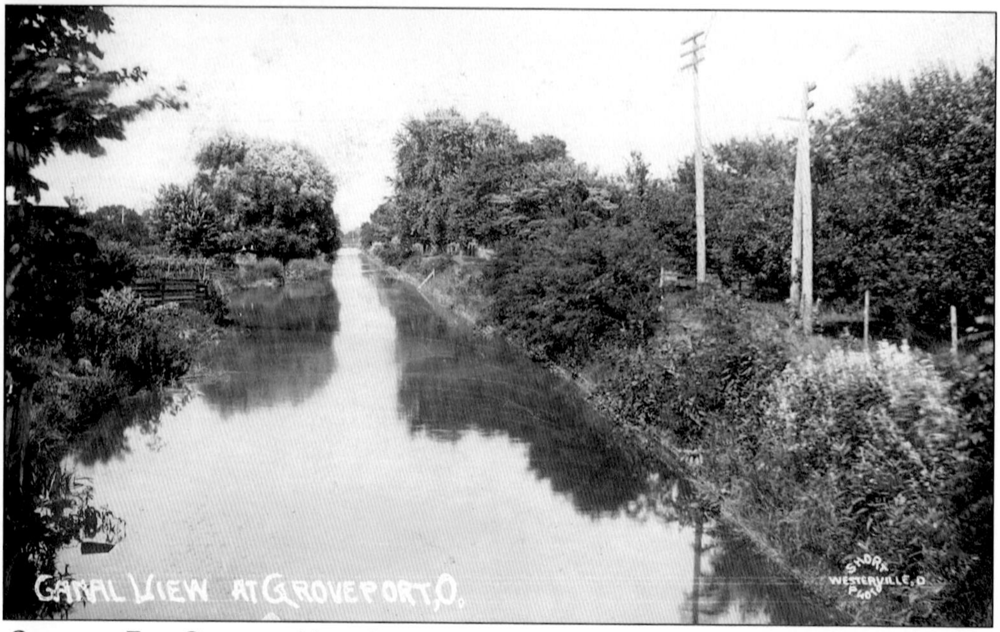

OHIO AND ERIE CANAL AT MAIN STREET, 1908. This is a view of the Ohio and Erie Canal in Groveport looking northeast from the Main Street bridge, which was located at the intersection of what is now Wirt Road and Main Street. The towpath is to the right and the gates to the canal boatyard are to the left.

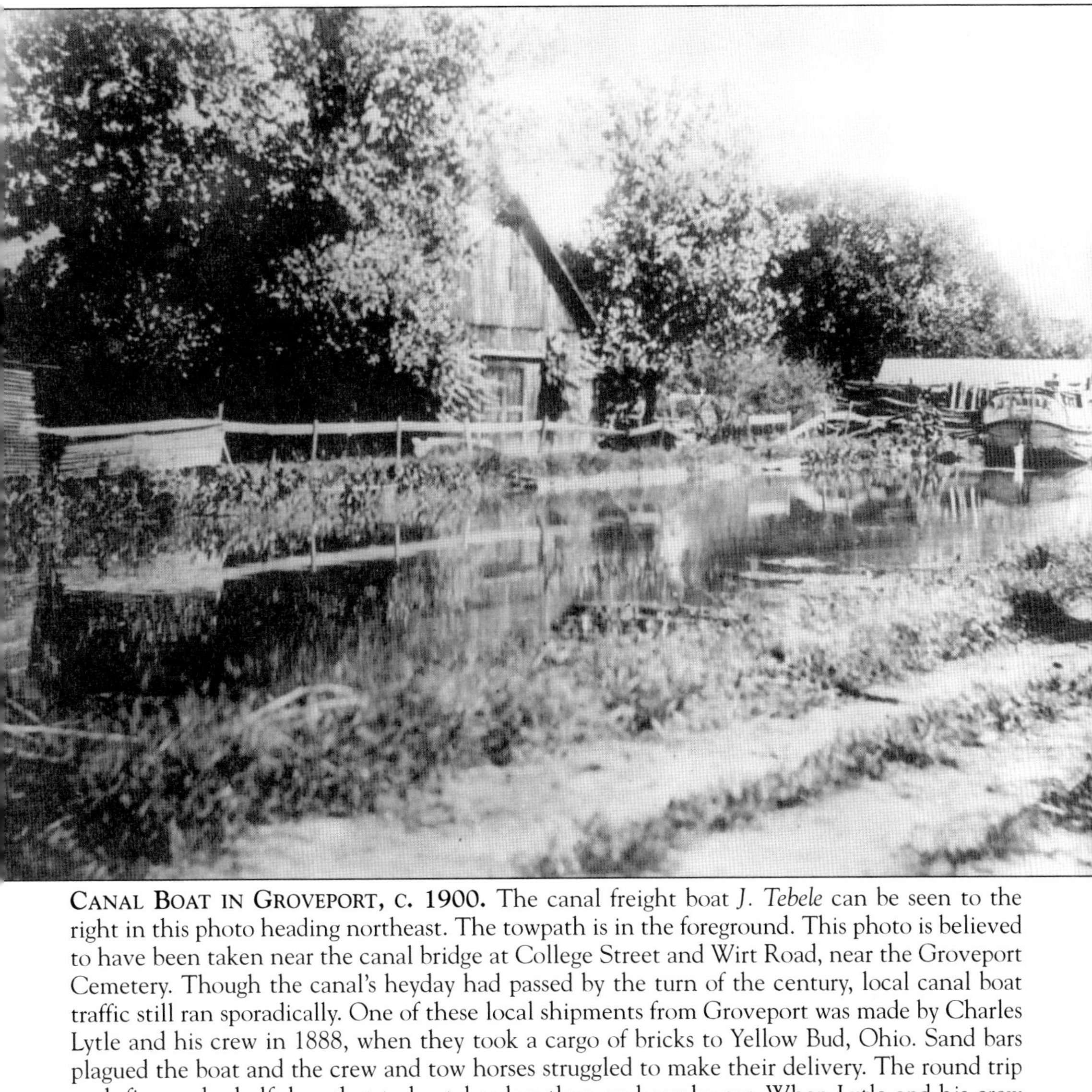

Canal Boat in Groveport, c. 1900. The canal freight boat *J. Tebele* can be seen to the right in this photo heading northeast. The towpath is in the foreground. This photo is believed to have been taken near the canal bridge at College Street and Wirt Road, near the Groveport Cemetery. Though the canal's heyday had passed by the turn of the century, local canal boat traffic still ran sporadically. One of these local shipments from Groveport was made by Charles Lytle and his crew in 1888, when they took a cargo of bricks to Yellow Bud, Ohio. Sand bars plagued the boat and the crew and tow horses struggled to make their delivery. The round trip took five and a half days that today takes less than an hour by car. When Lytle and his crew returned they tied their boat to the dock and never took it out again. Another canal boat was actually beached on the canal bank at the east end of Elm Street and used as a private residence for a time.

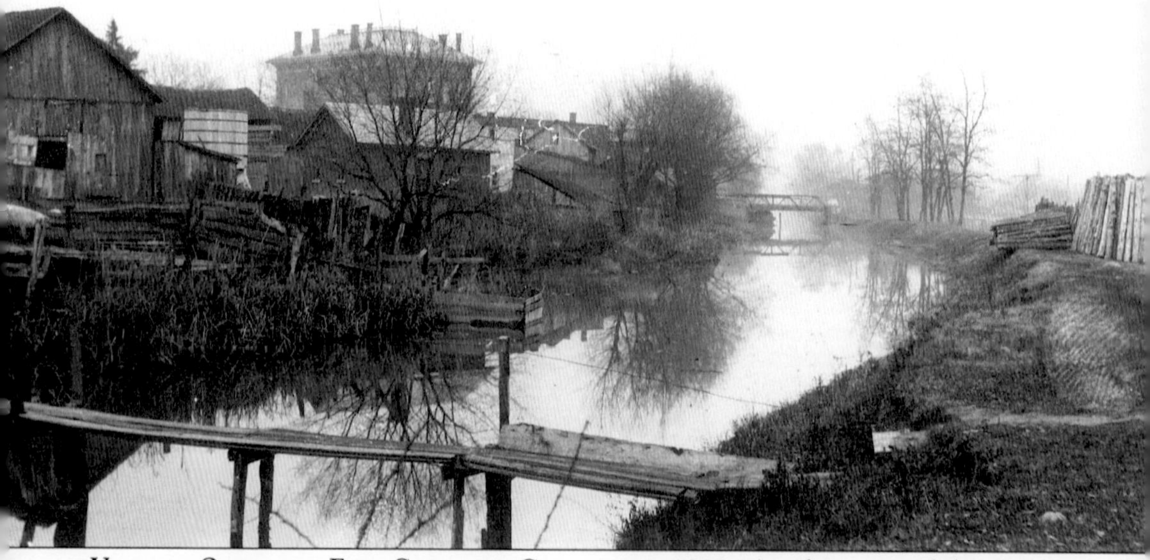

View of Ohio and Erie Canal in Groveport, 1908. Another view of the canal in Groveport from what is now the intersection Wirt Road and Walnut Street shows the iron turn bridge on Main Street (center right background), Groveport Town Hall (background), as well as various storage buildings and sheds that lined the canal banks. A large white hog can be seen in the left of the photo. (It was not unusual for hogs to roam freely about town in the nineteenth and early twentieth century.) A stack of lumber sits on the towpath to the right. The iron turn bridge on Main Street was erected in 1887, replacing a frame covered bridge. The bridge had to be turned by hand to allow boats to pass. Some bridge turners included John Cramer, Joe Miller, Erasmus Friend, W. E. Thompson, and A. H. McBriar. In 1911, the canal channel in Groveport was drained and filled in.

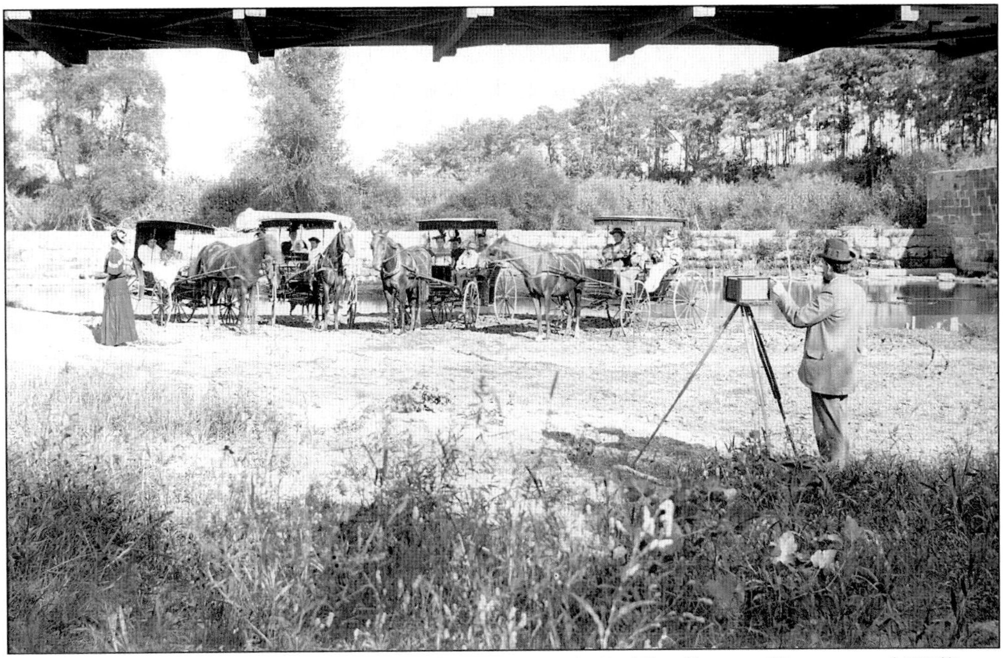

OUTING ALONG THE OHIO AND ERIE CANAL, C. 1900. The Bareis, Chaney, and Williams families pose in their buggies for a photographer near the state canal dam on Little Walnut Creek. The frame structure at the top of the photo is a covered bridge. An historian, George Bareis is noted for his book on the history of Madison Township, published in 1902.

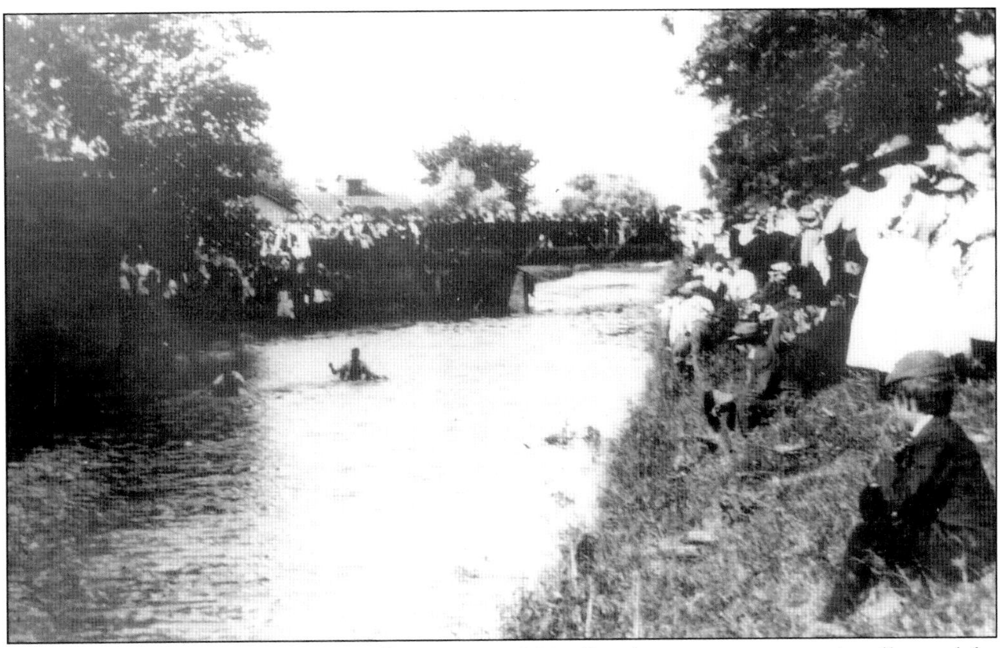

BAPTISM IN THE OHIO AND ERIE CANAL, C. 1900. Canal waters were occasionally used for baptismal services. A canal ford located at the east end of Groveport's Cherry Street was the scene of several baptisms. This photo shows a baptism believed to have taken place near the Cherry Street ford. The Main Street bridge is in the background.

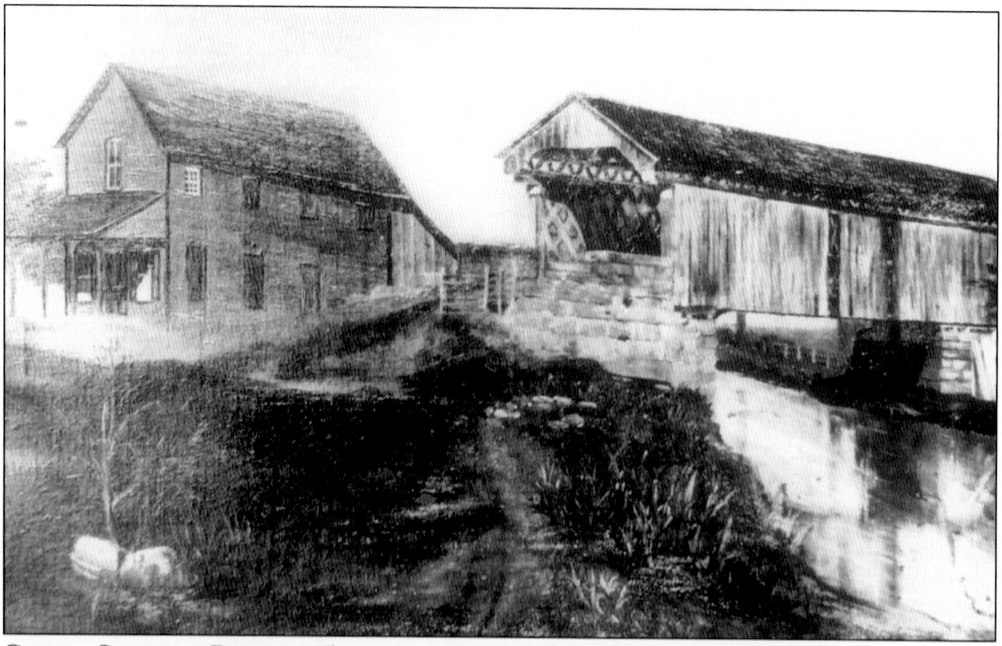

CANAL COVERED BRIDGE. This is a painting of the covered bridge over the canal on Groveport's Main Street. Built in 1847, it replaced a wooden bridge built by Adam Rarey. This bridge sat high on stone abutments to allow boats to pass easily underneath. It was replaced in 1887 by an iron turn bridge. The building to the left was used at various times as a saloon and also once was a meat shop.

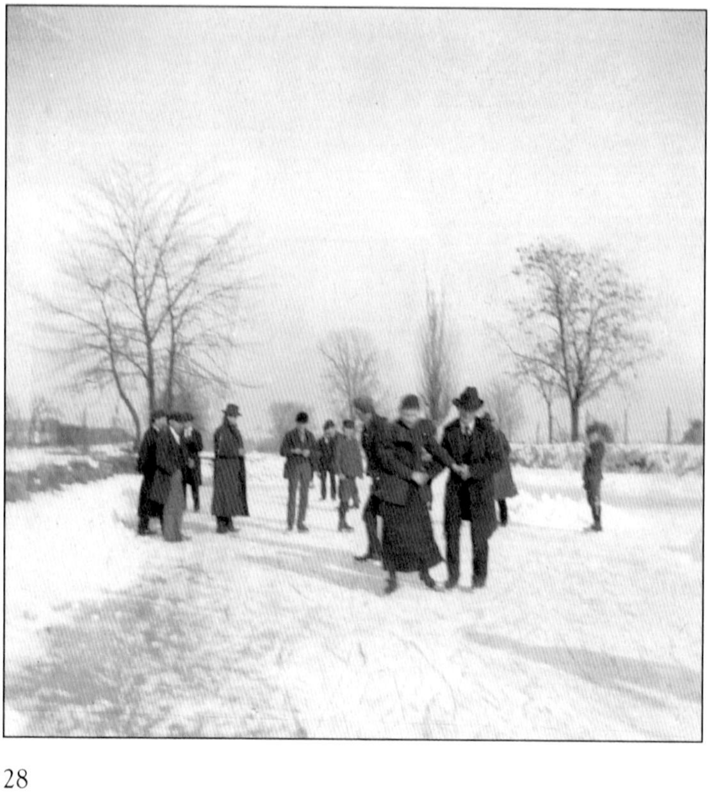

ICE SKATING ON THE CANAL, MADISON TOWNSHIP, C. 1910. Though the canal declined commercially in the twentieth century, it still played a role in the community as residents made recreational uses of its waters. Skating parties were common and fires would be built along the banks to warm the revelers. Skaters could glide along the canal's course for miles, stopping only to walk around the locks.

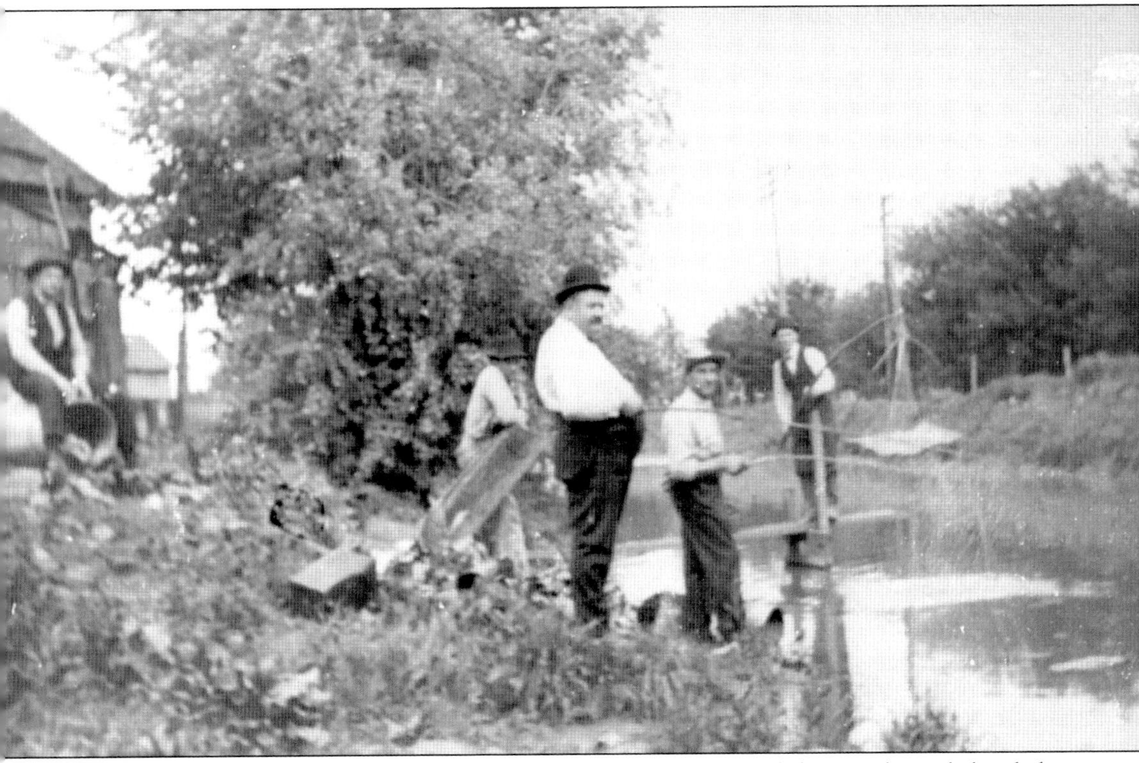

FISHING IN THE CANAL, C. 1908. These fishermen make use of the canal just behind the saloon that was located at Groveport's Main and Front streets just north of the Main Street bridge. Fishing was a popular pastime, with the basin at lock 22 considered a good location for catching black bass, while other parts of the canal yielded bullheads, rock bass, sunfish, and carp. In 1893, a small break in the canal bank temporarily drained a portion of the canal and Groveport boys "fished" by scooping stranded fish from the muck. Other recreational uses for the canal included ice skating, row boating, and swimming. Row boaters had to yield to canal boats and usually portaged around locks. Swimmers had to keep a watchful eye out for the marshal because taking a cool dip in the canal was illegal.

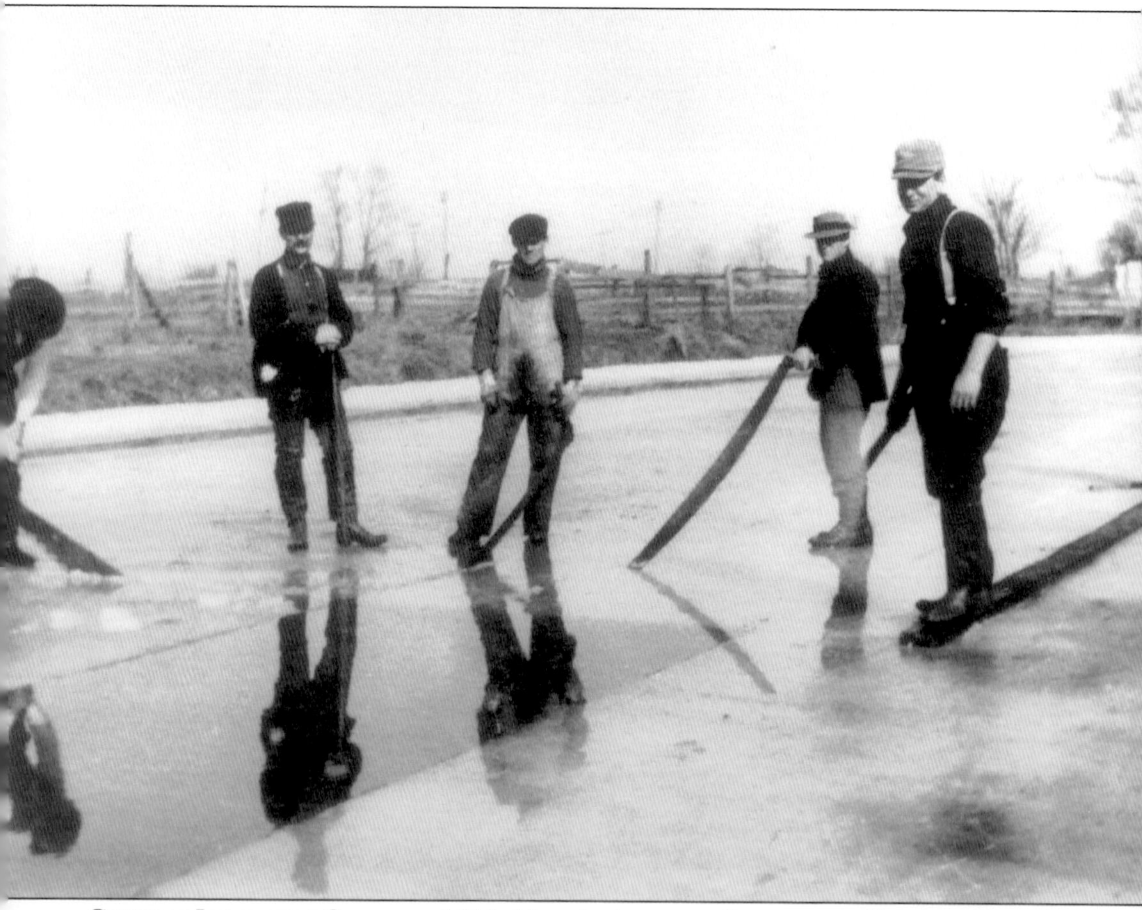

Cutting Ice on the Canal, c. 1910. Many businesses in Groveport and Madison Township evolved to serve the agrarian economy. Soon other enterprises emerged that were linked to the canal itself, including the harvesting of ice from the frozen canal in the winter for refrigeration purposes. Workers cut large blocks of ice from the canal with hand saws. The blocks were then covered with sawdust for insulation and stored in either the underground locker plant on Blacklick Street or in cool warehouses for warm weather use. This photo shows five workers in Groveport harvesting ice. The three men to the right have been identified as Hen Carter, Rich Mone and Bill Hanstine. The two men to the left have been identified as either Martin Kinsel, Malty Sandy, Jim Larison, Harve Rarey, or Clark Carter.

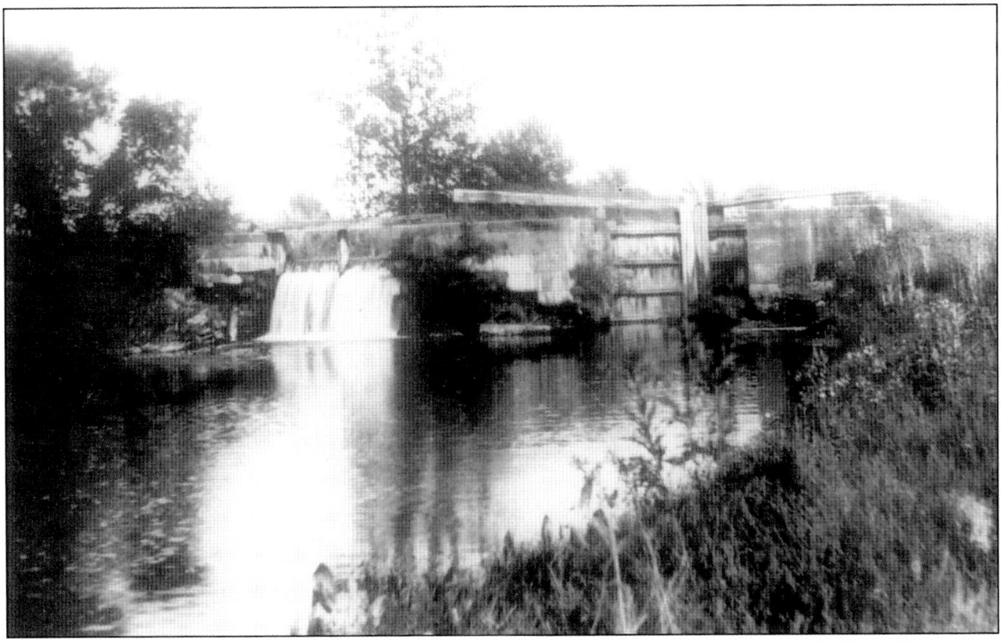

LOCK IN OPERATION. This lock is thought to be either lock 19, 20, or 21 in Madison Township and Canal Winchester, or lock 22 in Groveport. However, it is representative of all four locks in its construction and operation. Local locks were made mostly of sandstone and measured 90 feet in length and 15 feet in width. A lock's function was to lift or lower boats to meet the changing terrain.

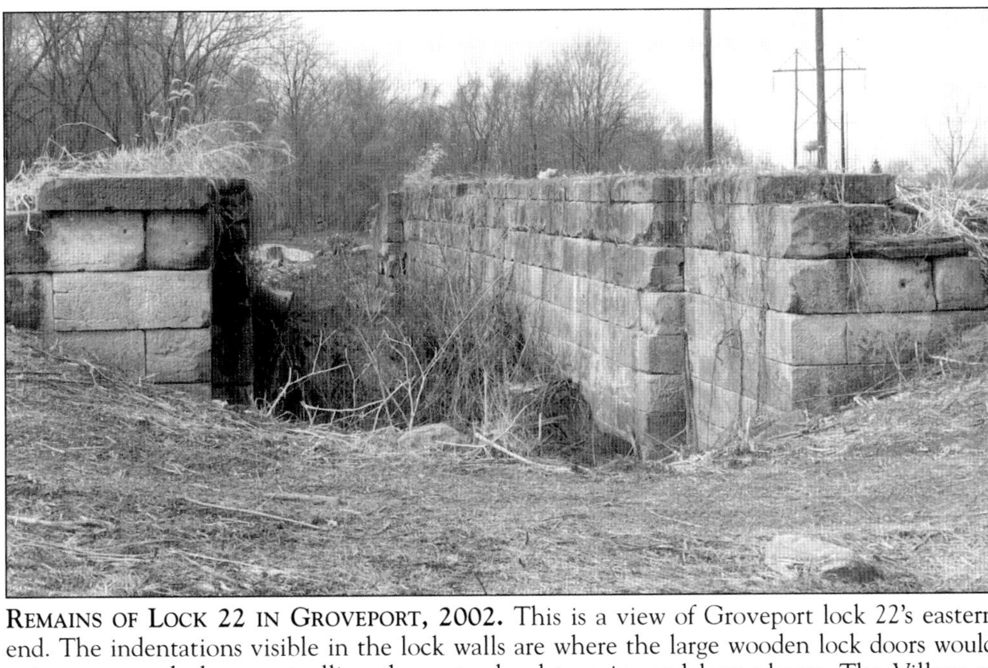

REMAINS OF LOCK 22 IN GROVEPORT, 2002. This is a view of Groveport lock 22's eastern end. The indentations visible in the lock walls are where the large wooden lock doors would swing open and close controlling the water level to raise and lower boats. The Village of Groveport is clearing brush from around this lock with plans to incorporate the structure into its park system.

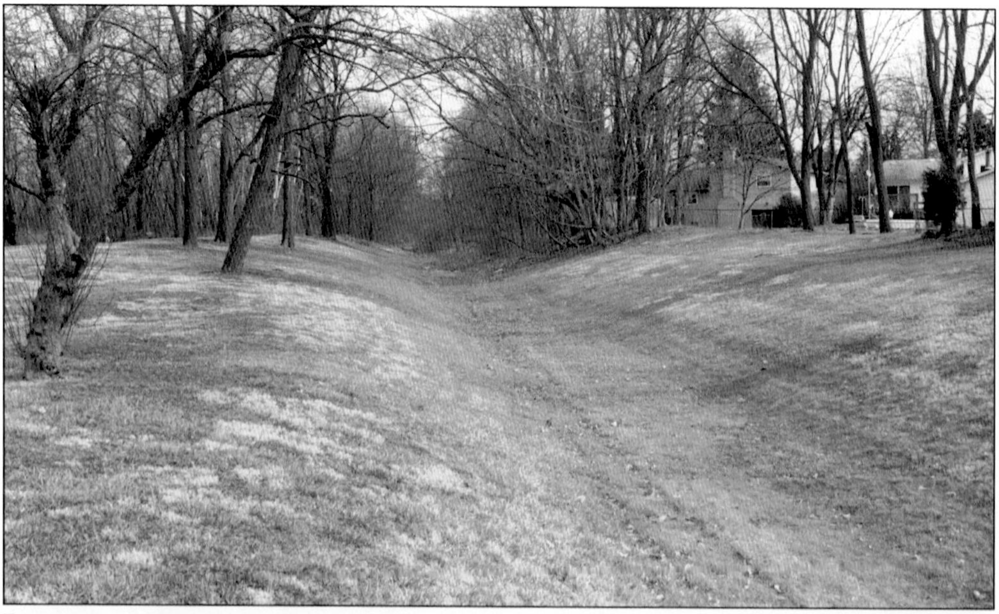

REMAINS OF OHIO AND ERIE CANAL, BLACKLICK PARK, GROVEPORT, 2002. The canal channel was typically 40 feet wide at the top and four feet deep. A canal boatyard and dry dock where boats were built and repaired once sat in what is now Blacklick Park. Boats were floated through the dry dock gate and then water was released to allow the boats to rest on trestle to be worked on. This operation was considered the first notable such operation below Baltimore, Ohio.

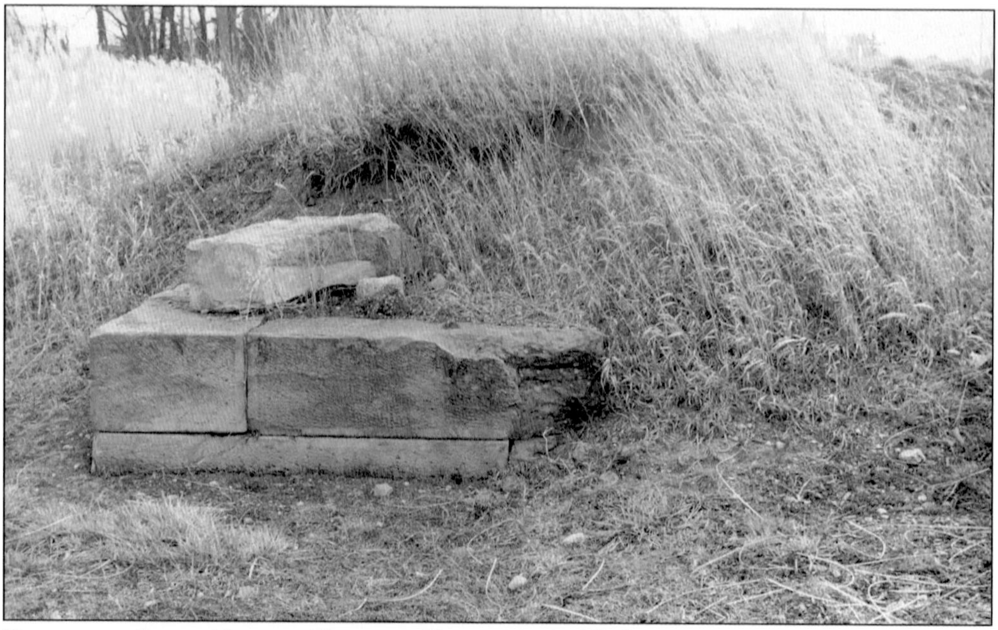

REMAINS OF LOCK 19, NEAR HANNERS PARK, 2002. All that remains visible of lock 19, near Canal Winchester, are a few sandstone blocks peeking out of the ground. This lock helped bring the water level of the canal to that of the average level of Little Walnut Creek. The Empire Mills operated near lock 19 from 1852 to 1895.

CANAL CULVERT, 2002. This culvert located in Madison Township along Groveport Road allowed the Scioto Valley Traction Line to pass over George's Creek. This site also was where a canal boat wooden "water" bridge once stood that floated boats over George's Creek.

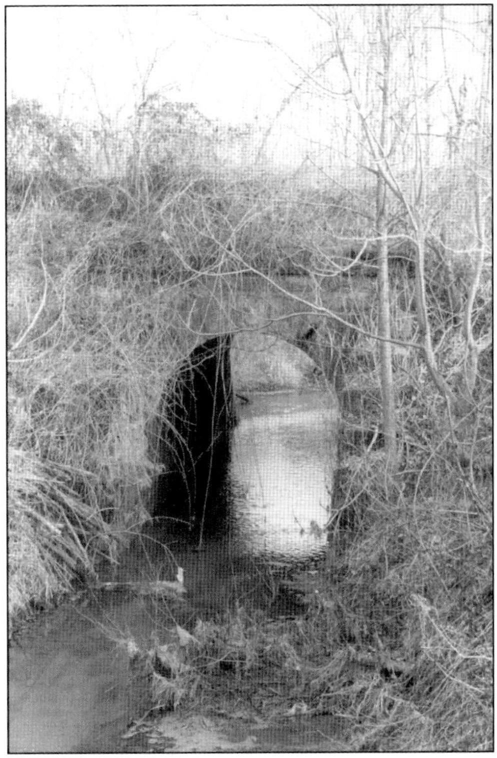

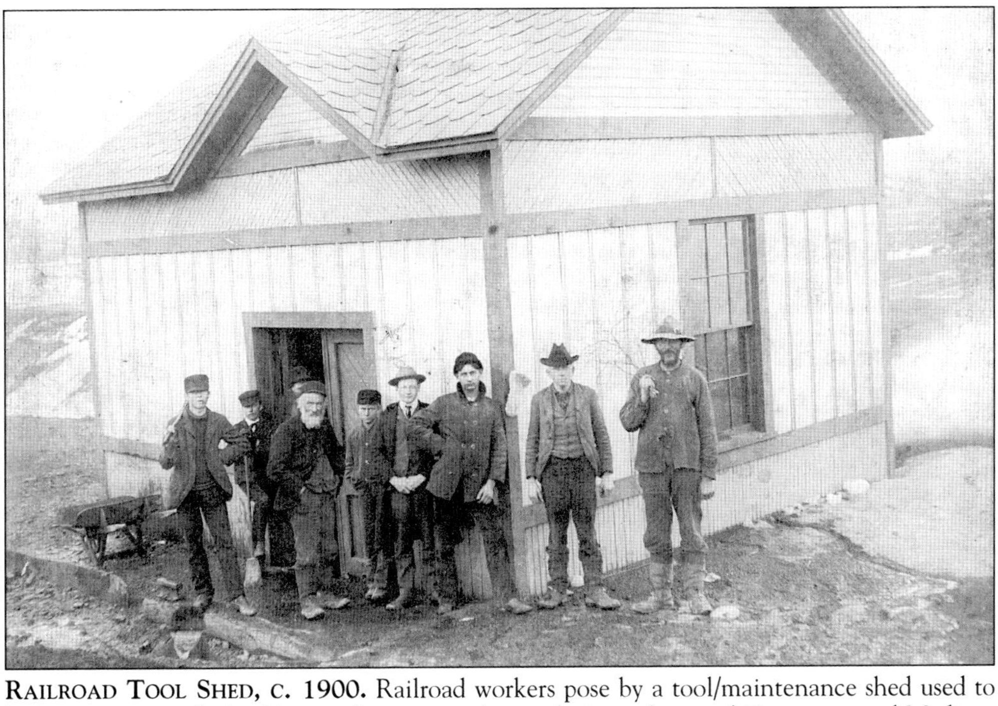

RAILROAD TOOL SHED, C. 1900. Railroad workers pose by a tool/maintenance shed used to house equipment for building and repairing the tracks in and around Groveport and Madison Township. The high amount of rail traffic on the line meant the tracks suffered much wear and tear and needed regular maintenance and repair.

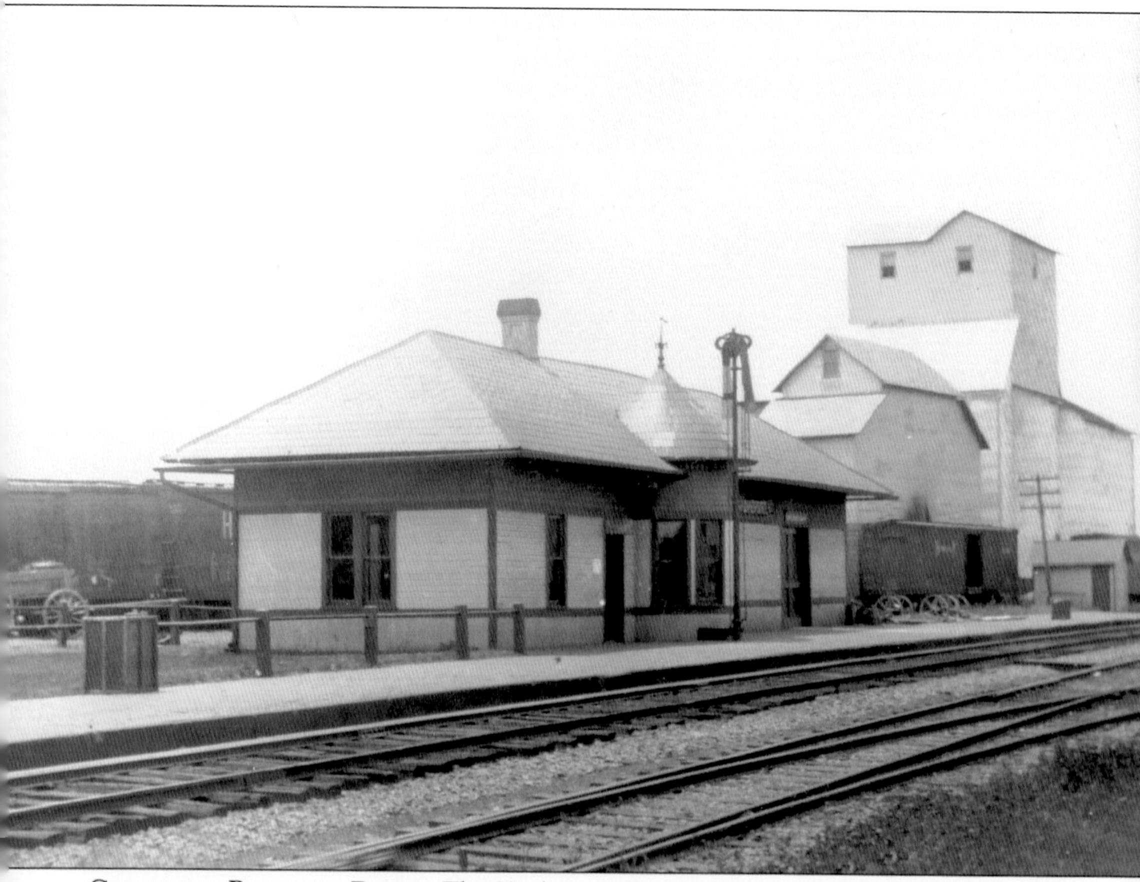

Groveport Railroad Depot. The Hocking Valley Railroad came to Groveport in 1868, spelling the doom of the canal system. The original plan called for running a rail route east from Columbus to Asbury and on to Canal Winchester, then southeast to Lancaster and Nelsonville. Groveport leaders realized that if the railroad bypassed their town it would have a devastating impact on the village's economy. Michael Corbett led the way to attracting the railroad by donating some of his land in Groveport for a rail right of way, and local leaders managed to raise $25,000 in stock subscriptions and then sweetened the deal with an additional $7,500 to secure the railroad through Groveport. The railroad depot pictured here was built around 1900 and demolished in the late 1950s. The building in the background is the old North Grain elevator, which was torn down in the 1970s. The depot sat along the south side of the tracks near Front Street.

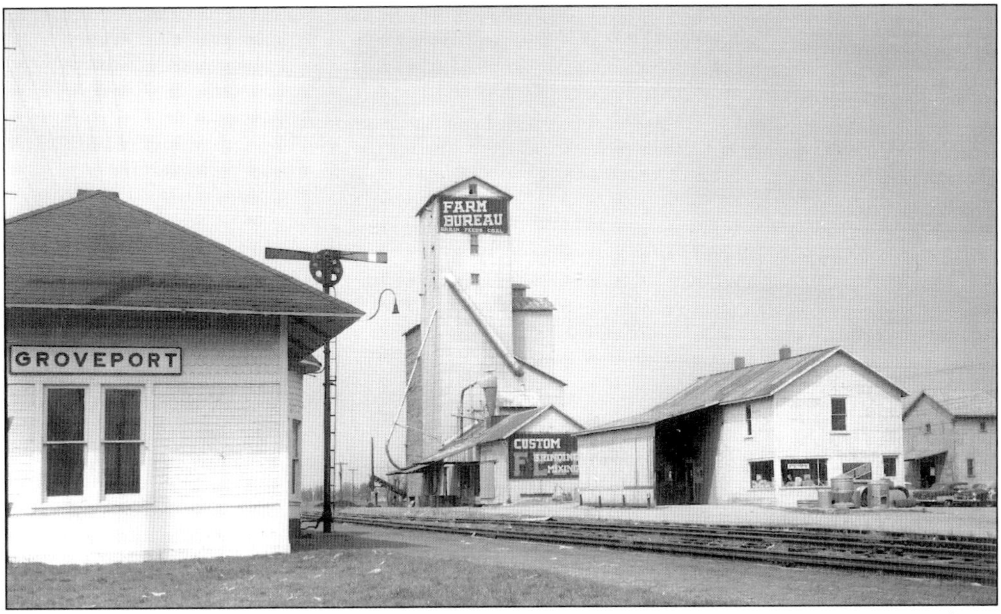

FARM BUREAU, GROVEPORT RAIL YARD C. 1958. The railroad had strong ties to Madison Township's agricultural economy. Along with the North Grain elevator there was also a Farm Bureau elevator, pictured here. In 1875, during its early heyday in the area, the railroad shipped over five-million pounds of freight from the township and over five-thousand passengers passed through the Groveport depot.

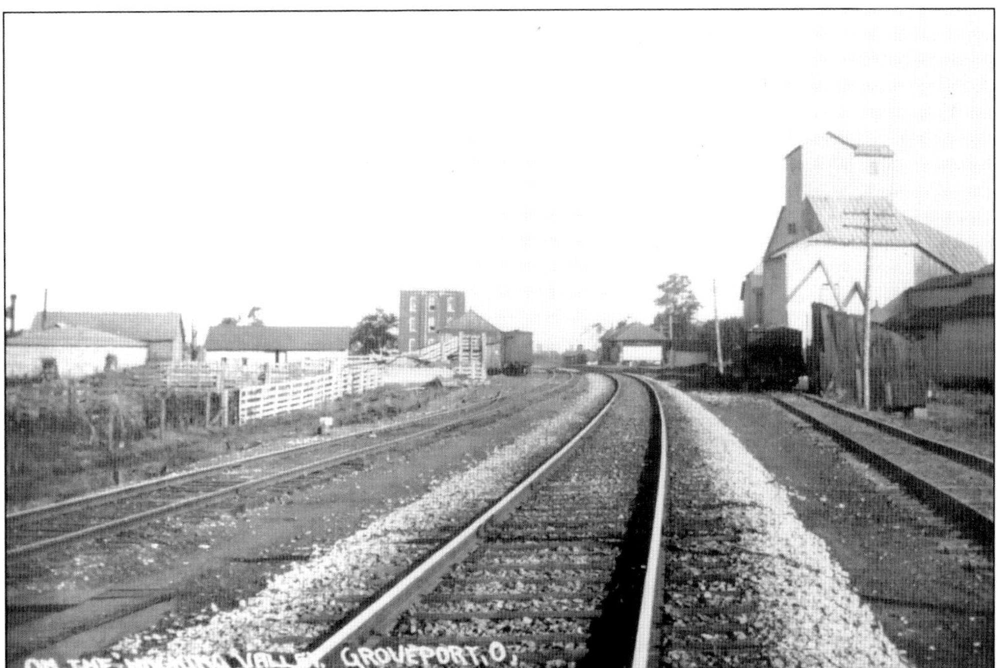

GROVEPORT RAIL YARD, C. 1958. A view of the Groveport rail yard looking to the east reveals livestock pens to the left, the North Grain elevator to the right, and three sets of tracks running through the town. The depot can be seen at the center rear of the photo.

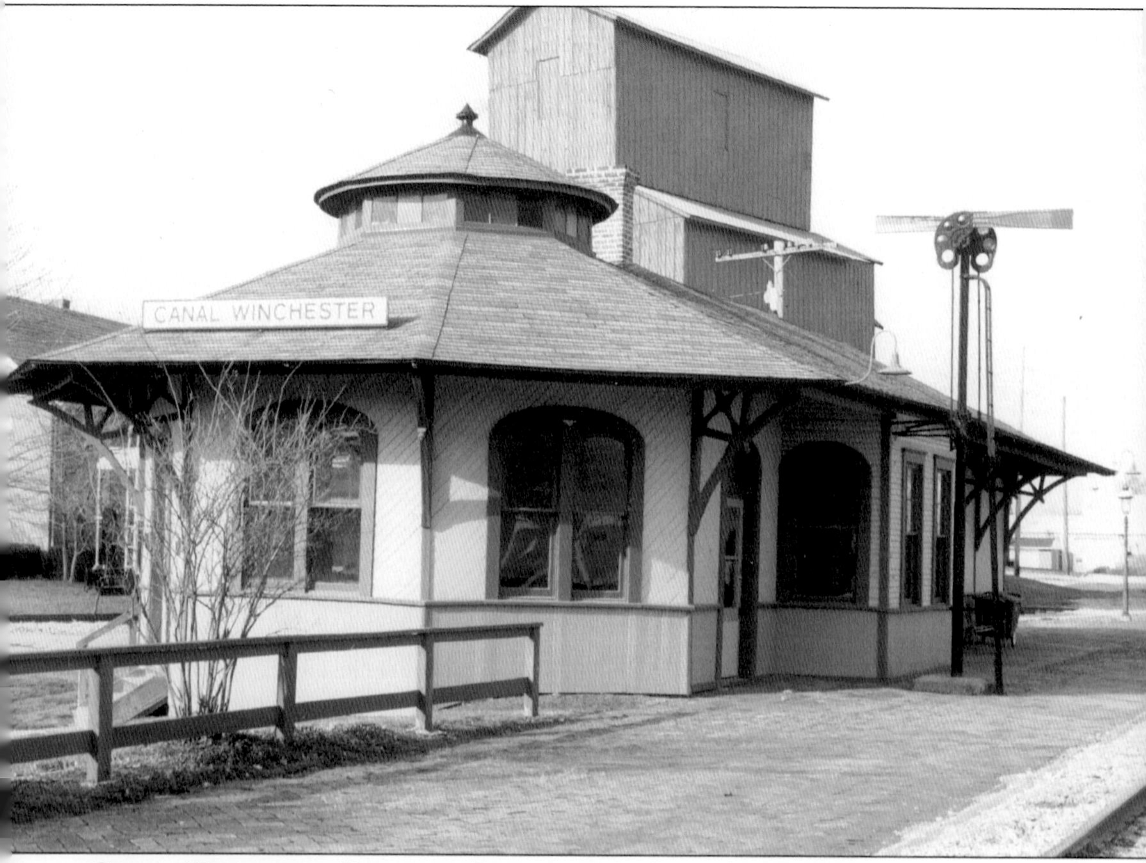

CANAL WINCHESTER RAILROAD DEPOT, 2002. Recently restored to its original 1894 design, the Canal Winchester railroad depot features an octagonal domed waiting room with colorful windows. Known as the "Queen of the Line," the depot reflects Stick/Eastlake-style construction. This depot replaced the original depot, built in 1869, which burned after a spark from a passing locomotive caught the roof afire. Madison Township farmers also shipped goods and traveled from Canal Winchester. In 1877, 108 cars of grain were shipped from Canal Winchester in one week. The depot now houses Canal Winchester railroad artifacts and is part of a historical complex in the village at Oak and High streets featuring the renovated O. P. Chaney grain elevator and the Prentiss School, a one room school house.

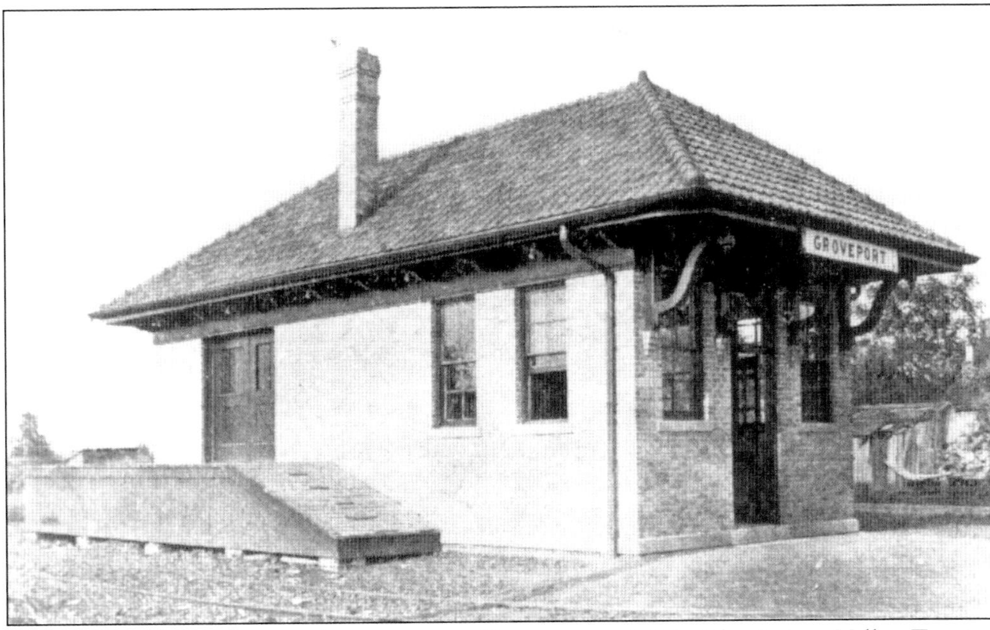

Scioto Valley Traction Line Depot, Groveport, 1908. The Scioto Valley Traction Line Depot sat on what is now a vacant lot on the northwest corner of Blacklick Street and Brooke Alley. The traction line, an electric railroad, opened in Groveport in 1904 and operated passenger service in the area until 1930, when cars and buses made it obsolete.

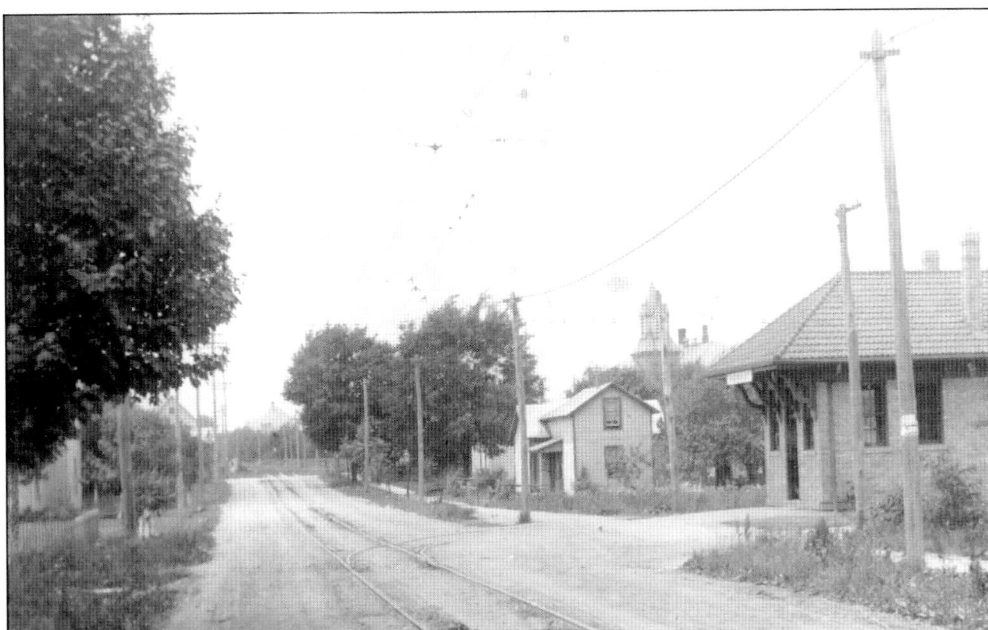

Scioto Valley Traction Line, Groveport, c. 1908. This view of Groveport's Blacklick Street looking west shows the Scioto Valley Traction Line tracks on the street before it was paved with bricks. The traction line depot is to the right. The tower in the center rear is the former Groveport School that once stood on College Street.

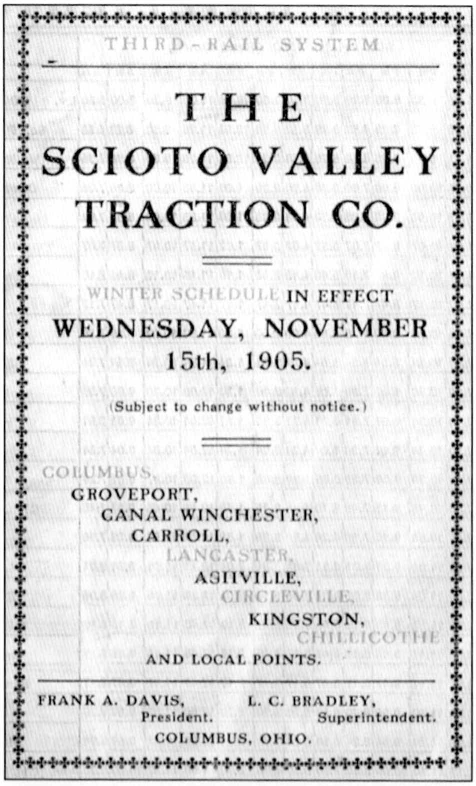

THIRD-RAIL SYSTEM

THE SCIOTO VALLEY TRACTION CO.

WINTER SCHEDULE IN EFFECT
WEDNESDAY, NOVEMBER 15th, 1905.

(Subject to change without notice.)

COLUMBUS,
GROVEPORT,
CANAL WINCHESTER,
CARROLL,
LANCASTER,
ASHVILLE,
CIRCLEVILLE,
KINGSTON,
CHILLICOTHE
AND LOCAL POINTS.

FRANK A. DAVIS, President.
L. C. BRADLEY, Superintendent.
COLUMBUS, OHIO.

SCIOTO VALLEY TRACTION LINE SCHEDULE. The traction line made Columbus and the surrounding area easier travel destinations for jobs and shopping for Groveport and Madison Township residents. It marked the beginning of Groveport becoming a Columbus suburb as people no longer had to live close to where they worked or shopped.

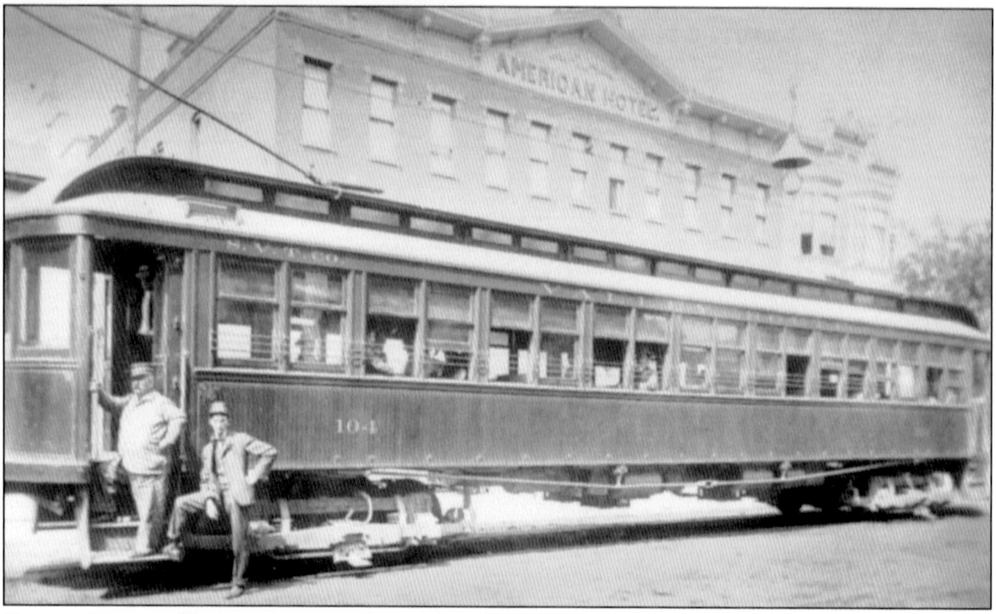

SCIOTO VALLEY TRACTION LINE CAR. This photo is representative of the type of traction line passenger cars that came through Madison Township. Scioto Valley Traction Line cars could reach speeds of up to 60 miles per hour. On July 19, 1904, the first car ran on the line from Columbus to Canal Winchester. The five mile trip between Groveport and Canal Winchester took a mere five minutes, much to the delight of the riders.

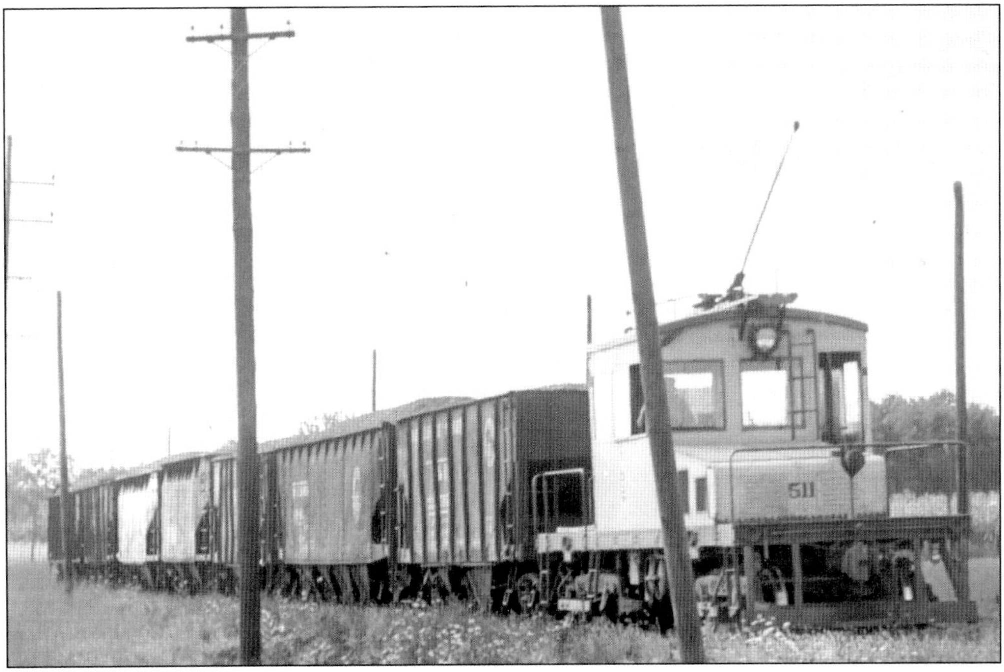

SCIOTO VALLEY TRACTION LINE COAL TRAIN AND ENGINE. After passenger service waned, the traction line still hauled freight until the mid 1950s. This freight included coal delivery from Groveport to the Pickaway Power Plant. A loaded coal train is pictured above. Below is a traction line engine used to haul freight on the line until the electric rail system was shut down in the 1950s.

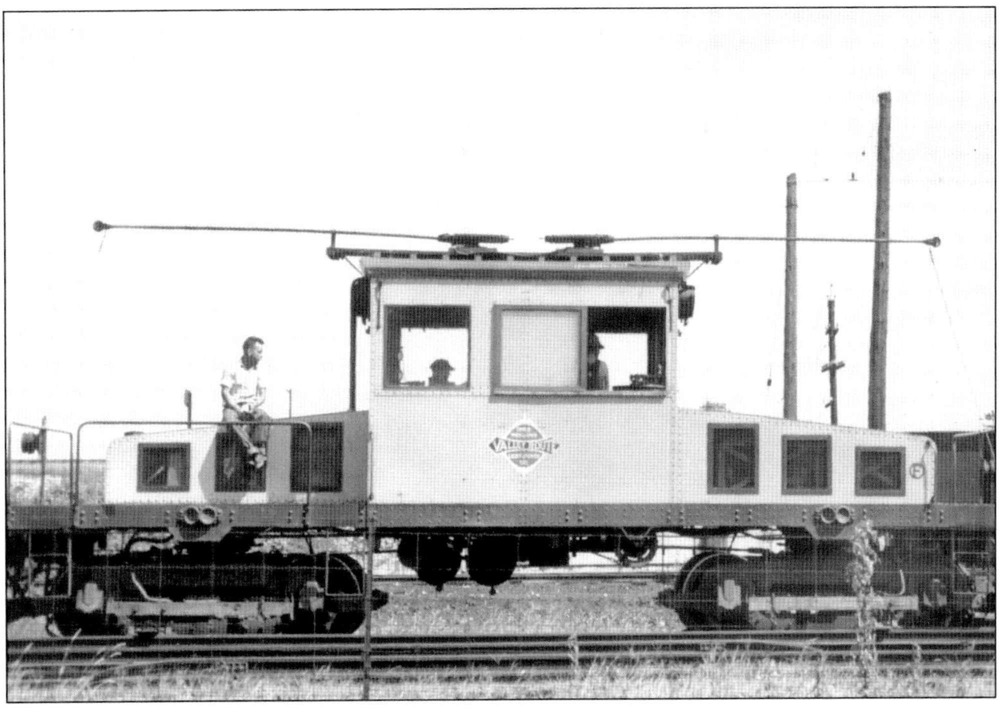

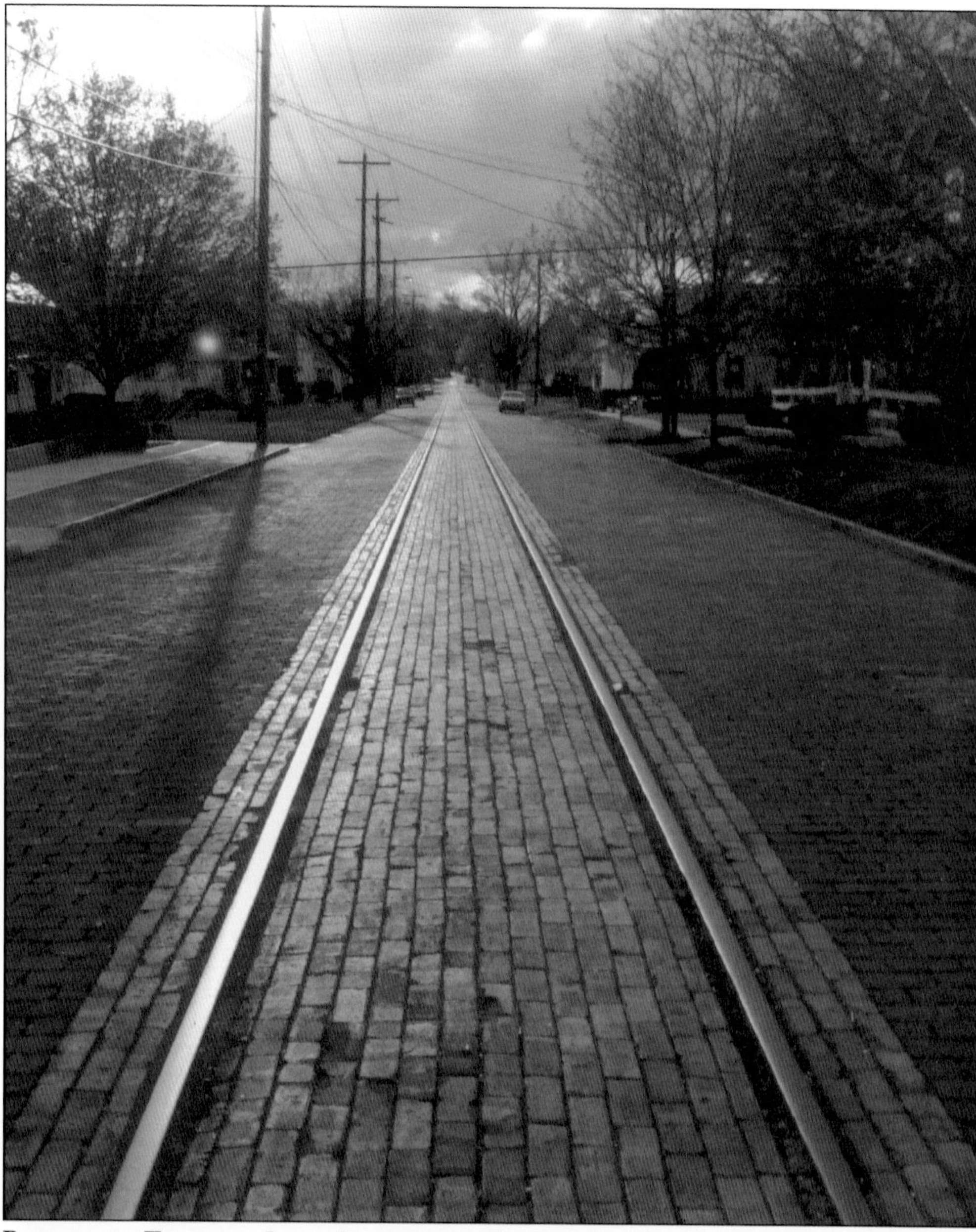

REMAINS OF TRACTION LINE, GROVEPORT. The Scioto Valley Traction Line tracks remain preserved embedded in Groveport's Blacklick Street. The electric railway played a major role in the growth of the village as the town's population nearly doubled from 519 in 1900 to 946 in 1930. The village's newfound accessibility via the traction line—or as it was also known, the "interurban"—opened new options for residents. Originally, the traction line right of way was planned to go directly down Groveport's Main Street. Village council decided to move it to the lesser traveled Blacklick Street to lessen the potential danger to traffic. Remnants of the traction line right-of-way can still be seen on the south side of Groveport Road west of Groveport, and on the north side of Groveport Road near Canal Winchester. Portions of the former traction line depot in Canal Winchester can be partially seen at the rear of some High Street commercial buildings just south of Waterloo Street.

Three

SCHOOLS

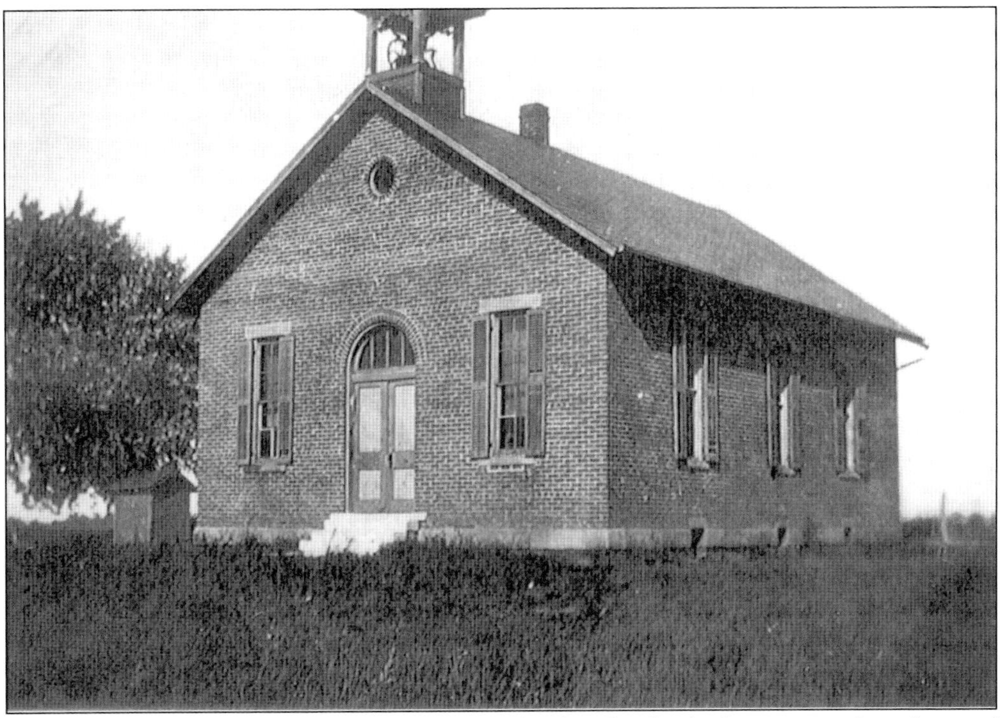

MUDSOCK SCHOOL, MADISON TOWNSHIP. Mudsock School, which once stood southeast of Groveport, is typical of the one-room schoolhouses that dotted rural Madison Township in the nineteenth and early twentieth centuries. Before public schools came into being in the township in 1848, most educating was done in private academies such as Richardson's Academy at Groveport and Richardson roads or the Rarey Academy just southwest of town.

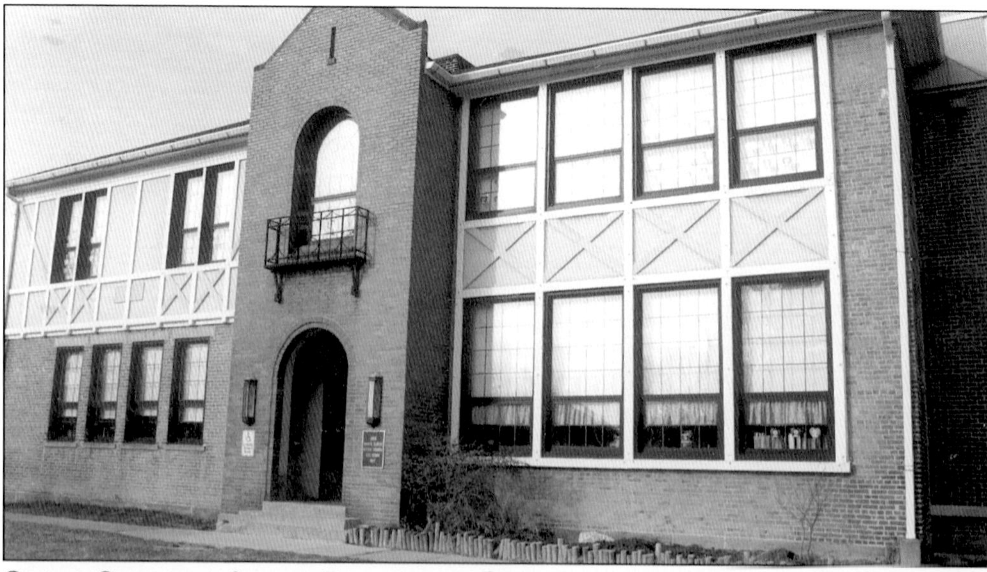

OLDEST OPERATING SCHOOL BUILDING IN OHIO, CANAL WINCHESTER. The oldest school building in continuous operation in Ohio, this building opened in 1862, and is now connected to Canal Winchester Middle School on Washington Street. While most Madison Township students attend Groveport Madison schools, some, along with students from Fairfield County, attend Canal Winchester schools.

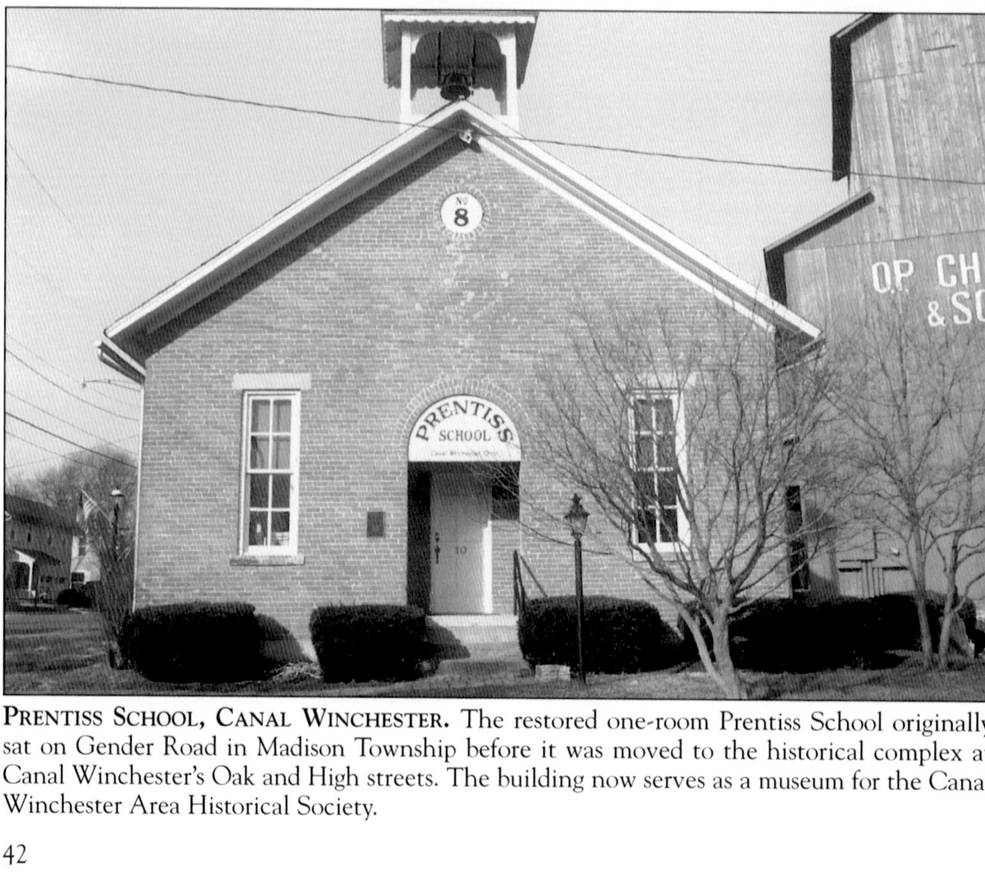

PRENTISS SCHOOL, CANAL WINCHESTER. The restored one-room Prentiss School originally sat on Gender Road in Madison Township before it was moved to the historical complex at Canal Winchester's Oak and High streets. The building now serves as a museum for the Canal Winchester Area Historical Society.

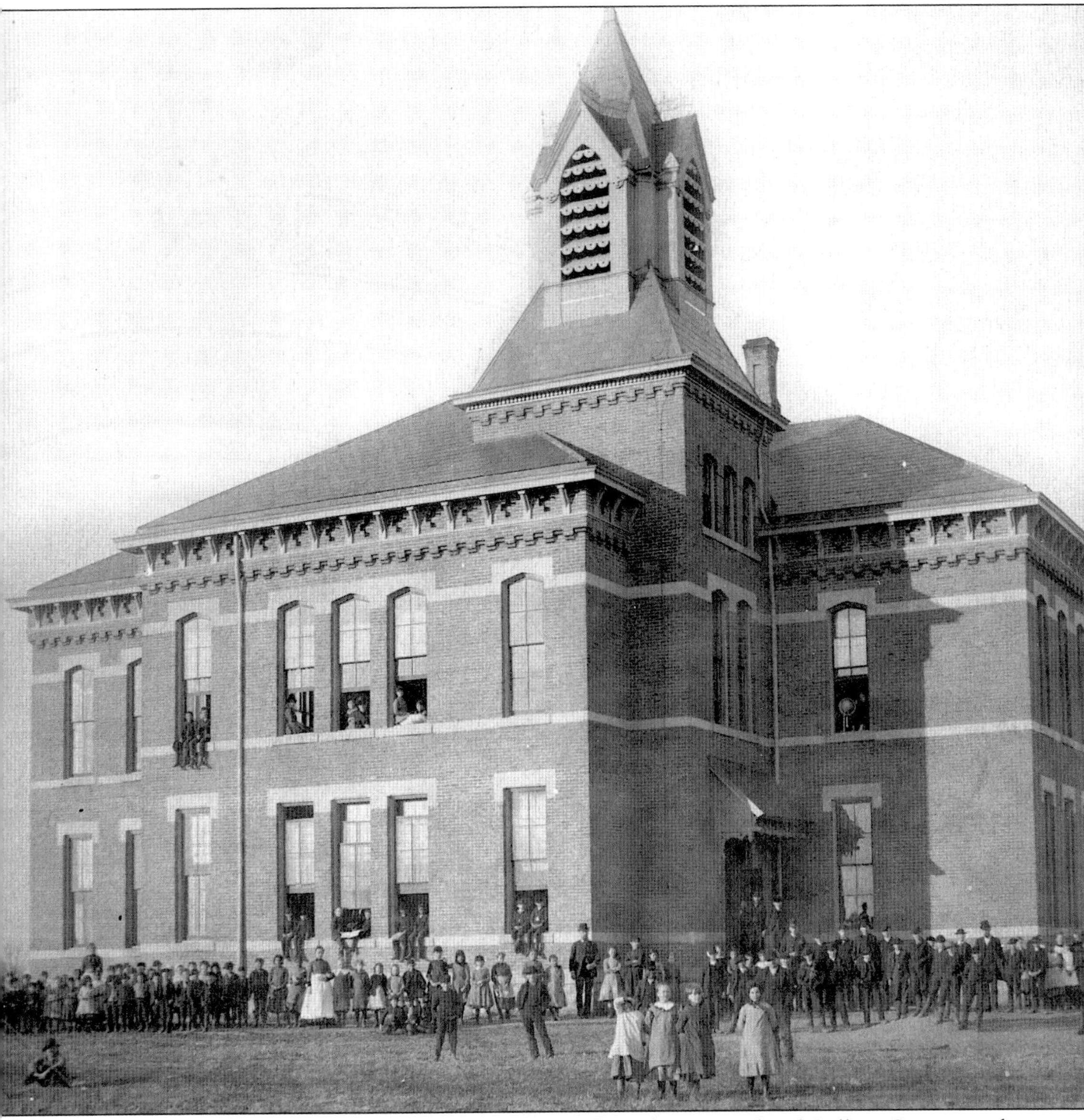

GROVEPORT SCHOOL, C. 1910. This school, located on the west side of College Street north of Blacklick Street and built in 1884 at a cost of $10,634, housed all 12 grades. It was expanded in 1912, when two classrooms and a laboratory were added, and in 1919 two portable rooms were attached to accommodate the growing Groveport Madison school district. The school was surrounded by a large playground with athletic fields for football, baseball, and track and field. According to Groveport Madison Alumni Association records, 411 students earned their high school diploma at this school during its years of operation. Students walked or rode horses or carriages to school and stabled their horses at a livery on nearby Blacklick Street. At noon each school day the students went to the stable to tend to their horses. By 1921, the school became too small and the district's citizens voted to maintain three elementary schools—one each in Groveport, Edwards Station, and Brice—and a high school in Groveport. This decision was also in harmony with the State of Ohio's desire in the post-World War I era to see more school districts consolidated and centralized.

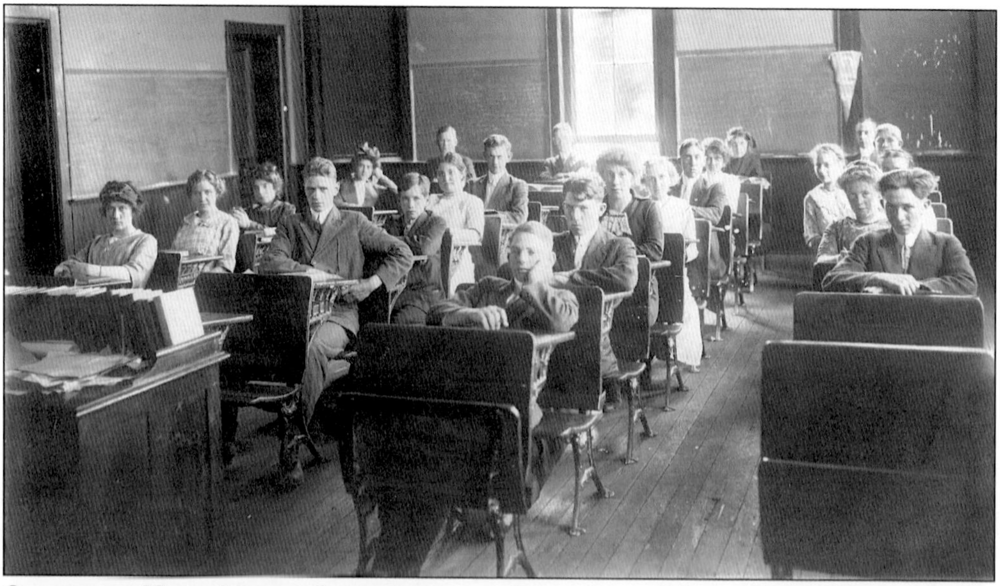

Groveport High School Classroom, c. 1910. This is a high school classroom at the Groveport School on College Street. Note the formal attire and serious countenances of the students. The room is sparse and relied heavily on natural light from the windows. Though a heat stove is not visible, one must have been present. Chalkboards lined the room.

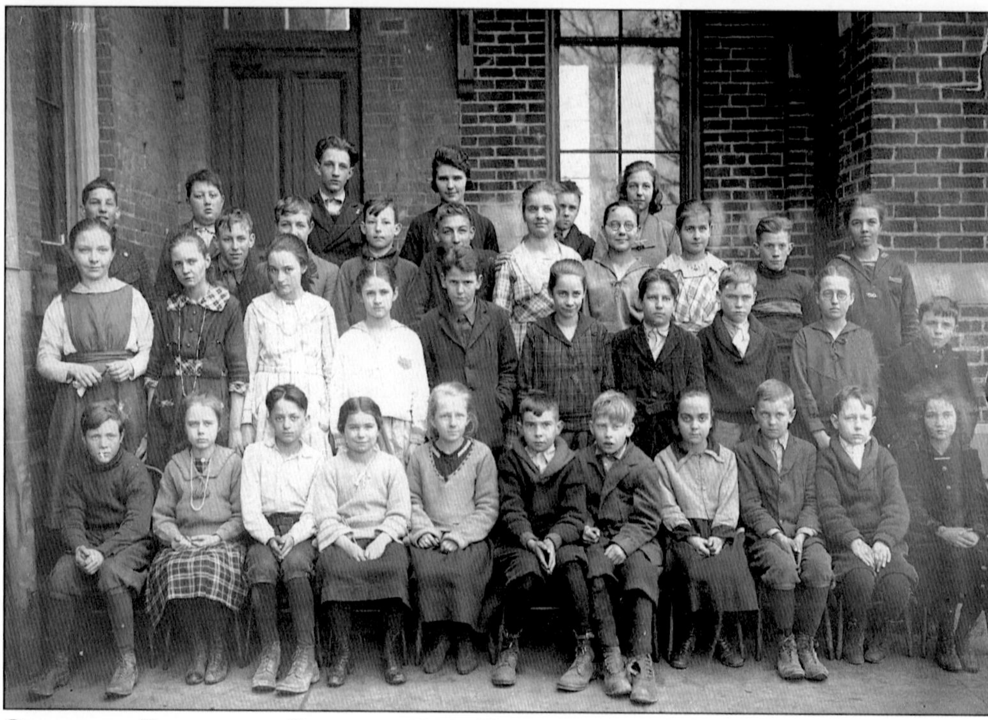

Groveport Elementary Class, c. 1910. This is a group of elementary school students at the Groveport School on College Street. Once again note the formal clothing and serious outlook of the children. Many of these students were farm children who had to wedge their studies between completing farm chores before and after school.

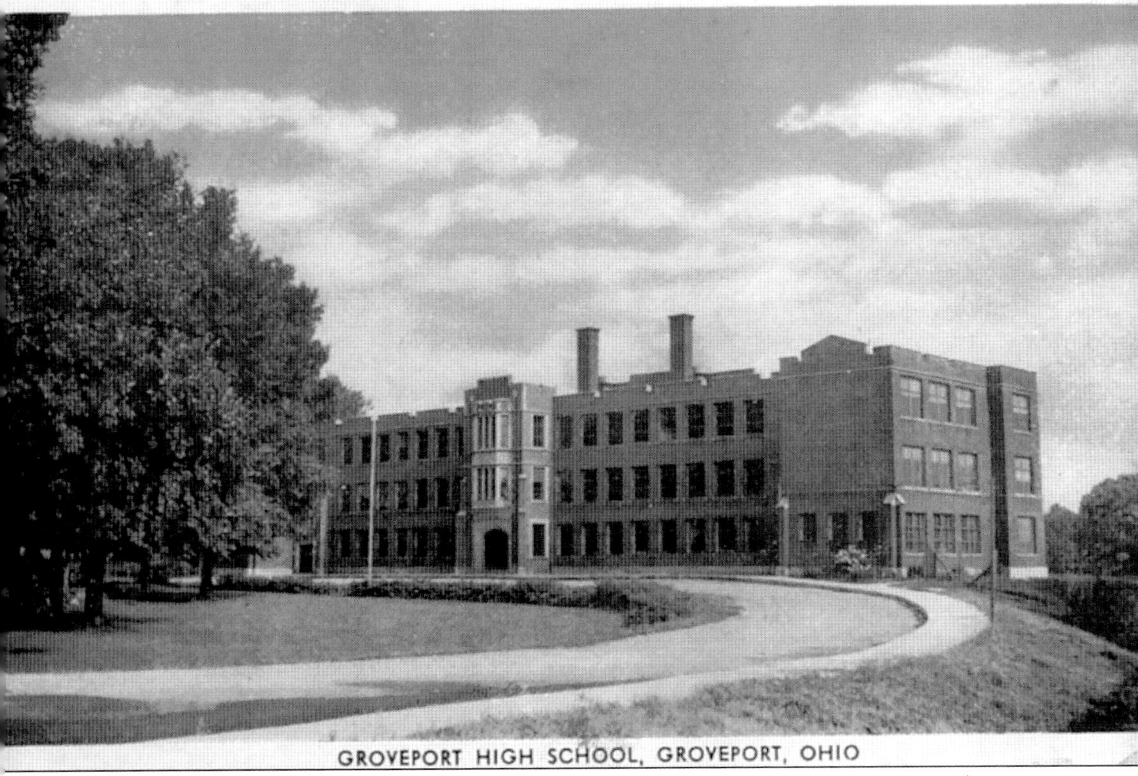

GROVEPORT SCHOOL, C. 1940. Built in 1923 on Groveport's Main Street at a cost of $225,000, this three-story red brick building housed all 12 grades until the mid 1950s. The school was built at the eastern edge of Groveport's business district on pasture land once owned by the Rarey family. The structure features interior glazed brick walls as well as a separate gymnasium and auditorium, which is unique for buildings of its era that often combined the auditorium and gymnasium into one room. Ten acres of playground and athletic fields ring the structure. A large, tree-filled courtyard with an attractive stone fountain fronts the building. For many years the school, along with Groveport Town Hall, was the hub of the community's social life. Farmers' exhibits, lyceum courses, plays, musical performances, as well as a variety of school functions kept this building full of the energy of community life. The building remains in use as an elementary school and has recently undergone extensive restoration.

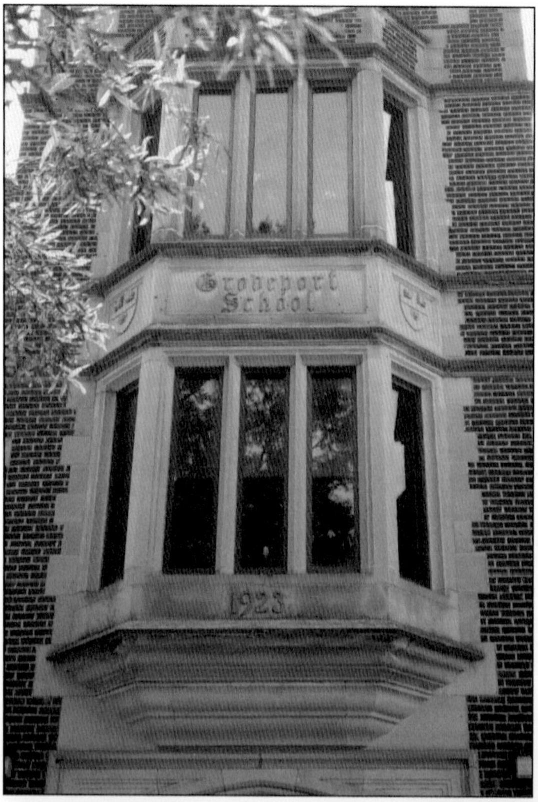

GROVEPORT SCHOOL FACADE. This photo shows some of the decorative architectural features of the Groveport School on Main Street. Many Ohio schools built in the nineteenth and early twentieth centuries exhibited architectural flourishes that set the buildings apart. In many ways the early schools almost have a design similar to simple churches while post-World War II school buildings tend to look more like office buildings, perhaps reflecting a culture change from a more philosophical viewpoint to one of commercial practicality.

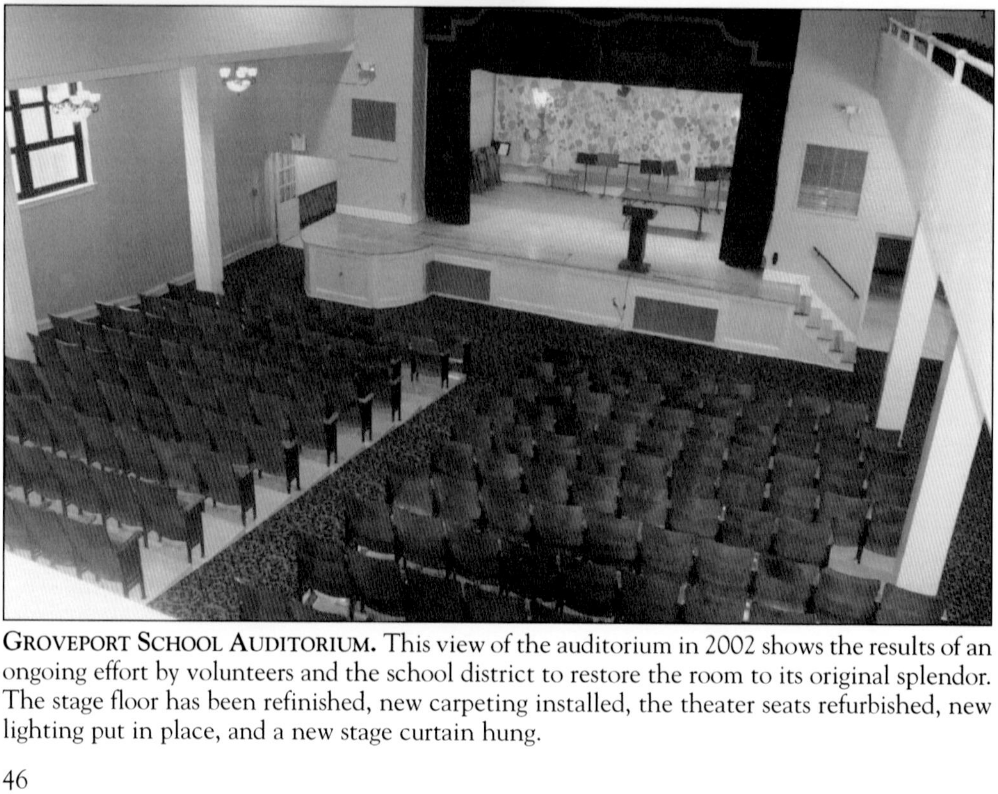

GROVEPORT SCHOOL AUDITORIUM. This view of the auditorium in 2002 shows the results of an ongoing effort by volunteers and the school district to restore the room to its original splendor. The stage floor has been refinished, new carpeting installed, the theater seats refurbished, new lighting put in place, and a new stage curtain hung.

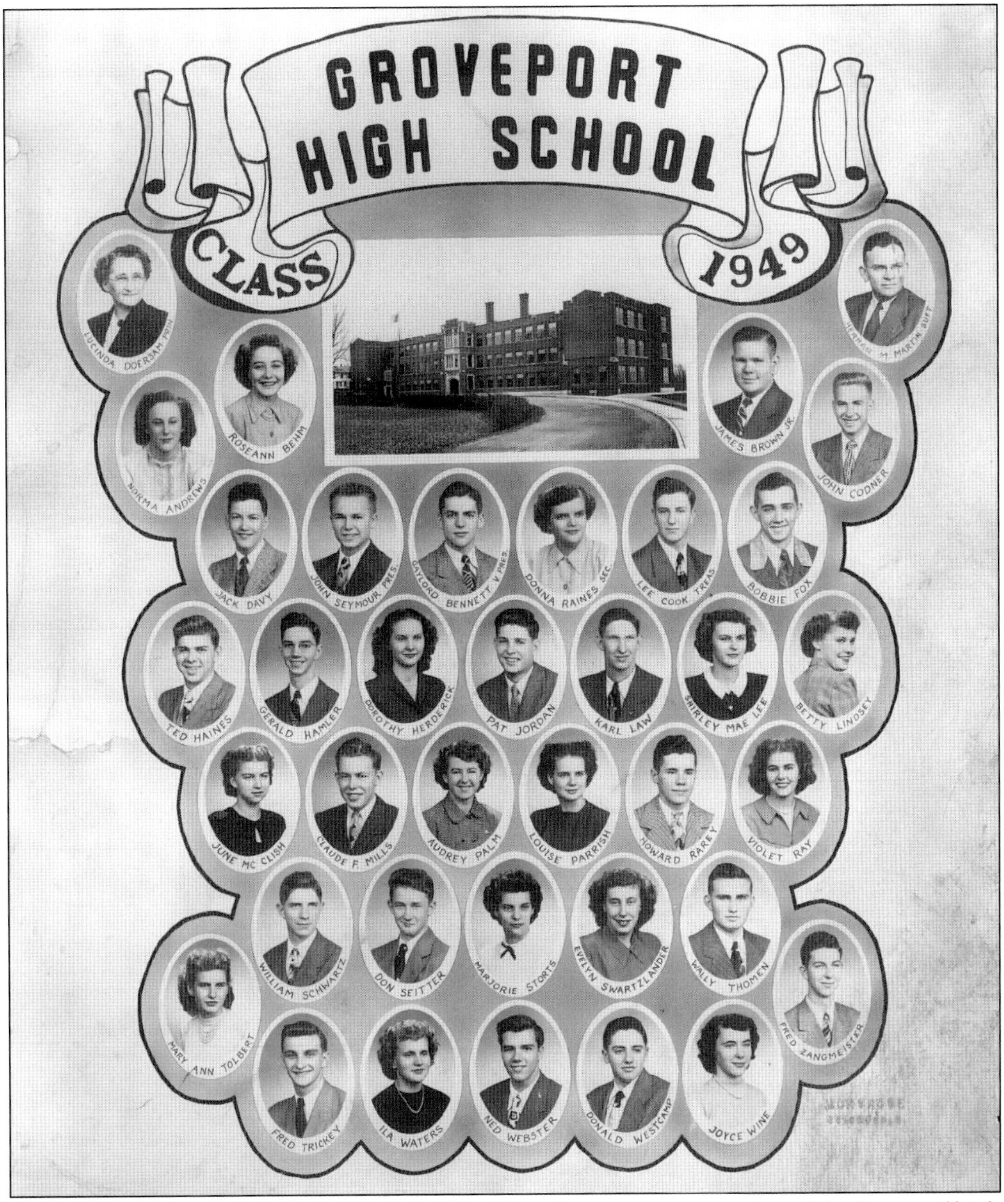

GROVEPORT HIGH SCHOOL CLASS OF 1949. This photo is representative of the layout of high school class pictures through much of the school district's history. The population growth of the school district can be easily tracked by looking how the number of photos on these placards grew from just a handful of faces in the district's early days to modern graduating classes of more than three hundred. Reading from the top left, from left to right, then down, are Lucinda Doersam, principal; Herman Martin, superintendent; Norma Andrews, Roseann Behm, James Brown Jr., John Codner, Jack Davy, John Seymour, Gaylord Bennett, Donna Raines, Lee Cook, Bobbie Fox, Ted Haines, Gerald Hamler, Dorothy Herderick, Pat Jordan, Karl Law, Shirey Mae Lee, Betty Lindsey, June McClish, Claude Mills, Audrey Palm, Louise Parrish, Howard Rarey, Violet Ray, William Schwartz, Don Seitter, Marjorie Storts, Eveyln Swartzlander, Wally Thomen, Mary Ann Tolbert, Fred Trickey, Ila Waters, Ned Webster, Donald Westcamp, Joyce Wine, and Fred Zangmeister.

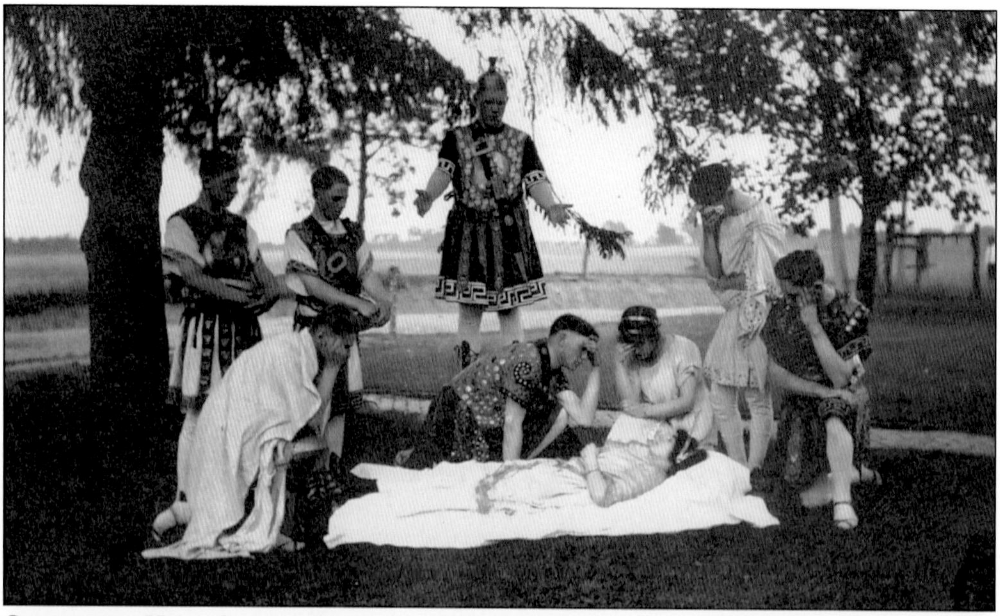

GROVEPORT HIGH SCHOOL PLAY, C. 1912. The Latin class at Groveport Madison High School rehearses a play on the lawn of the Elmont Hotel. Here, student Lawrence Leyshon's character delivers a eulogy. The only other identified actor is Howard Hanstein, on Leyshon's right. Students often made their own costumes for plays.

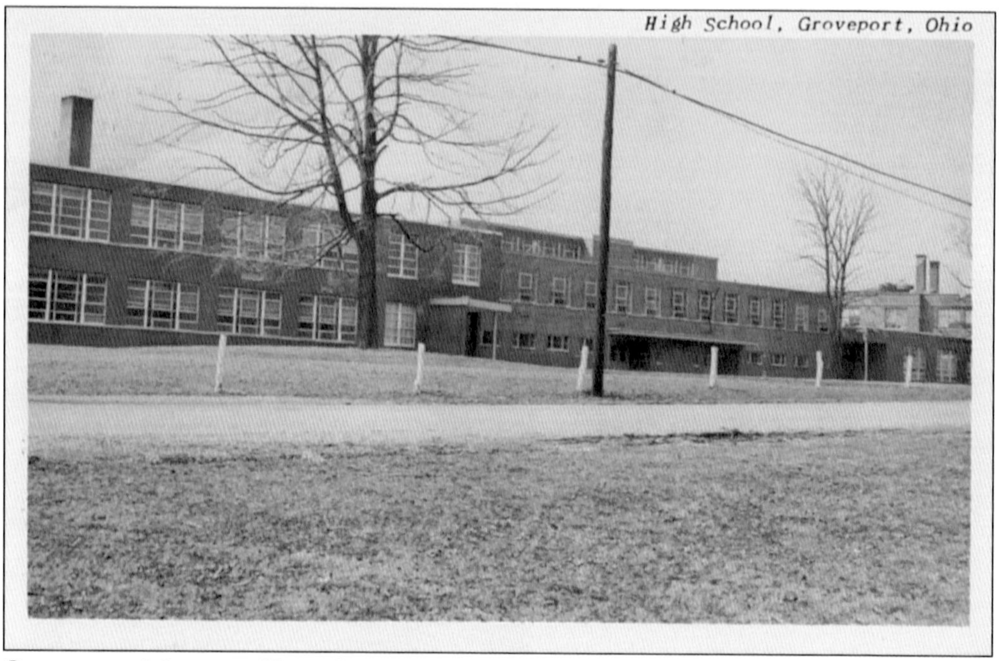

GROVEPORT MADISON HIGH SCHOOL, C. 1958. The Groveport Madison School District constructed this building in stages throughout the 1950s to accommodate its growing number of students, first building the gymnasium and then adding classrooms as funds became available. It is located on Main Street in Groveport, next to the Groveport Elementary. It served as the district's high school until 1971.

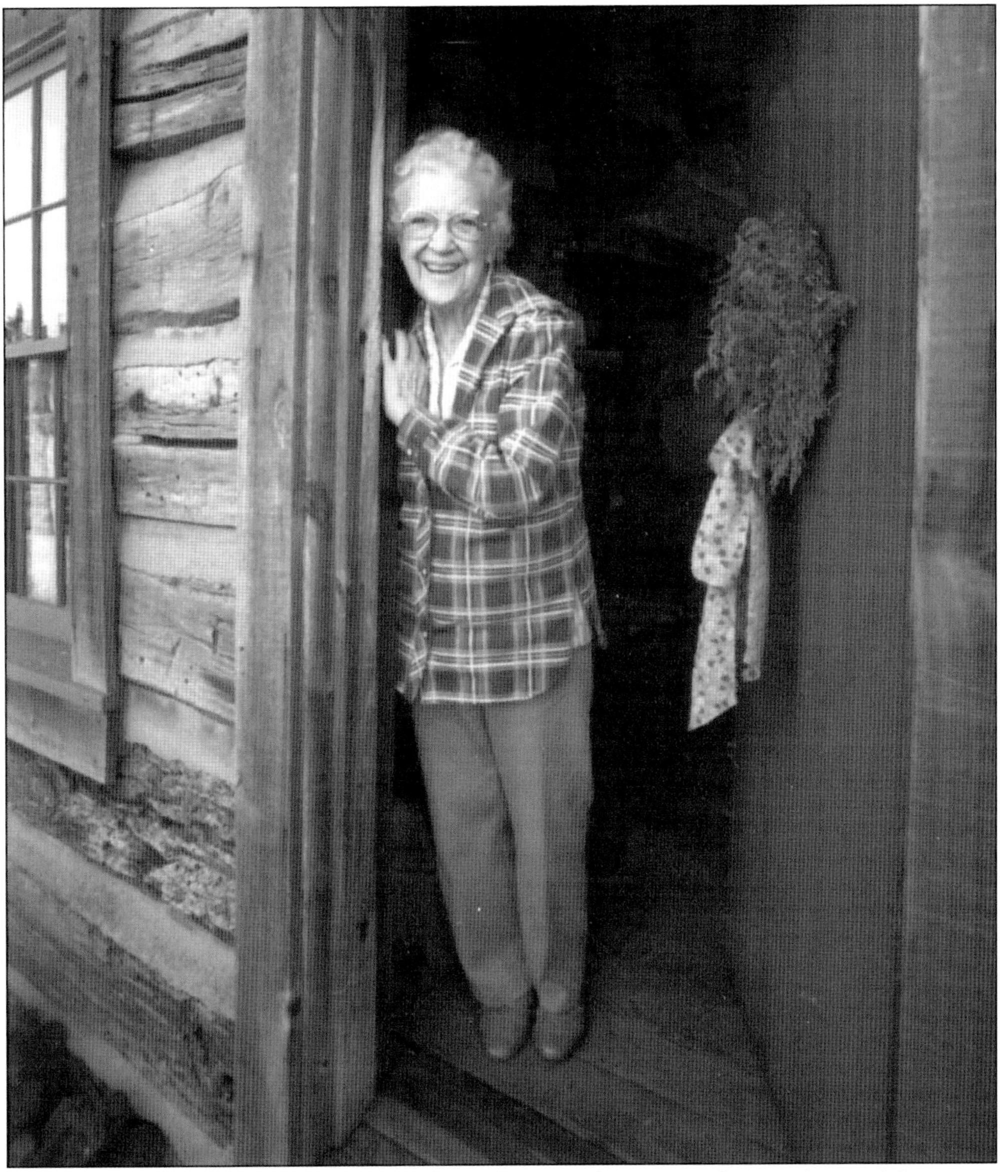

NORA CARRUTHERS. She was born Nora Dowler in Madison Township southeast of Groveport in 1903. Nora excelled at academics as well as sports, being a member of the 1919 undefeated Groveport girls basketball team. Married in 1928 to Carol Carruthers, Nora began her teaching career in a one room schoolhouse and was a teacher in the Groveport Madison School District for most of her career. She, along with Naomi McGuire, started the first kindergarten in the district in 1955. (She also taught Sunday School at the Lutheran Church from time she was 18 until age 87.) She retired from the school district in 1965, but she never stopped teaching. Following her retirement she immersed herself in community activities. Of particular note is her work with the Groveport Heritage and Preservation Society (which she helped form in 1972) where she conducted a one-room school house program at the log house in Heritage Park for elementary students. Through this program she was able to give modern students a feel for how children of the past learned using slate chalkboards and other simpler materials. Nora passed away in 1994. (Photo courtesy of Mary Circelli.)

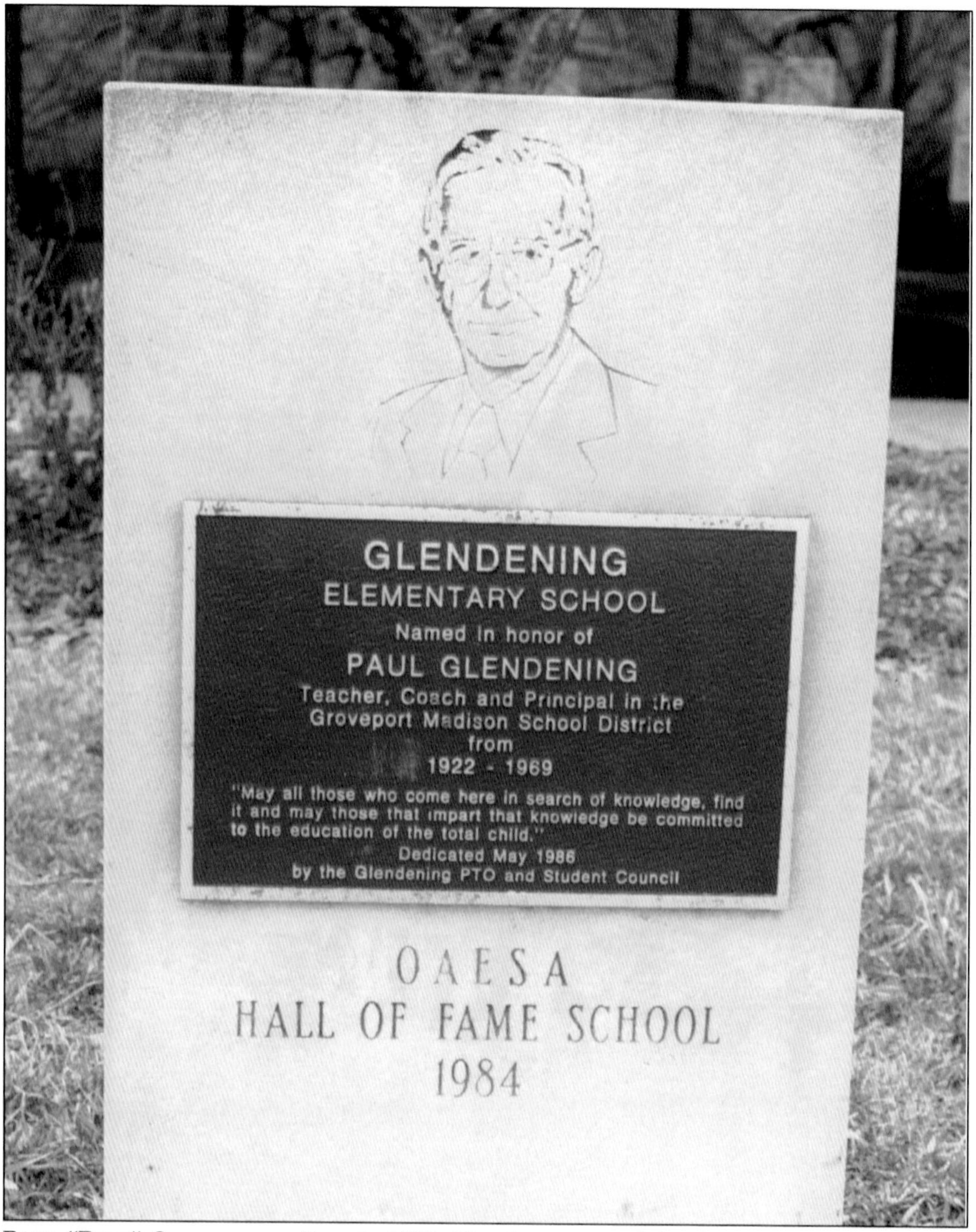

PAUL "PETE" GLENDENING. Born in 1898, Glendening served the Groveport Madison school district as a teacher, coach, and principal for 47 years from 1922 to 1969. Glendening was capable of teaching a variety of subjects and coached boys football, basketball, and baseball squads as well as girls basketball and softball teams at all grade levels. Glendening also worked as a house painter in the summers (as teaching was not a well paid profession) and enjoyed a good reputation for his work. He ended his career as the principal of Groveport Elementary. Glendening Elementary School, built in 1971, and Glendening Drive in Groveport are named in his honor. Glendening, and his wife Lillian, lived in a home they purchased in 1948 on Groveport's east Main Street, just a few houses down from Groveport School where he spent his career. He passed away in 1978 at the age of 80.

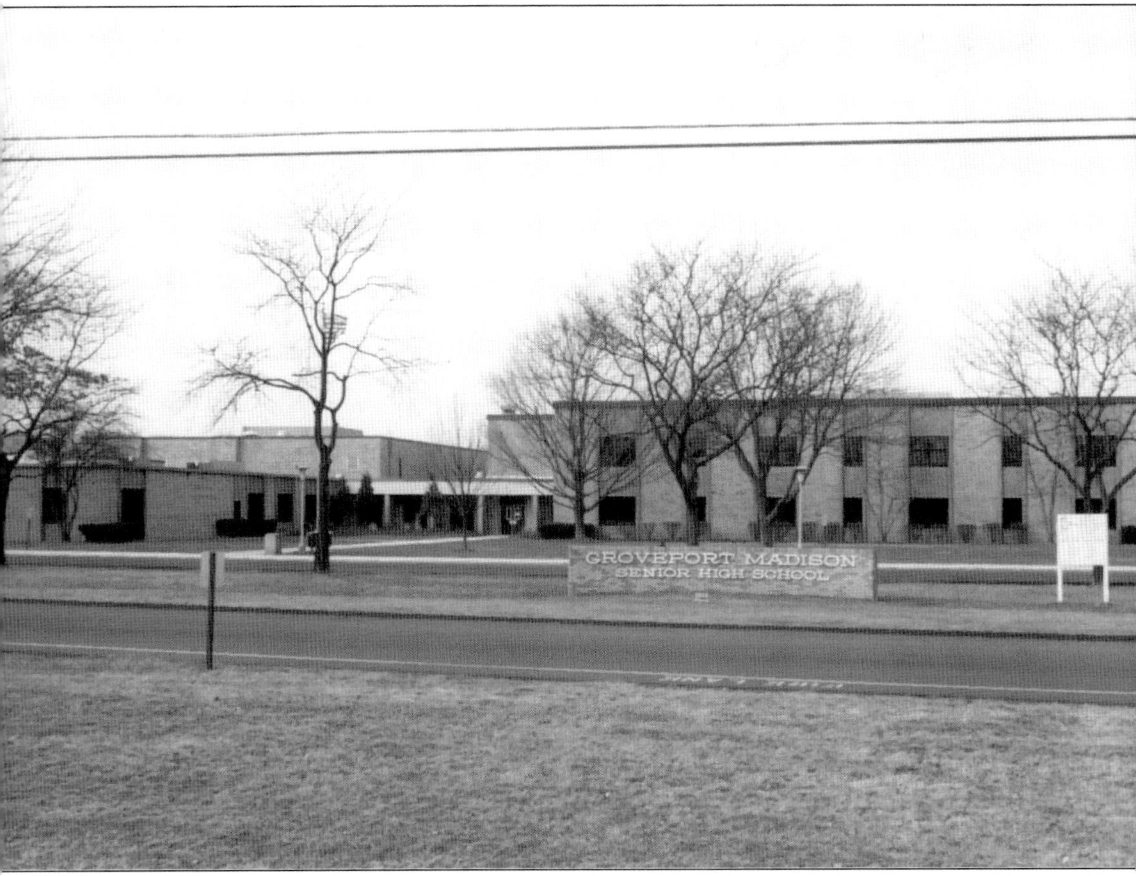

GROVEPORT MADISON HIGH SCHOOL, 2002. Built originally as a junior high school on South Hamilton Road in 1968, this building became Groveport Madison High School in 1971 and still serves the district in this capacity. Besides its classroom space, the school boasts an auditorium, gymnasium, library, laboratories, Cruiser Stadium, baseball and soccer fields, and tennis courts. The building is centrally located in Madison Township as the school district made use of its township section 16 land along the northern banks of Blacklick Creek that was set aside for schools' use when the township was originally formed. Rapid growth and crowding in the school district in the latter half of the twentieth and early twenty-first centuries has necessitated that high school freshman attend a separate school, the former high school on Groveport's Main Street.

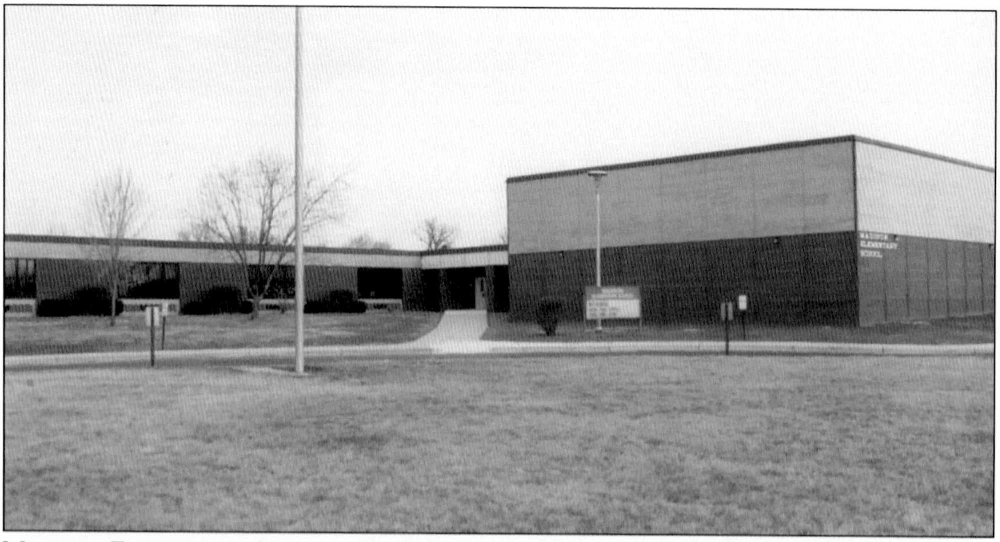

Madison Elementary School. The baby boom of the post-World War II era had a significant impact on Madison Township. The demand for housing led to the development of acres and acres of township farm land into residential subdivisions and commercial entities. To meet this need the school district built five elementary schools in the late 1960s and early 1970s. Located in Blacklick Estates, Madison Elementary, pictured here in 2002, is representative of the architecture of these schools.

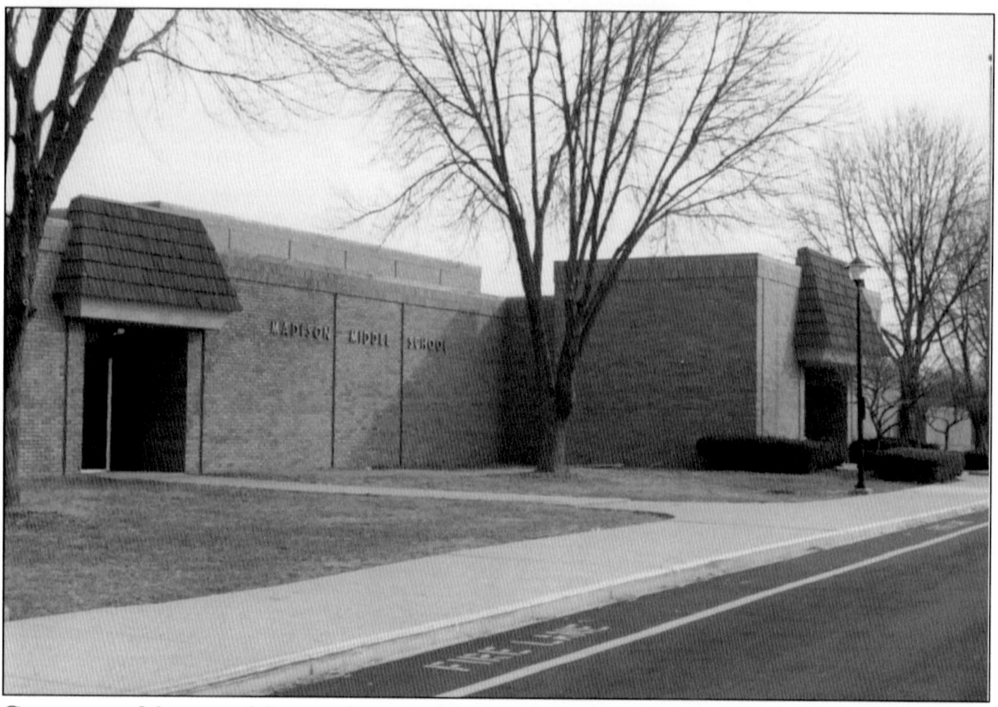

Groveport Madison Middle School North. Likewise, the growth in student population called for more middle school space in the district. In 1975, the district built Middle School South in Groveport and Middle School North in northern Madison Township (pictured here in 2002) to accommodate this rapid increase in students.

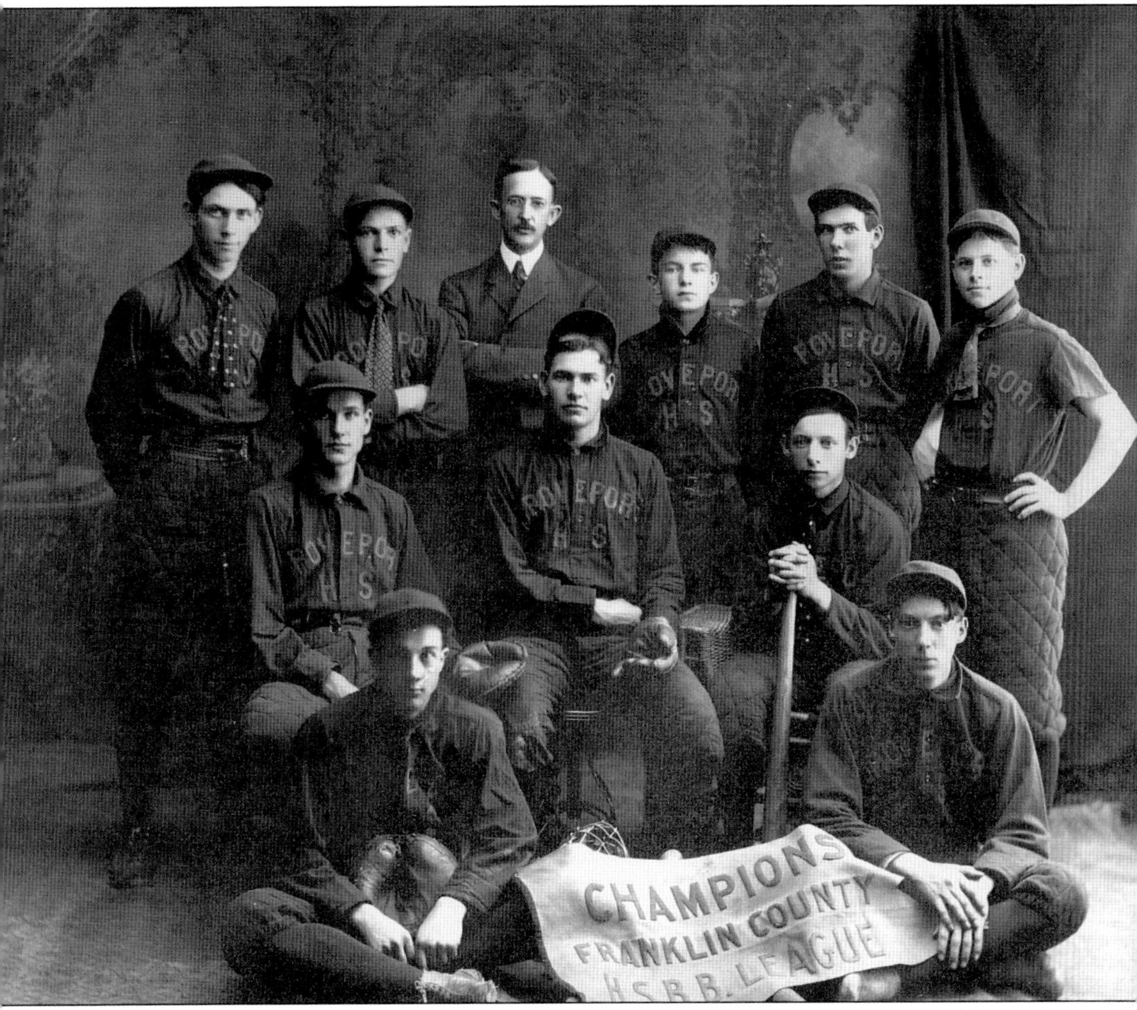

FRANKLIN COUNTY BASEBALL CHAMPIONS, 1906-07. Over the past one hundred years Groveport has competed in the Franklin County League (until 1957), the Mid Eight League (until 1974), and the Ohio Capital Conference (presently) in a variety of sports. Throughout its athletic history Groveport Madison High School has won its share it league championships both in team and individual sports. Baseball, a sport rooted in America's agrarian past, was one of the first sports to be embraced by the primarily agricultural community. Pictured here are the 1906-07 Franklin County League baseball champions, from left to right: (front row) Ernest Rarey and Ora Morehart; (middle row) Vernon Wildermuth, Elmer Weise, and Clem Lincoln; (back row) four unidentified members, Bert Wildermuth, and Claude Adell.

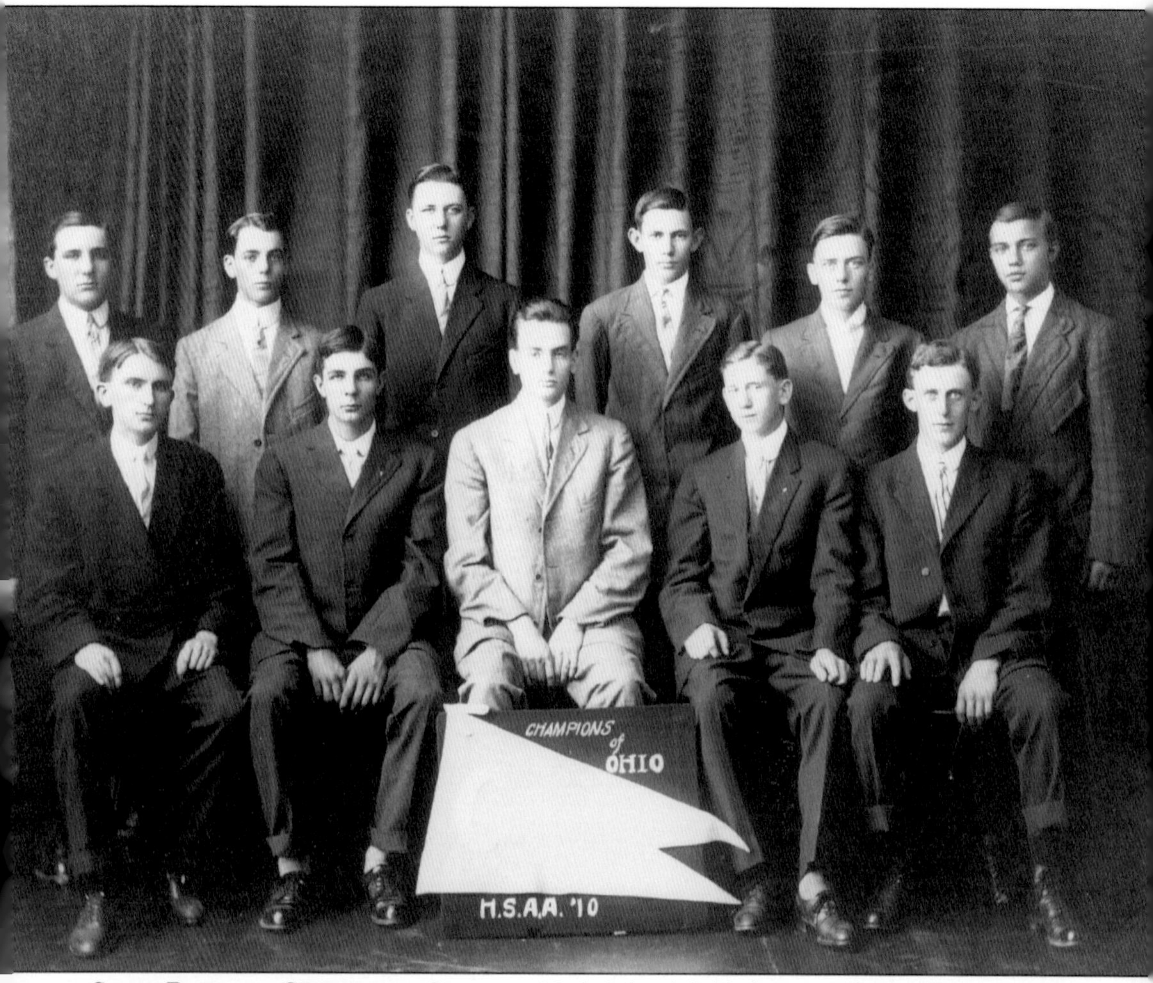

STATE BASEBALL CHAMPIONS. Groveport High School fielded a state championship baseball team in 1910. The team played its home games in a field by the former Groveport High School on College Street. Team members were, from left to right: (front row) Lester Peterman, Russell Wildermuth, Leo Kile, Grover Peters, and Clarence Wildermuth; (back row) Joseph Zwayer, Dorwin Sims, Walter Koebel, Ralph Rainier, Ray Nothstine, and Warren Rarey. Sims would later graduate from Ohio State University and return in 1919 as a teacher and assistant principal at Groveport. In 1920, he became principal and in 1924 rose to the position of school district superintendent. It was Sims, while serving as superintendent, who suggested that the Groveport Madison High School athletic teams be known as the Cruisers, in honor of John S. Rarey's fiery stallion.

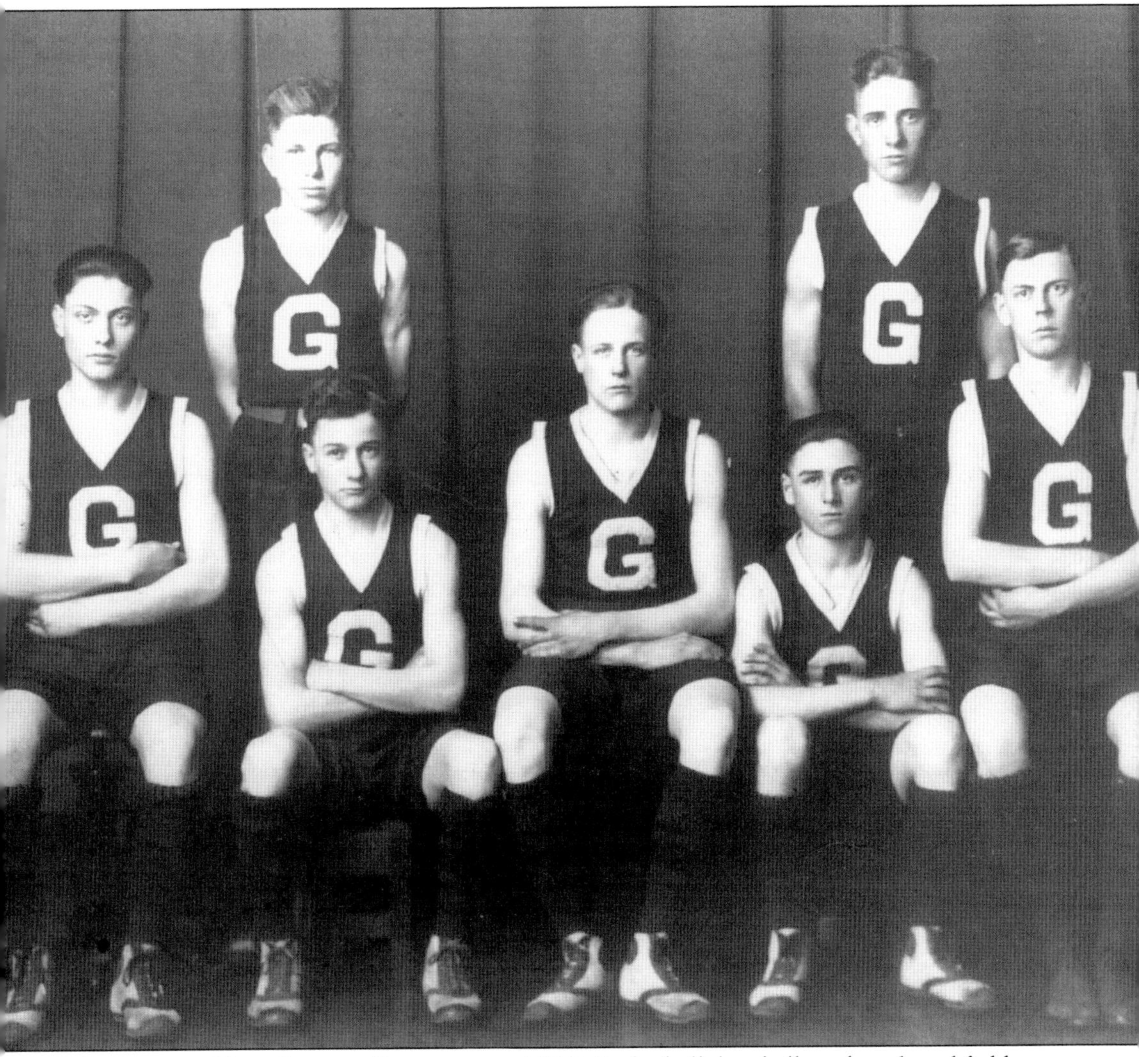

GROVEPORT HIGH SCHOOL BASKETBALL, 1918. Basketball, baseball, and track and field were the primary sports at Groveport High School in the early twentieth century (though football began to catch on in the World War I era). The 1918 basketball squad pictured here played its games in the second-floor auditorium of Groveport Town Hall. The ballroom floor of the auditorium served as the playing court for both boys and girls varsity basketball teams until 1923. Spectators would stand along the sidelines or sit on the auditorium stage. The Town Hall court had a distinct home court edge in that a support pole in the middle of the floor was used to great advantage by the Groveport players to pick off and screen visiting players not familiar with the pole's location. The members of the 1918 team were, from left to right: John Brantner, George Woerlein (standing), Dallas Brobst, Cliff McKee, Ted Steele, Ray Schwartz (standing)ß, and Charles Edwards.

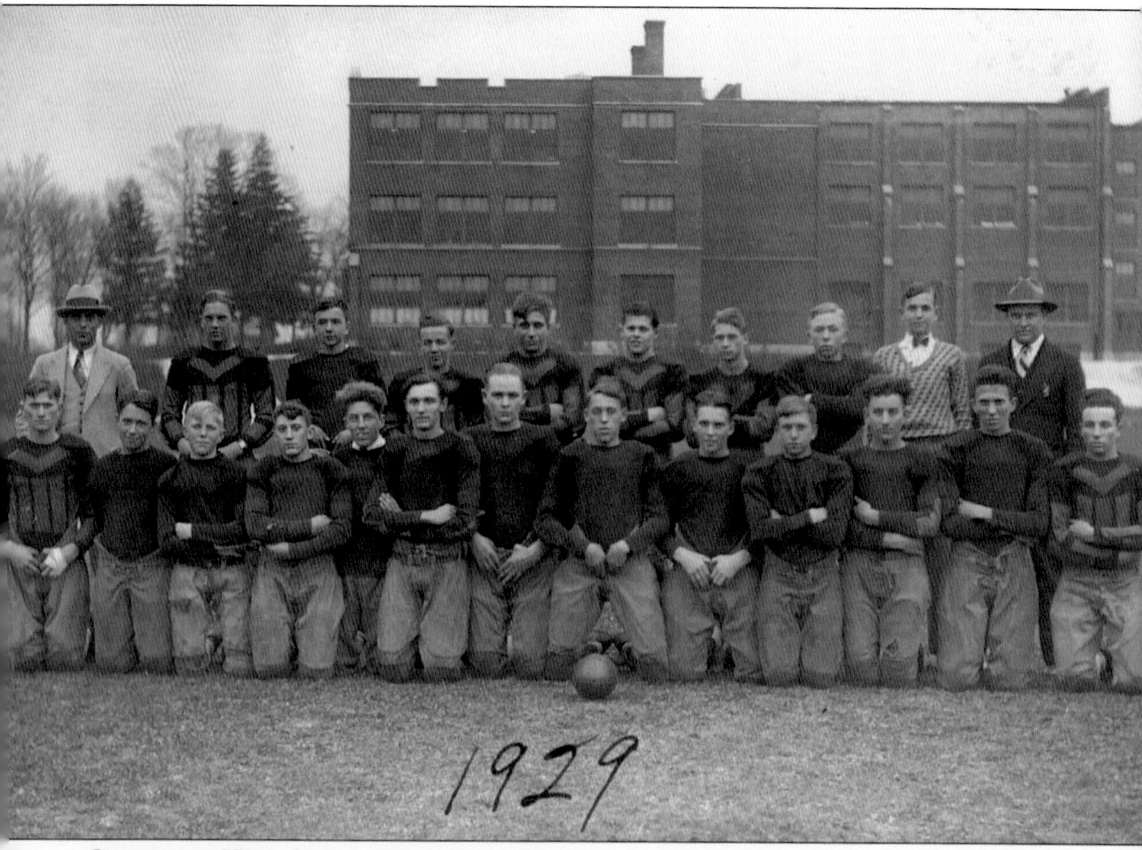

GROVEPORT HIGH SCHOOL FOOTBALL, 1929. The 1929 football squad was one of several in a string of teams that consistently finished at or near the top of the old Franklin County League. This team posed here on the field where they played their games located just west of Groveport School near the old canal route. Pictured here are, from left to right: (front row) Bill Alton, Delbert Simms, John Sachs, Charles Rohr, Paul Johnston, Floyd Heil, Arthur McCollister, "Sport" Vineyard, Kermit Nelson, Robert Kessler, Ob Morgan, Darwin Peer, Lawrence Simms, and Lynn Alkire; (back row) Dorwin Sims, Carl Keely, Leroy McClure, Harley Judy, Herb Rush, Ed Moore, John McCollister, and O. E. Smith. The squad went 7–1–1 and shut out six opponents. Scores were: Groveport 7 Grandview 0; Groveport 27 Mount Sterling 0; Groveport 6 Upper Arlington 6; Groveport 20 Ashville 13; Groveport 0 Bexley 33; Groveport 7 Worthington 0; Groveport 51 Gahanna 0; Groveport 6 Johnstown 0; and Groveport 24 Walnut Township 0.

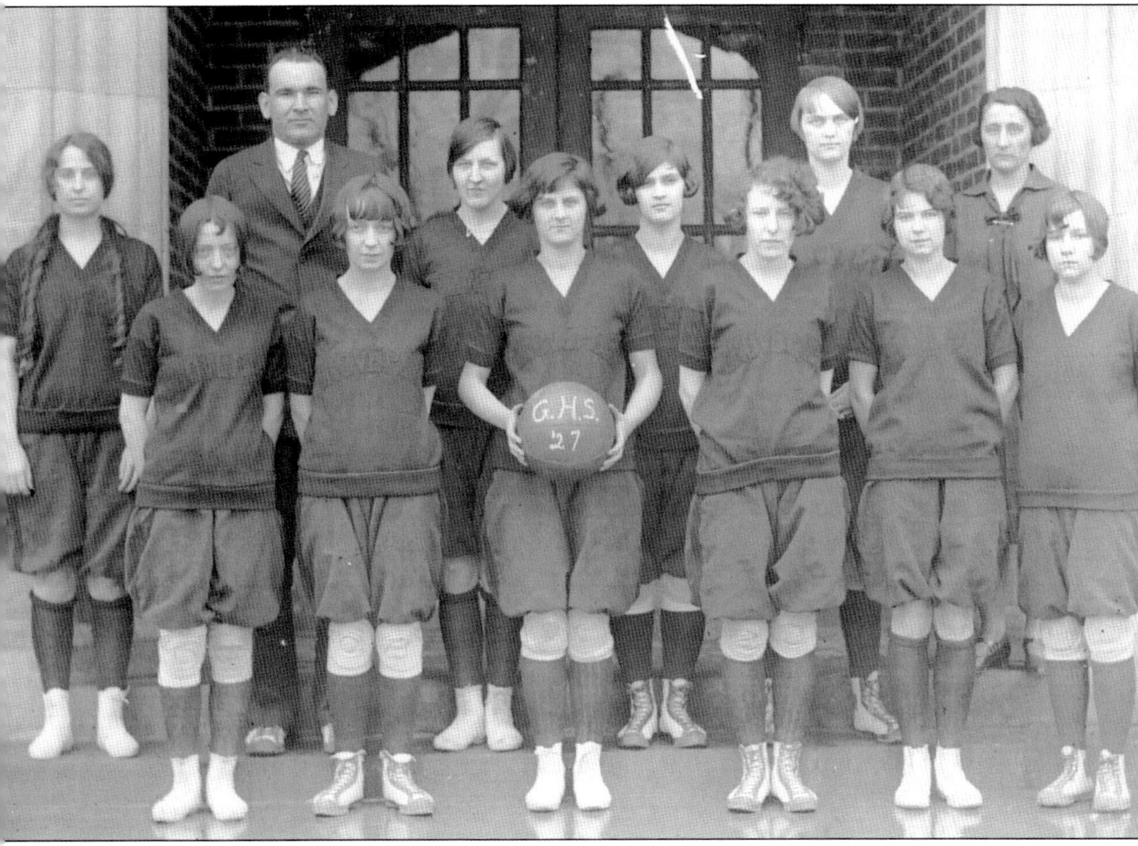

GROVEPORT HIGH SCHOOL GIRLS BASKETBALL, 1927. Groveport High School girls varsity basketball dominated the old Franklin County League in the post-World War I era and well into the 1920s and 1930s. For example, the 1919 team went undefeated winning 23 games in a row. The girls teams consistently drew large crowds to their Groveport Town Hall court and later to the Groveport School gym, where they rarely lost a home game. Team uniforms (which reflected the style of the time and appear cumbersome when compared to the sleek uniforms worn today) were often made by students at the school. This 1927 team took the county championship. Team members were (not in picture order): Irma White, Margaret Heil, Irene Miller, Vivian Knipe, Eloise Wilson, Oneida Mohr, Veva Vance, Electa Nothstine, Iretha Frettinger, Mary Nance, and Edith Nelson. They were coached by Lucinda Doersam.

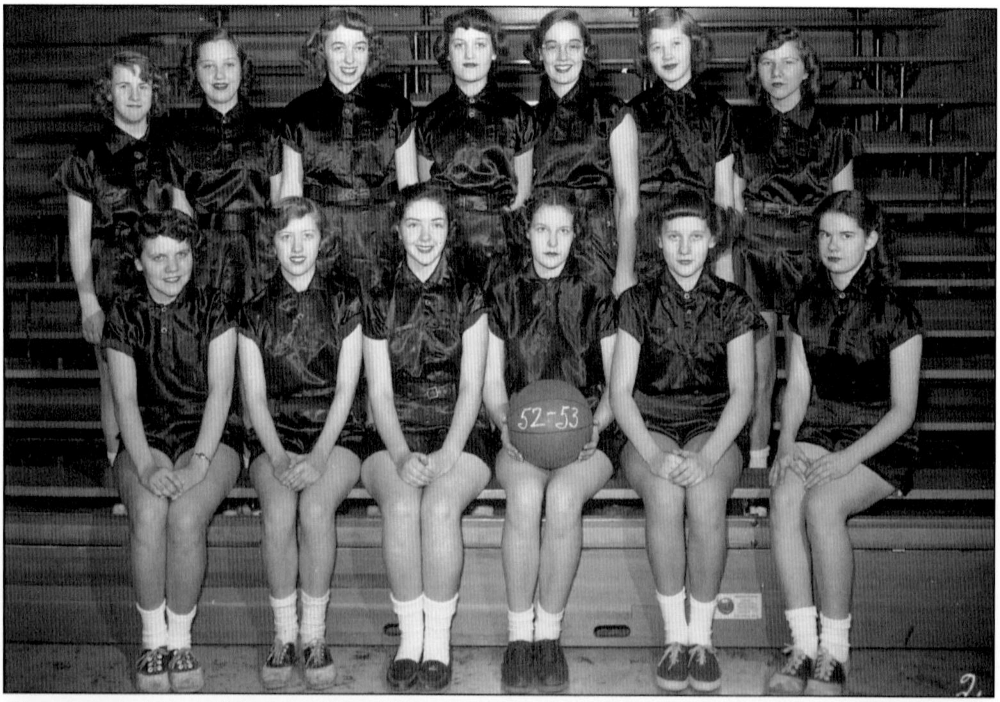

GROVEPORT HIGH SCHOOL GIRLS BASKETBALL, 1952-53. Following World War II, girls varsity basketball was replaced by the intramural girls athletic association. Basketball remained an intramural sport at Groveport and throughout Ohio until Title IX, enacted in the 1970s, reopened the opportunity for girls varsity sports. Groveport Madison High School girls have participated in interscholastic team sports such as basketball, softball, and volleyball in the Ohio Capital Conference since Title IX's inception.

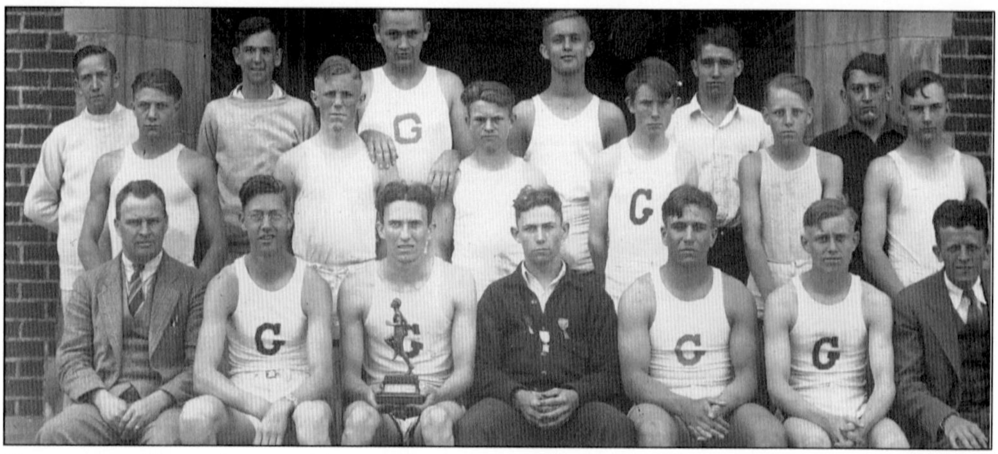

GROVEPORT HIGH SCHOOL TRACK TEAM, C. 1940. Groveport Madison High School has fielded some form of a track and field team throughout its history. One such team is pictured here displaying a trophy of victory. By the mid-1930s the school had a new track and field complex built around the football field located west of the school. The new cinder track, along with high jump, pole vault, and broad jump pits, as well as areas for shotput and discus, were a gift from the classes of 1929-33. The track was used until the late 1970s and the area is now is home to baseball fields.

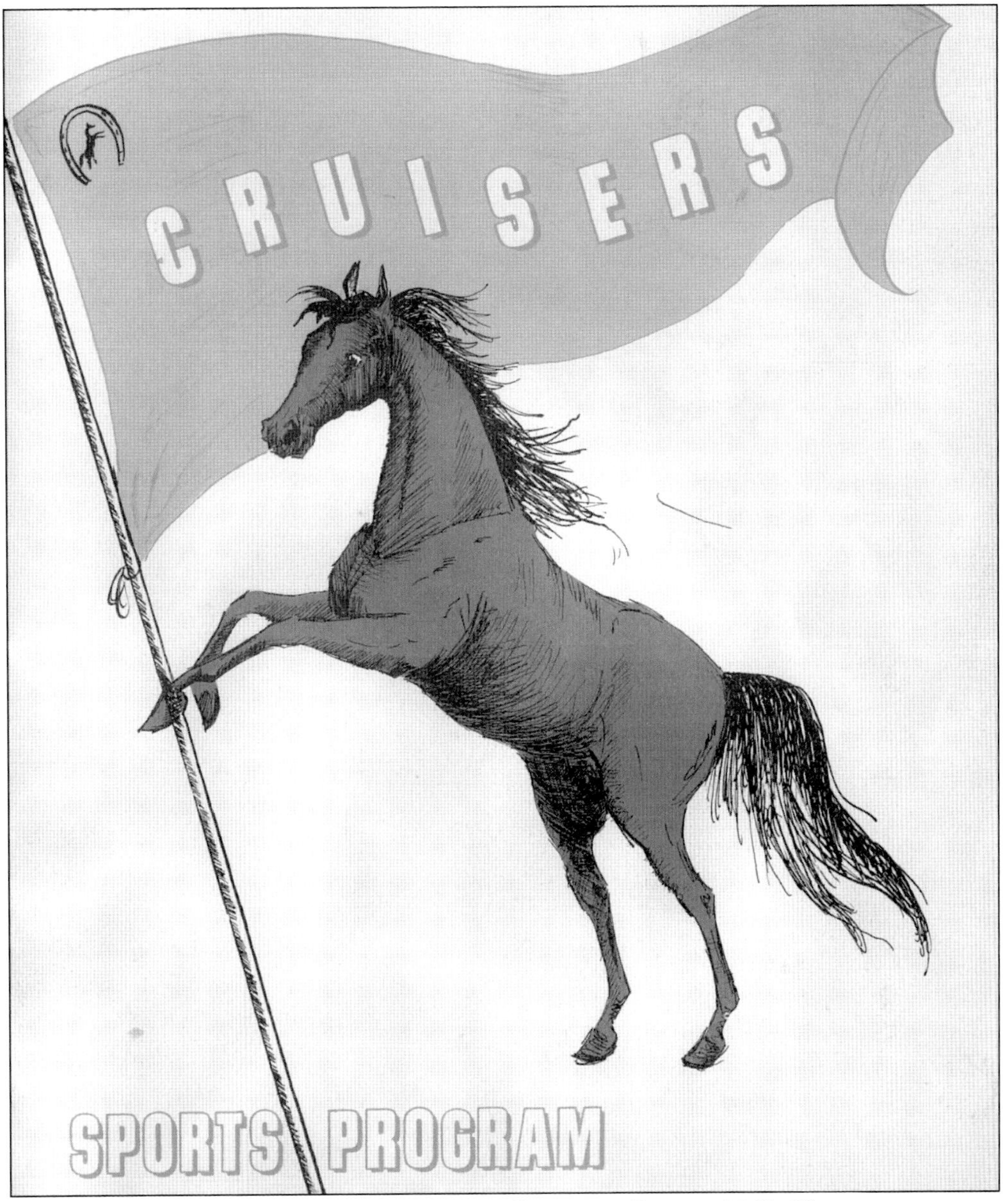

GROVEPORT MADISON HIGH SCHOOL SPORTS PROGRAM COVER, 1962. This sports program prominently features a portrait (drawn by Ed Rarey) of Cruiser, the Groveport Madison High School mascot. This design was used throughout the 1960s until the early 1970s for the school's athletic program. It was a departure from the standard, generic advertising based program covers that dominated the era. The program often included the story of John S. Rarey and Cruiser; the school fight song; the school alma mater; photos of teams, cheerleaders, the band, and school officials; local advertising, and sports schedules. The alma mater, written by Barbara Carpenter and J. T. Pence, goes: "All hail to Groveport High School; Thy praises we will sing; We'll join together hand in hand; And let our voices ring! Hail, all hail to the memories; We've shared throughout the years; They've all meant so much to us; Our hopes, our doubts, our fears; And now when we leave her; To go our separate ways; We'll always speak her reverent name; With honor, love, and praise!"

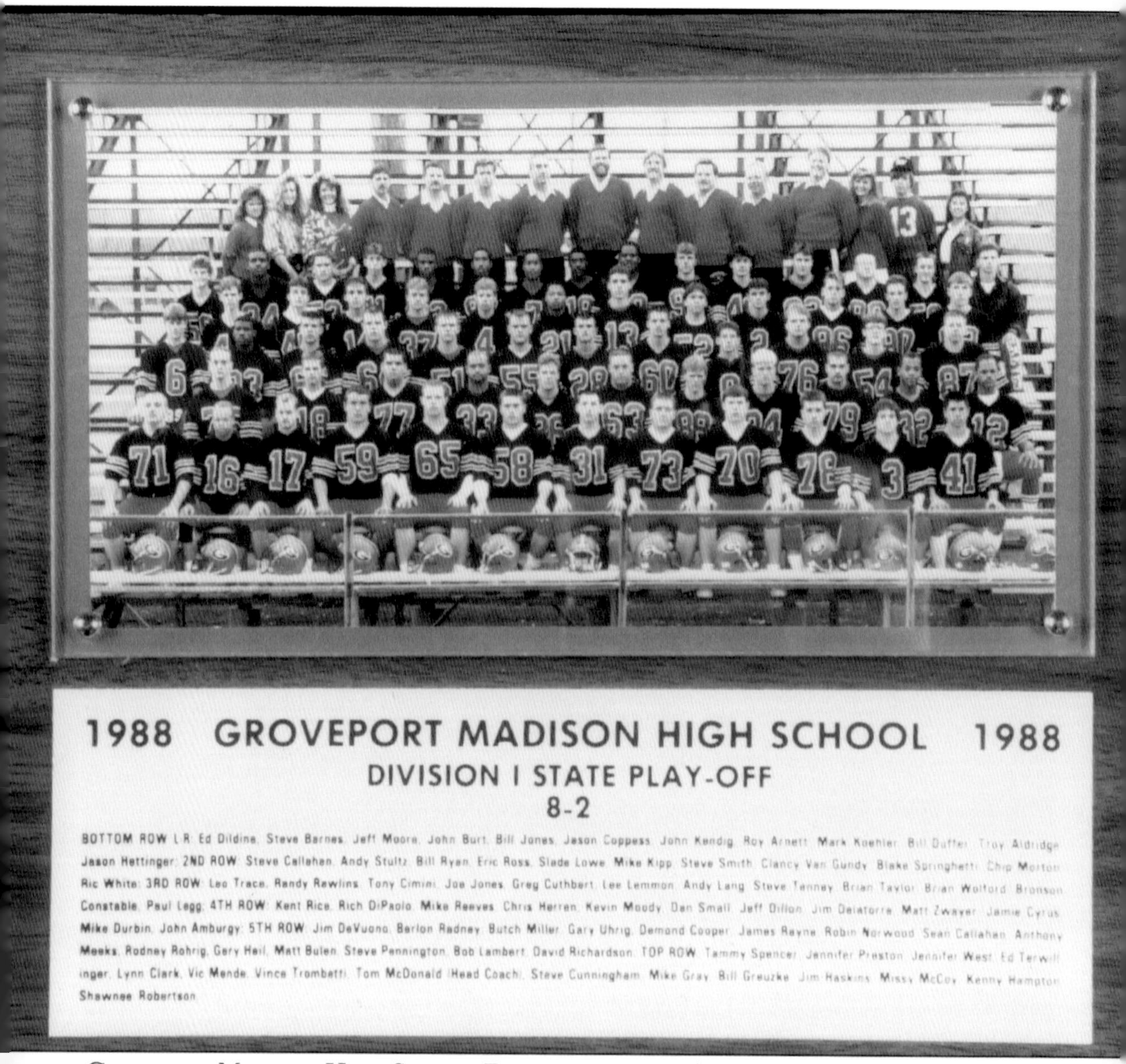

GROVEPORT MADISON HIGH SCHOOL FOOTBALL, 1988. This team finished 8–2 and qualified for the state Division I playoffs. Team members were, from left to right: (first row) Ed Dildine, Steve Barnes, Jeff Moore, John Burt, Bill Jones, Jason Coppess, John Kendig, Roy Arnett, Mark Koehler, Bill Duffer, Troy Aldridge, and Jason Hettinger; (second row) Steve Callahan, Andy Stultz, Bill Ryan, Eric Ross, Slade Lowe, Mike Kipp, Steve Smith, Clancy Van Gundy, Blake Springhetti, Chip Morton, and Ric White; (third row) Leo Trace, Randy Rawlins, Tony Cimini, Joe Jones, Greg Cuthbert, Lee Lemmon, Andy Lang, Steve Tenney, Brian Taylor, Brian Wolford, Bronson Constable, and Paul Legg; (fourth row) Kent Rice, Rich DiPaolo, Mike Reeves, Chris Herron, Kevin Moody, Dan Small, Jeff Dillon, Jim Delatorre, Matt Zwayer, Jamie Cyrus, Mike Durbin, and John Amburgy; (fifth row) Jim DeVuono, Berlon Radney, Butch Miller, Gary Uhrig, Demond Cooper, James Rayne, Robin Norwood, Sean Callahan, Anthony Meeks, Rodney Rohrig, Gary Heil, Matt Bulen, Steve Pennington, Bob Lambert, and David Richardson; (sixth row) Tammy Spencer, Jennifer Preston, Jennifer West, Ed Terwillinger, Lynn Clark, Vic Mende, Vince Trombetti, Tom McDonald, Steve Cunningham, Mike Gray, Bill Greuzke, Jim Haskins, Missy McCoy, Kenny Hampton, and Shawnee Robertson.

Four

COMMUNITY LIFE

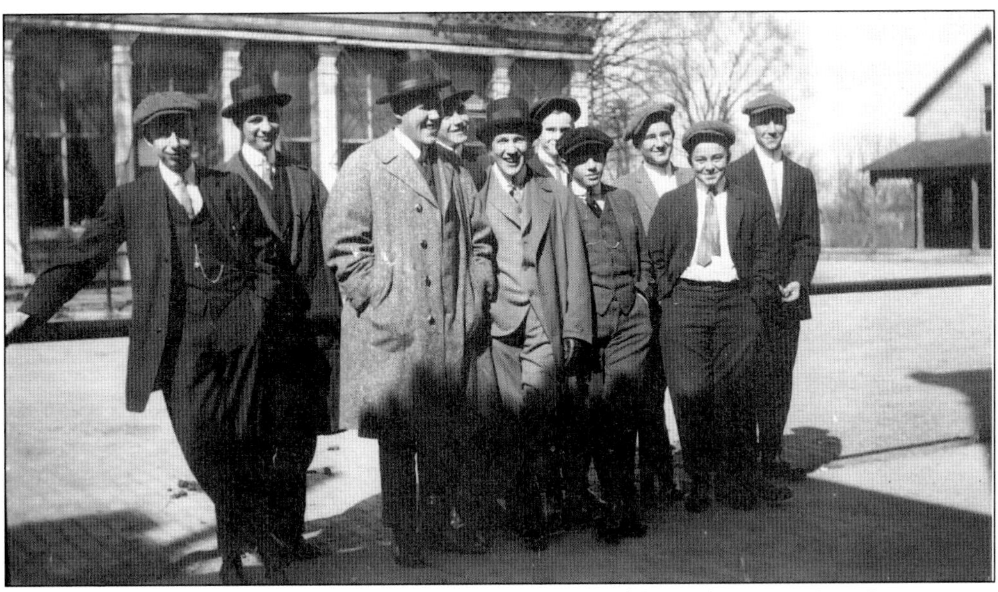

MEN ABOUT TOWN, C. 1912. These jaunty fellows posed for a photo on Main Street across from Groveport Town Hall. The building to the right is a saloon. Pictured here, from left to right, are: John Moody, Russell Rarey, Lawrence Leyshon, (unidentified), John Leyshon, (unidentified), Howard Hanstein, Carl Nafzger, (unidentified), and (unidentified). Moody (far left) is leaning on a hitching post.

TO-NIGHT!

WET OR DRY?

HON. JAMES A. WHITE

EX-MAYOR OF BARNSVILLE

Will address a Citizen's

Meeting at the

Town Hall

AT 7:00 O'CLOCK.

Everybody Come

TEMPERANCE DEBATES. From 1850 to 1910, temperance advocates petitioned Groveport Village Council to ban or regulate alcohol sales a dozen times. Each time they succeeded and each time within a short period of time the temperance ordinance was repealed when pro-alcohol rights supporters managed to accumulate enough votes to win elections. As this handbill indicates, the Groveport Town Hall auditorium was used as a forum for the "wet or dry" debates that surfaced in the village. The most notable conflict occurred in 1895, when a temperance ordinance passed 178–84. Closing notices were posted on the local saloons. Saloonkeeper Milton Miller defied the notices and kept operating, accumulating $360 in fines. Miller presented signed petitions to repeal the temperance ordinance but was ignored by council. He sued the village and won his case before the Franklin County Common Pleas Court. Groveport remained "wet" until national prohibition was instituted in the 1920s.

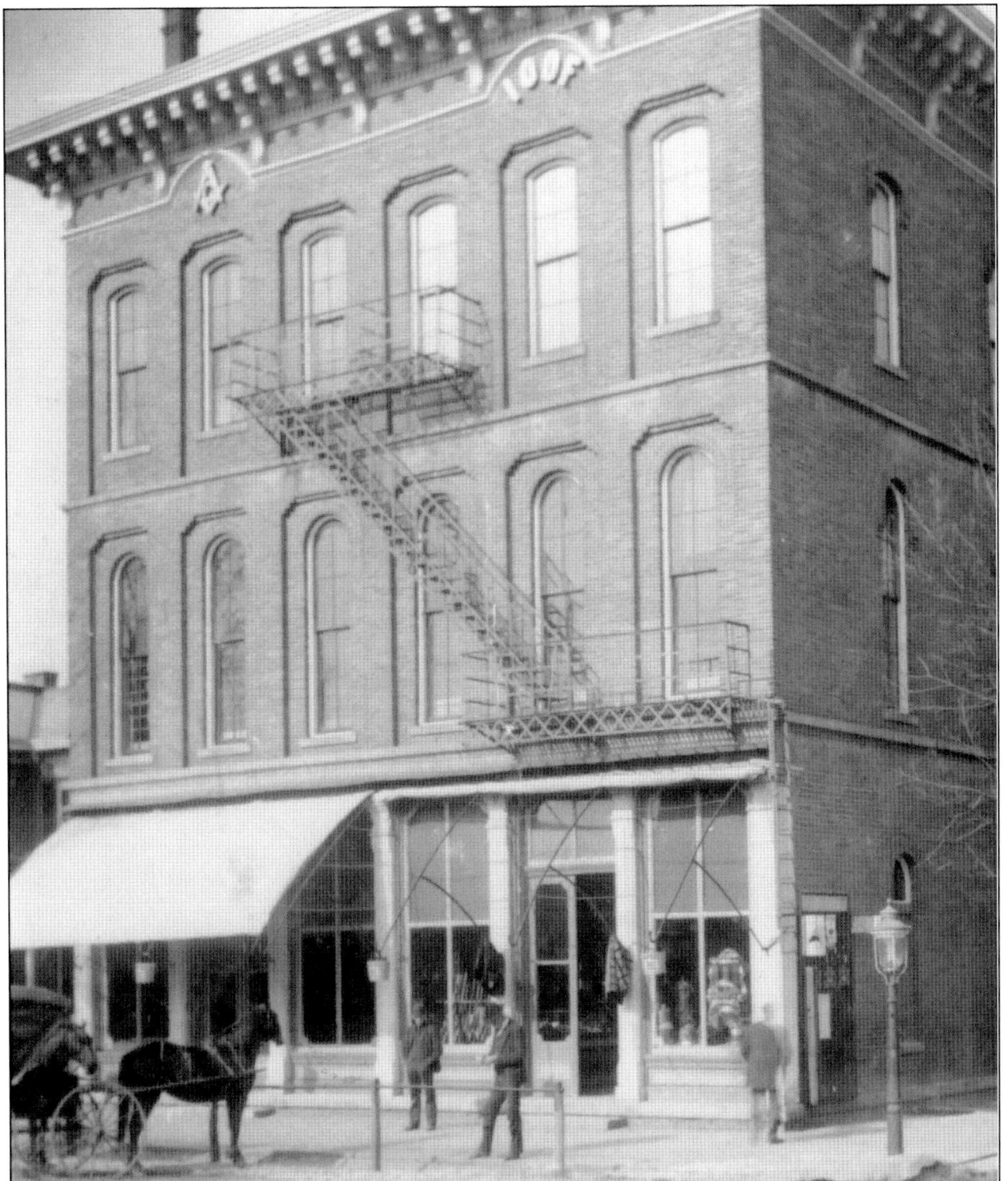

GROVEPORT TOWN HALL, C. 1900. One way a frontier town could show the world it was "civilized" was through the construction of public buildings and theaters. Groveport and Madison Township achieved this with the construction of Groveport Town Hall in 1876. The village and township teamed with the Masons and the Odd Fellows to build the three-story High Victorian Italianate hall at the corner of Main and Front streets, on land donated by William Rarey, at a cost of $10,745. The structure features tall windows, stone and wood moldings, and ornate metal ceilings. Originally the third floor meeting rooms were used by the Masons and Oddfellows organizations. The second floor held the auditorium and the first floor contained government offices to the rear and a grocery store and hardware in the two front rooms, which were rented out as a way helping to fund the building. The first floor was still being used for retail space until the 1960s. Today the building functions as a community center, art gallery, museum, meeting place, and concert hall.

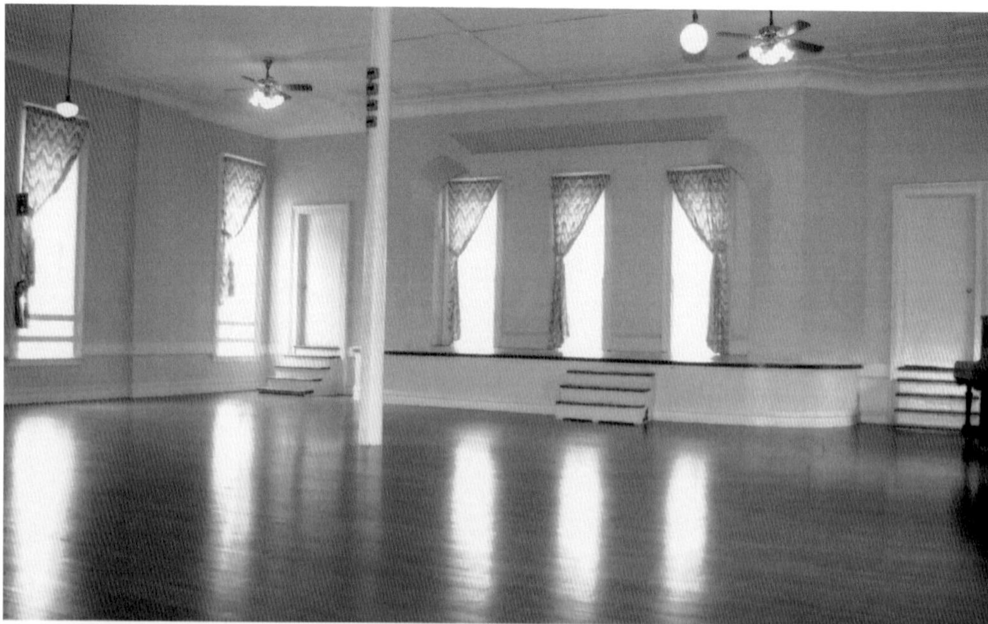

GROVEPORT TOWN HALL AUDITORIUM, 1996. This is a view of the auditorium prior to its being repainted and having its floor restored. The room has been used for concerts, lectures, dances, weddings, plays, and even for Groveport High School basketball games in the days before the school had its own gymnasium. Visible is the pole in the middle of the floor that was a decided advantage for the home team!

LOCAL

ORATORICAL CONTEST

TO BE HELD AT

Town Hall, Groveport, O.,

March 20, 1908.

To select a Representative to the Franklin County Interscholastic Oratorical Contest.

PROGRAM

Piano Solo, Capricante,..*Paul Wachs.*
Bert Williams.

Invocation...Rev, H. B. Cooper.

Vocal Solo, Asthore,...
Mrs. Clark Elliot.

Oration,.................................."Modern Slavery in America."
Leo A. Kile.

Piano Solo, Lost Paradise...
Edith Tussing.

Oration,.."American-Japanese War."
Ethel Wright.

Mysoli, When the Heart is Young,..
Mrs. Clark Elliot.

Oration,.."The Republic in Danger."
Roy Newberry.

Music.

Decision of Judges.

JUDGES.

Prof. David R. Major, O. S. U.
Rev. P. H. Chappelear, Columbus, O.
Att'y J. K. Henry, Lancaster, O.

Peterman Job Print, Groveport, O.

ORATORICAL NOTICE, 1908. This handbill is an example of one of the many activities that have taken place at Groveport Town Hall over the years. This event featured music and three orations: "Modern Slavery in America," by Leo Kile; "American-Japanese War," by Ethel Wright; and "The Republic in Danger," by Roy Newberry. Town Hall remains a community focal point and helps to preserve Groveport's sense of identity by maintaining a functional link to the past.

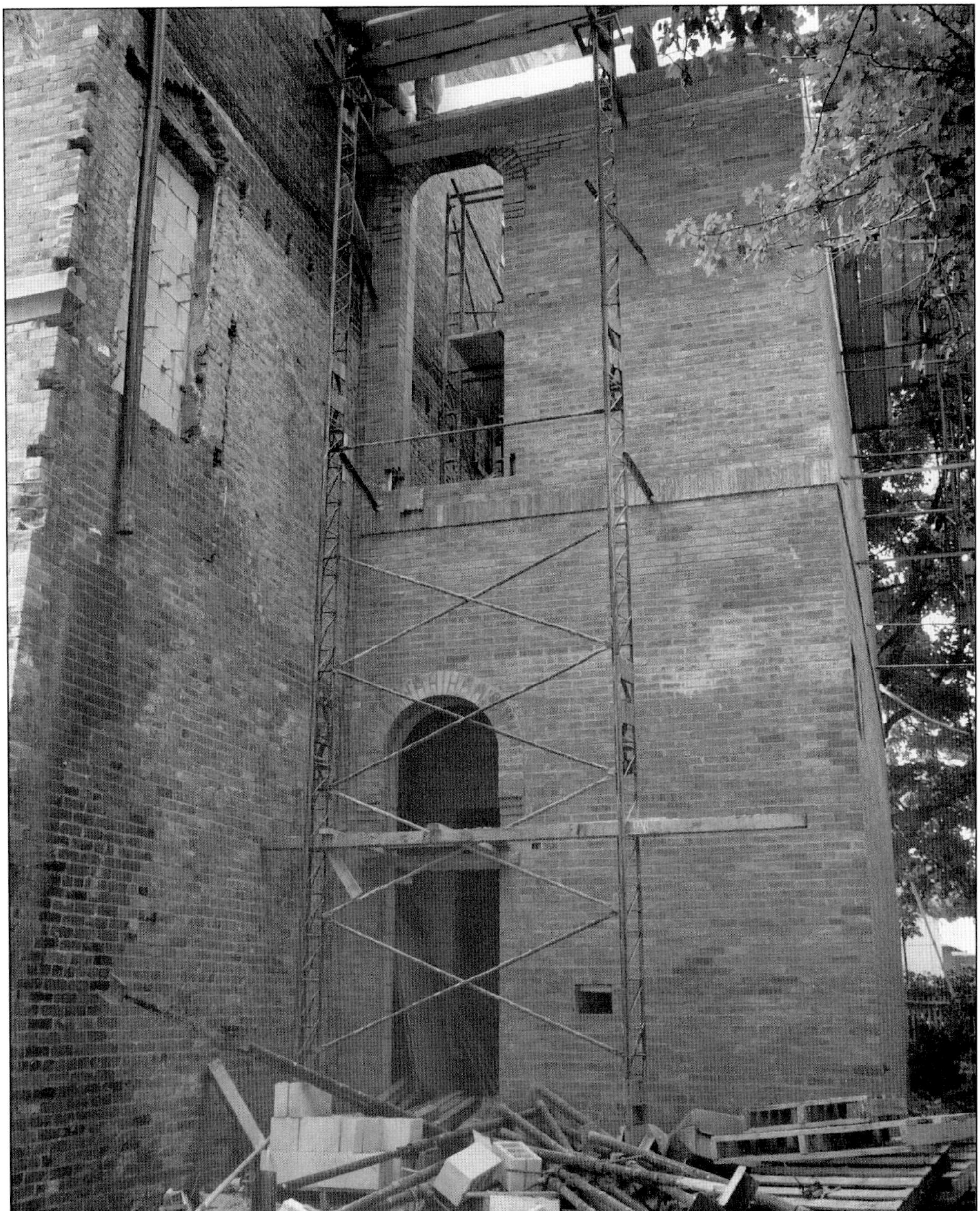

GROVEPORT TOWN HALL RENOVATIONS. The building has undergone two major periods of renovations—from the late 1970s to the early 1980s and from 1998 to the present. This photo shows the addition of the elevator shaft and lobby at the rear of the building in 1979. Other work completed over the years has included the refurbishing of the auditorium floor, installation of modern heating and air conditioning units, roof repairs, electrical work, plumbing replacement, and repainting the interior to match a color consistent with the era of its construction. Groveport purchased Madison Township's share of the building in 1996. (The township built its own building in 1996.) The village's efforts to maintain the structure as a functioning facility is a reflection of the town's desire to keep pace with the modern world while preserving what it can of its past.

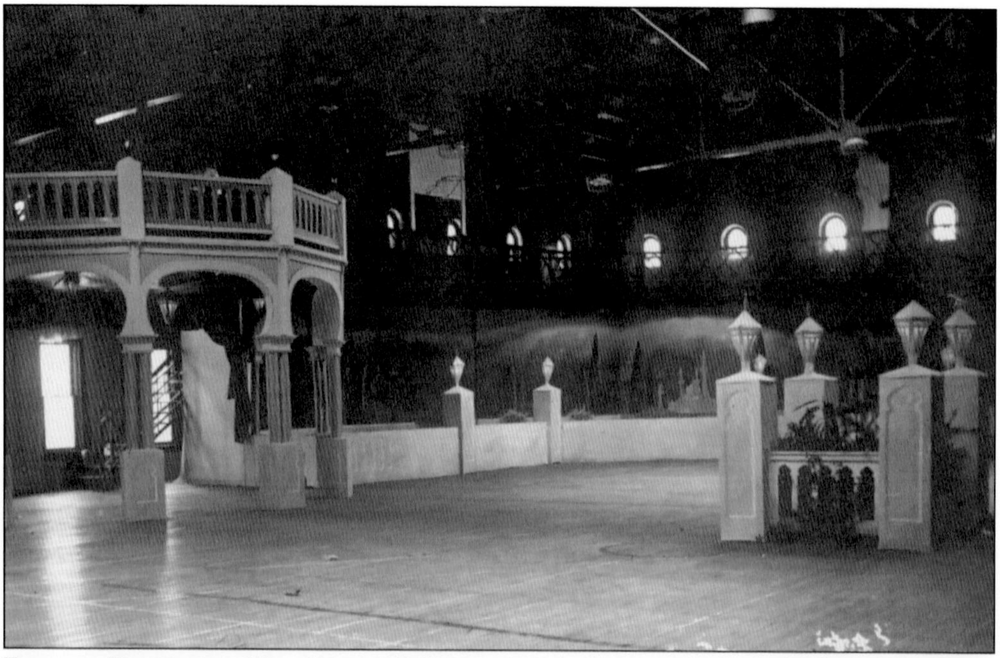

ELMONT BALLROOM. The Elmont Ballroom was large enough to hold dances, wedding receptions, and other galas. The elegant ballroom featured decorative plaster festoons and a highly polished cherry wood dance floor, sanded with finely ground glass to keep it smooth.

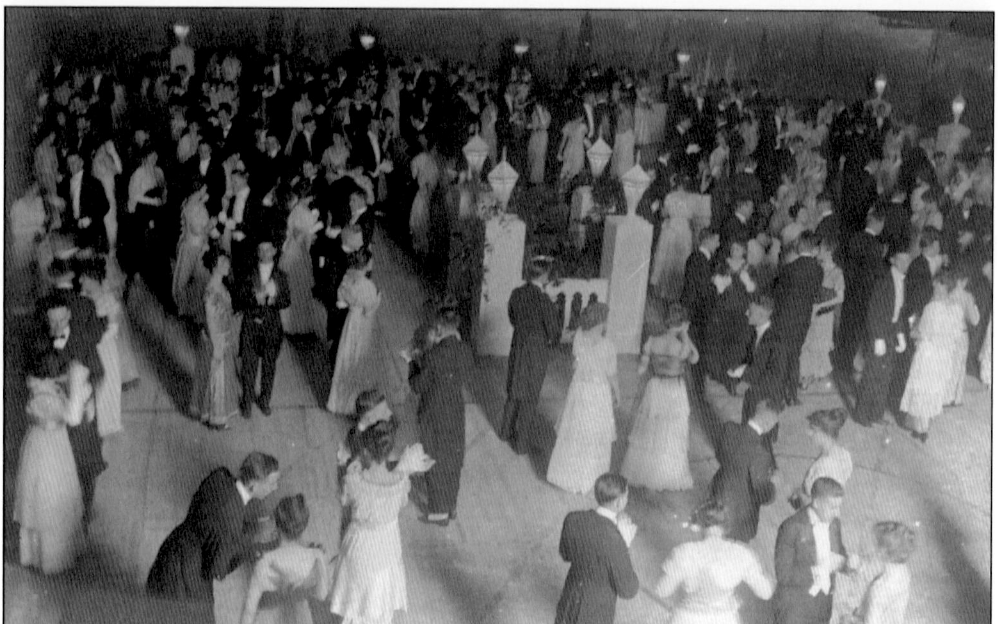

DANCING AT THE ELMONT. Social life in Groveport often revolved around the schools, Town Hall, and the churches. But the Elmont Hotel was also a major player through the first half of the twentieth century when it came to social activities. Here the Elmont Ballroom is packed with guests at a formal dance.

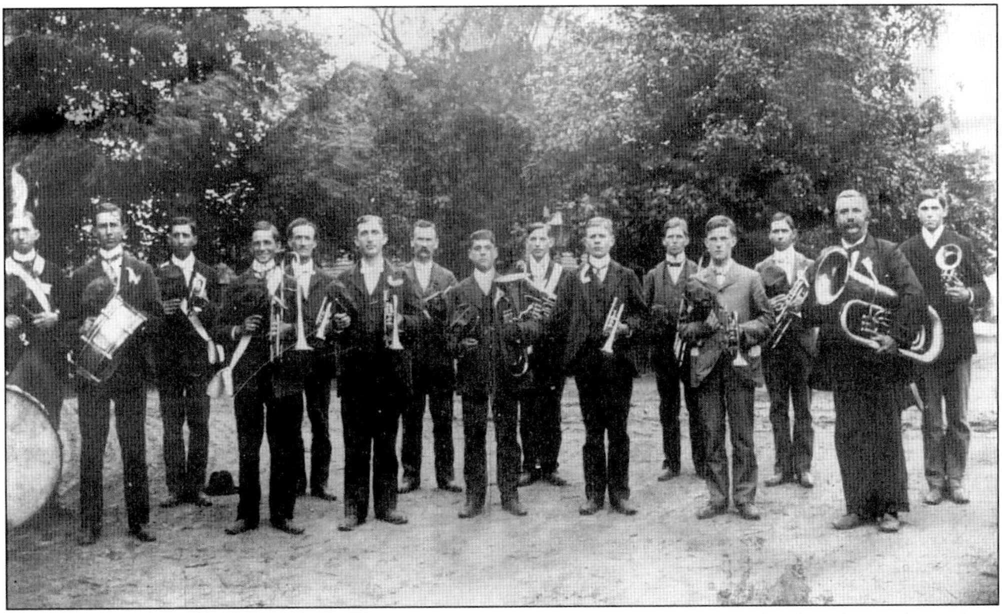

Groveport Band, c. 1900. The band performed weekly concerts at the band stand at Main and Front streets until disbanding after World War I. Members of the band, from left to right, were: Charles Dolby, Byron Seymour, Clifford Jordan, Millard Jordan, Kirk Carruthers, Sturgis Davis, L. W. Carruthers, Jesse Bateson, Lucius Davis, R. Kitzmiller, Louis Sims, Ray Teegardin, Arthur Jordan, John Dunklee, and Vernon Lowery.

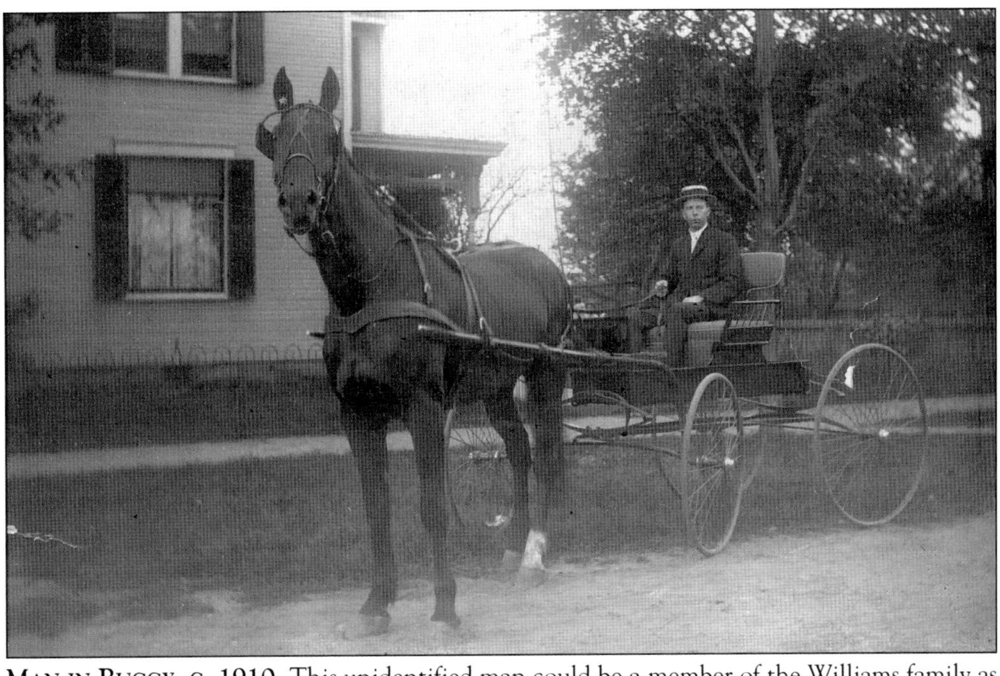

Man in Buggy, c. 1910. This unidentified man could be a member of the Williams family as he is parked before the Williams home on Groveport's Main Street, near Center Street. This photo is a fine example of demonstrating how most folks traveled by horse and buggy in the days before automobiles.

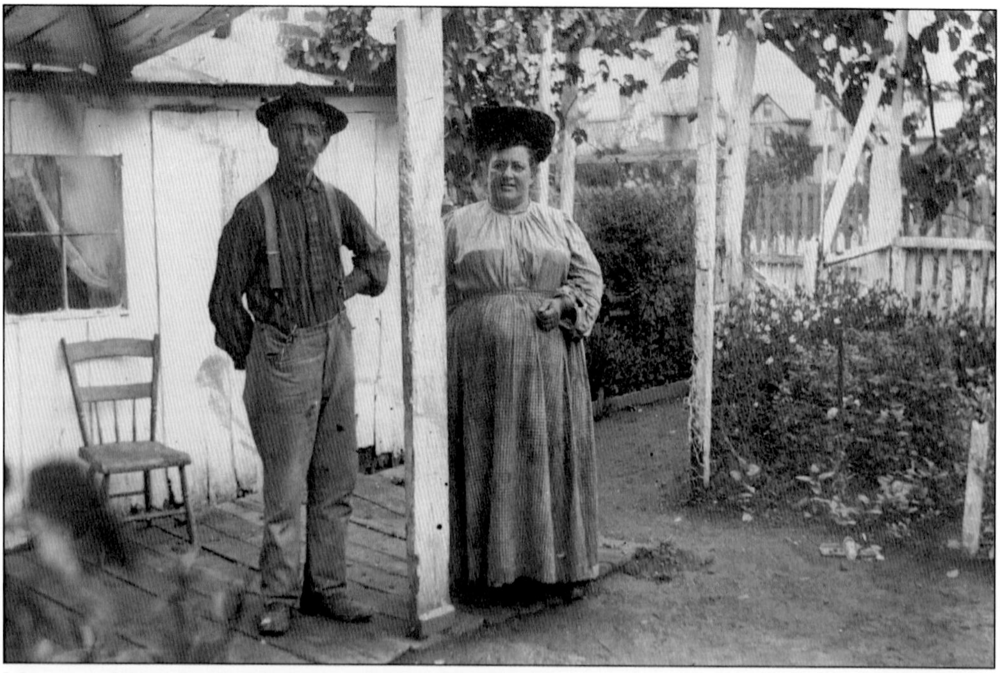

Mr. and Mrs. Dave Decker, 1908. This photo was taken in the backyard of the Decker home on Groveport's Elm Street. Large residential lots were platted in Groveport to allow room for big gardens. Though people lived in town, they still raised a good portion of their own food just as those in the surrounding farm community did.

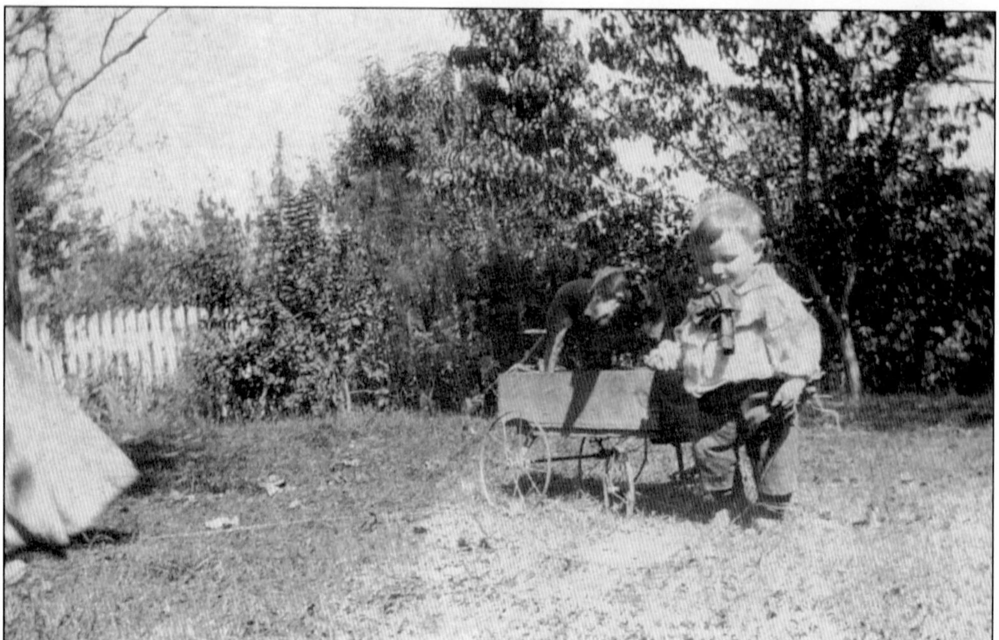

Bert Williams, c. 1910. Bert Williams as a young lad pulls his dog in a cart in the front yard of his Main Street Groveport home. Williams grew up to work as the symphony director at the Ohio Theatre in Columbus beginning in 1926. He was a master organist and composer.

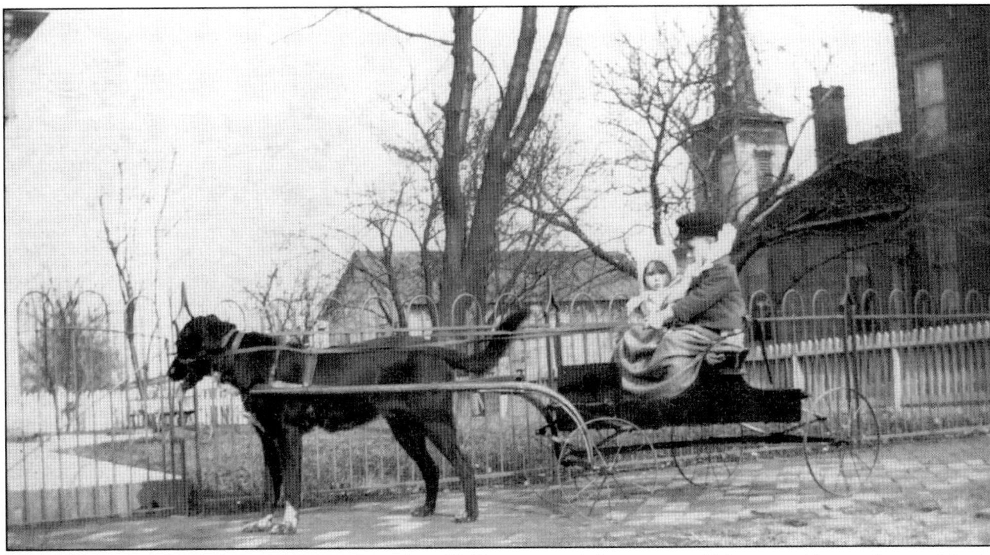

CHARLES WILLIAMS, C. 1910. Charles Williams and his sister (Margaret?) go for a ride in their yard on Groveport's Main Street. The windmill in the rear of the photo pumped water for the neighboring Saylor residence. The wrought-iron fence was made by the children's father, Frank, a blacksmith.

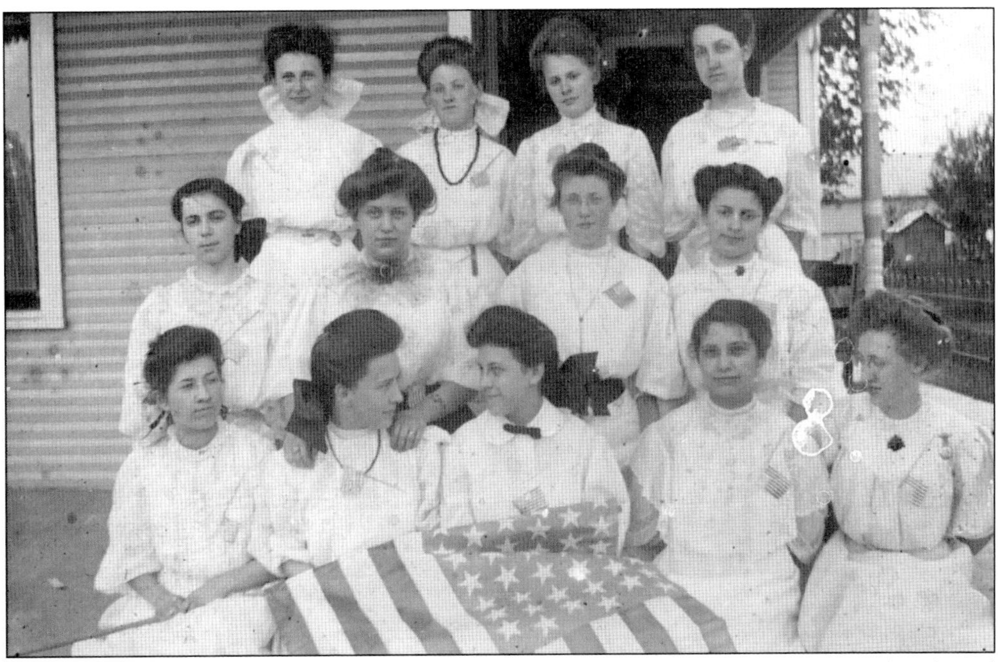

WOMEN WITH FLAG. Bonds of community are formed when people form groups be they formal organizations or as informal as friends gathering on street corners or porches. Groups breathe life into a community and reflect its heart. Here some Groveport and Madison Township women gather on a front porch on a patriotic holiday. Pictured here, from left to right, are: (front row) Goldie Schleppi, Edith Tussing, Mary Stevenson, and Gertrude Adel; (middle row) Ethel Long, (unidentified), (unidentified), and Anna Coon; (back row) Amy Wildermuth, Irma Myers, (unidentified), and (unidentified).

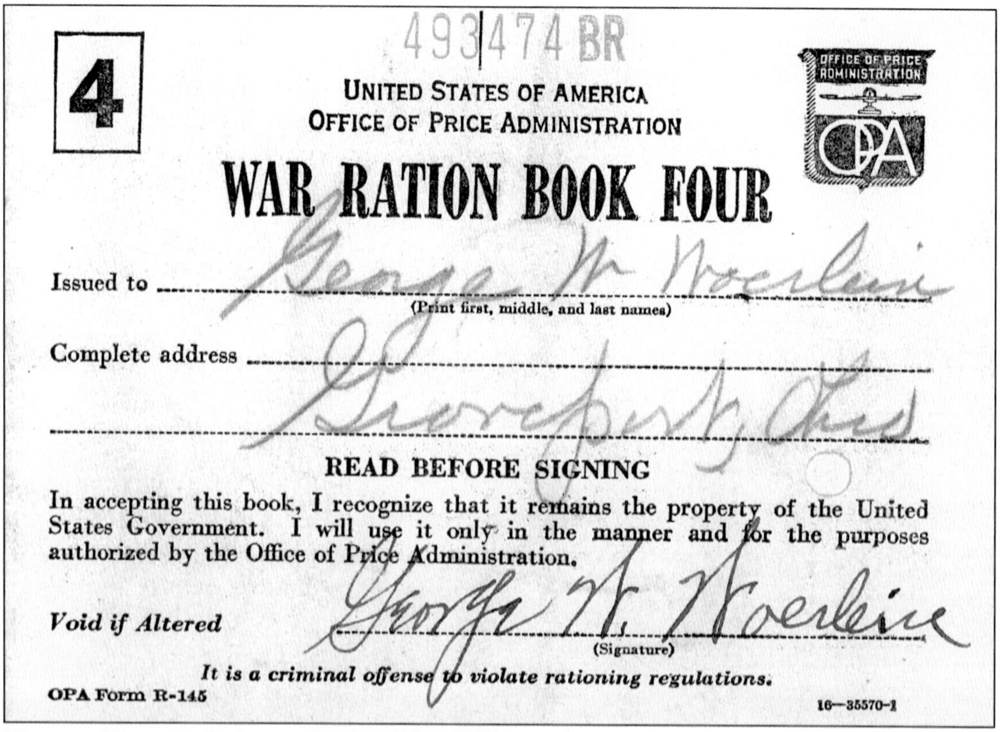

4

493474 BR

OFFICE OF PRICE ADMINISTRATION

OPA

UNITED STATES OF AMERICA
OFFICE OF PRICE ADMINISTRATION

WAR RATION BOOK FOUR

Issued to George W. Woerlein
(Print first, middle, and last names)

Complete address Groveport, Ohio

READ BEFORE SIGNING

In accepting this book, I recognize that it remains the property of the United States Government. I will use it only in the manner and for the purposes authorized by the Office of Price Administration.

Void if Altered George W. Woerlein
(Signature)

It is a criminal offense to violate rationing regulations.

OPA Form R-145 16—35570-1

WORLD WAR II RATION BOOK. This ration book was owned by George Woerlein of Groveport. Rubber, gasoline, shoes, scarce food items, and a variety of other goods and services were rationed to citizens to support the war effort.

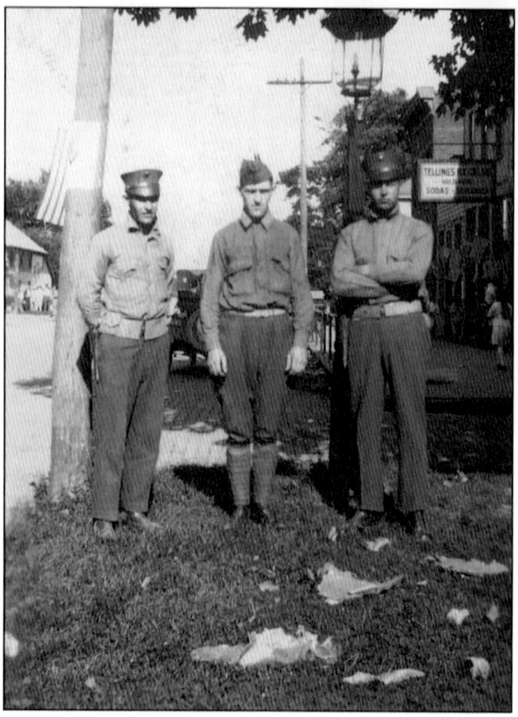

THREE SOLDIERS (DATE UNKNOWN). These local military men pose for a photo at the corner of Crooked Alley and Main Street in Groveport. They are believed to be, from left to right, Forest "Finn" Jordan, Merle Howison, and Alva "Boots" Carr. An old gas streetlight can be seen rising behind them between Howison and Carr.

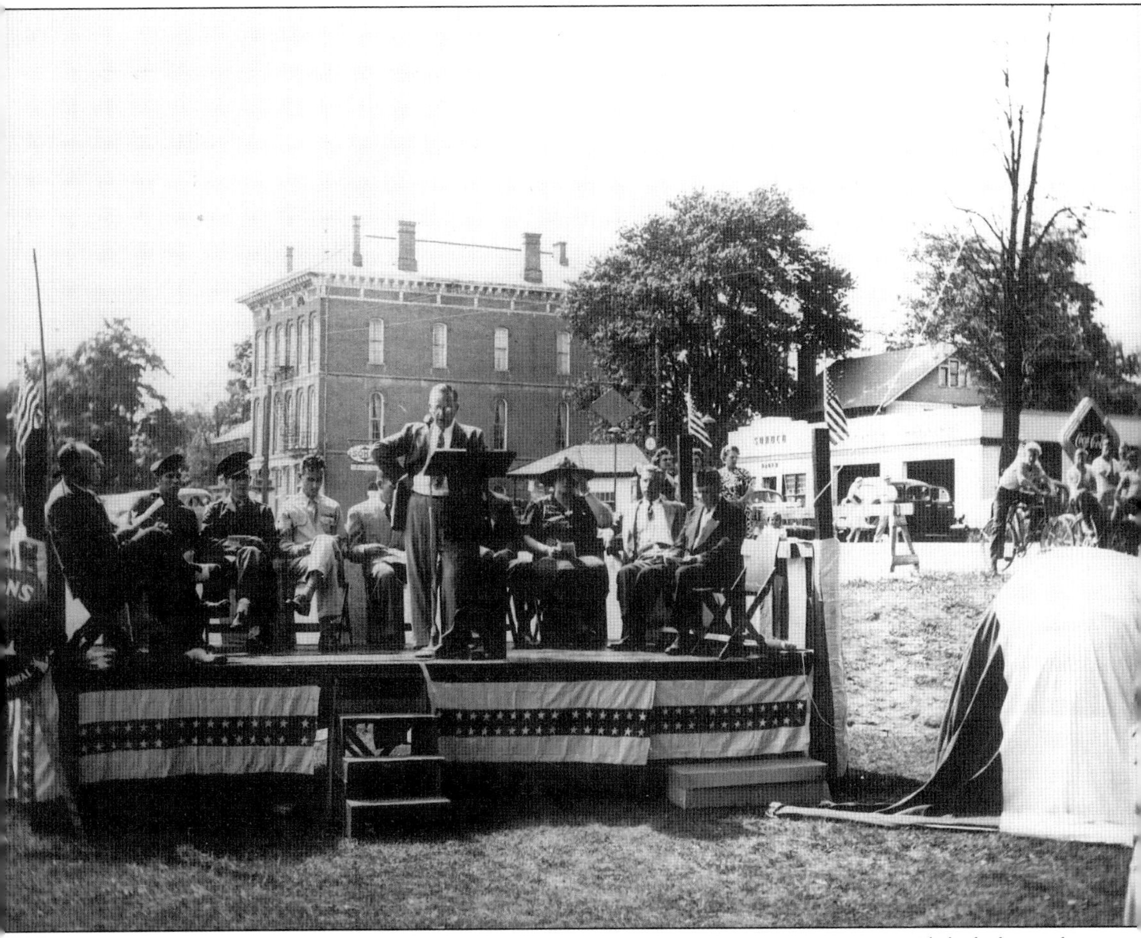

MEMORIAL STONE DEDICATION, MEMORIAL DAY 1946. The Groveport Lions Club dedicated a stone memorial to those area men and women who served in World War II on Memorial Day, 1946. Groveport has no town square, so the courtyard of the Groveport School on Main Street was chosen as the memorial's site. The courtyard was the most appropriate setting as the school was the one place all the local veterans shared a common experience in life. The ceremony included music by the high school band; as well as speeches by Mayor J. R. Buchman, American Legion Commander Carl Benson, Spanish American War veteran Frederick Mills, World War I veteran Stephen McClish, Malcolm Sims of the Army, and State Senator Roscoe Walcutt. Gold Star mother Mazie Palsgrove presented a floral offering. (Gold Star mothers were women who had lost a son or daughter in the war.) The memorial stone is under a cover to the right of the photo. Groveport Town Hall can be seen in the background.

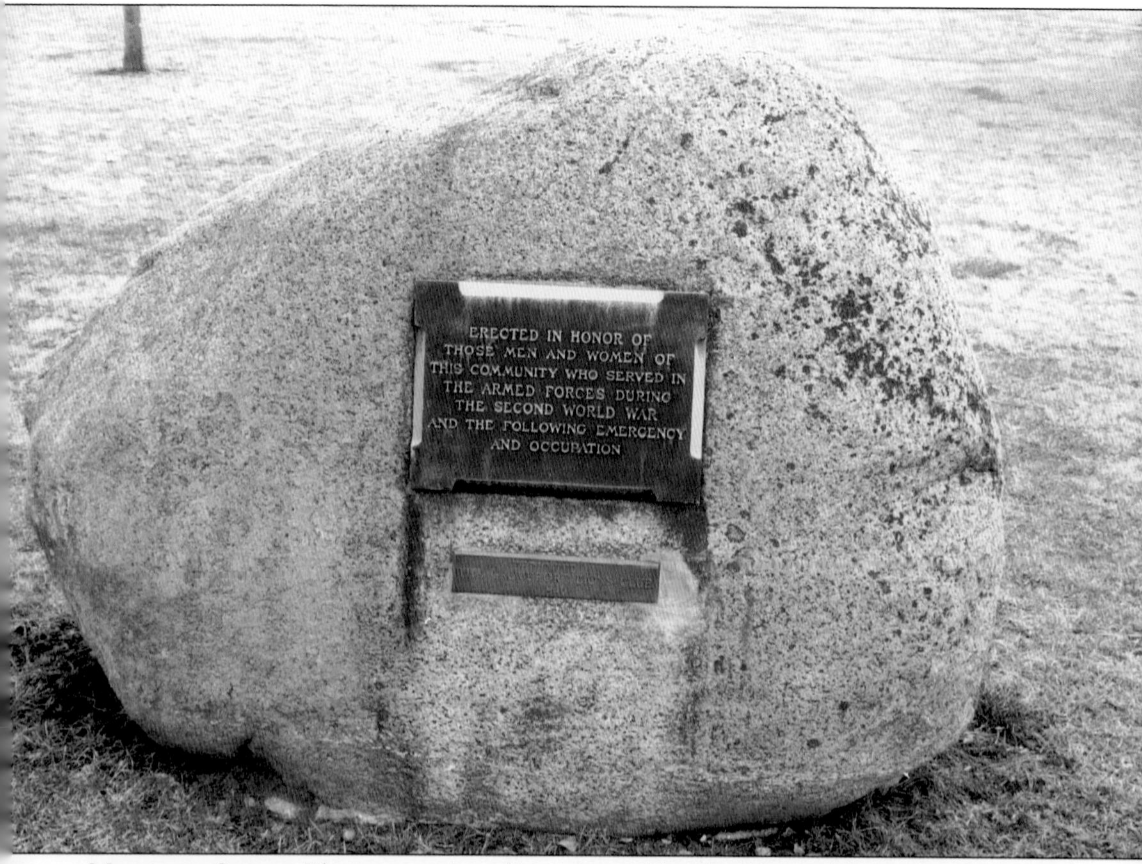

MEMORIAL STONE. The memorial itself is a large Ohio boulder emblazoned with a simple plaque: "Erected in honor of those men and women of this community who served in the armed forces during the Second World War and the following emergency occupation." The stone rests in the northwest corner of the Groveport School courtyard near the intersection of Main Street and Wirt Road. Placing the stone here ensured it would be seen by many people. Nestled in the soft green grass, the stone is an elegantly simple reminder of the profound sacrifice made by the members of the Groveport Madison community in service to their country. Coupled with the stone memorial is a list of those who served in the war. This "Roll of Honor" is located in the foyer of Groveport School. A gold star is affixed beside the names of those who lost their lives during the war.

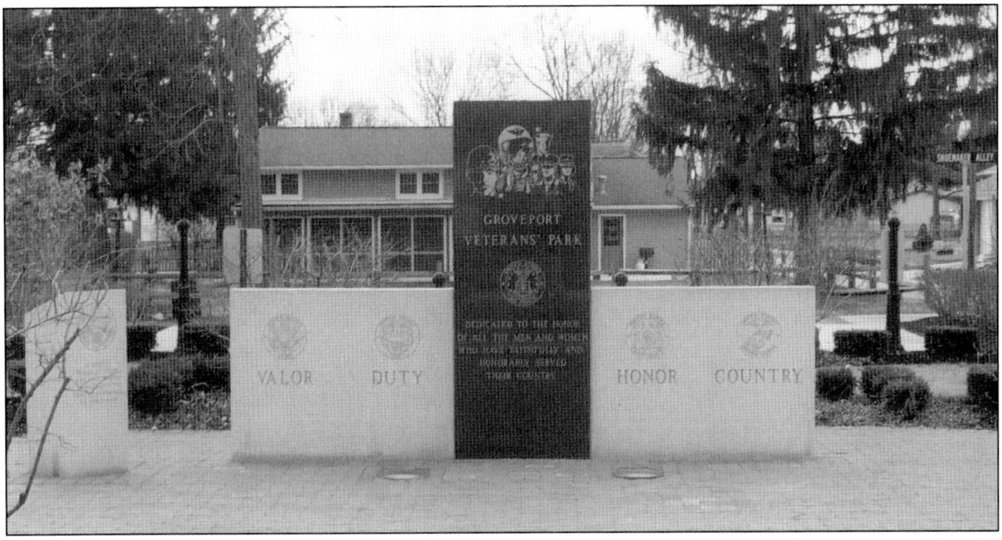

GROVEPORT VETERANS PARK. Opened in 1997, Veterans Park is located on the south side of Main Street at Hilly Alley. Each Veterans Day a special ceremony is held at the park in recognition of those from the community who have served in the armed forces. Memorial bricks are installed in the park's plaza with the names of area veterans.

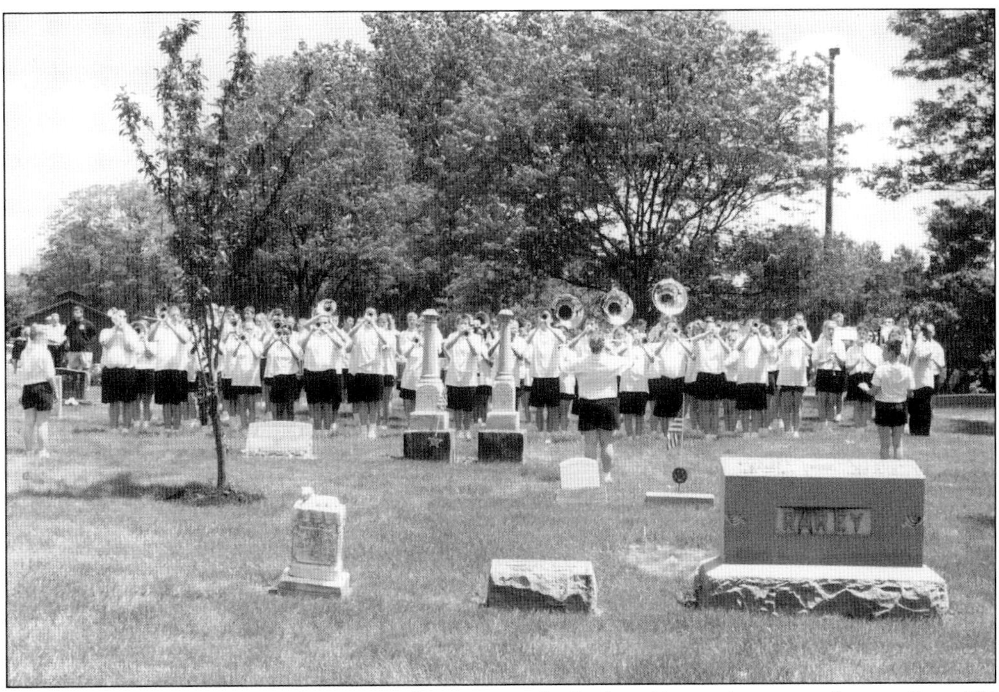

MEMORIAL DAY, 2001. Each Memorial Day since the Robert Dutro American Legion Post 486 was formed in 1921, post members have led a parade of children carrying flowers to be placed on the graves of veterans in the Groveport Cemetery. Here the Groveport Madison High School Marching Band performs patriotic music while standing among the decorated graves.

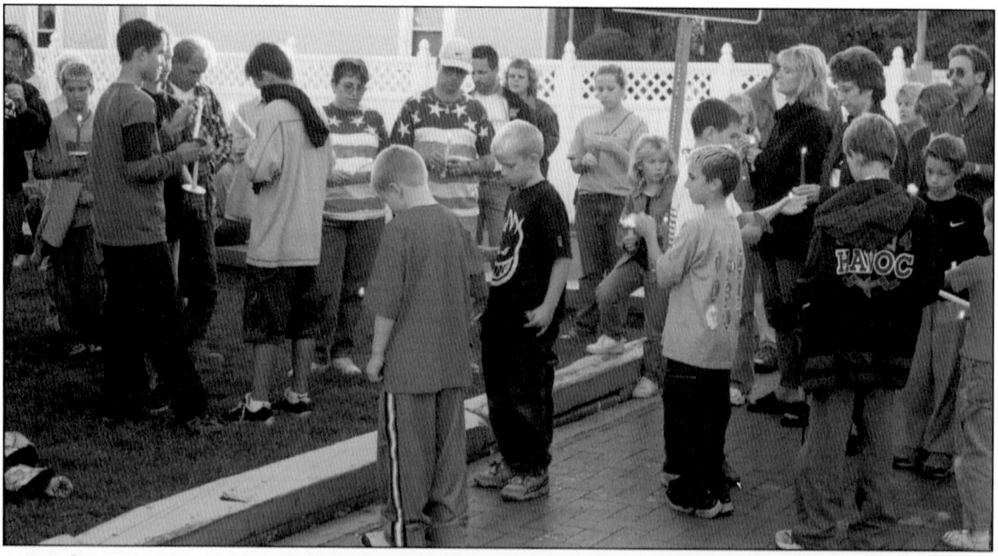

9-11 GATHERING. A few days following the tragedy of September 11, 2001, when terrorists hijacked four planes—two destroying New York's World Trade Center, one damaging the Pentagon in Washington, D.C., and one crashing in a Pennsylvania field after the passengers revolted—Groveport residents held an informal candlelight vigil at the corner of Crooked Alley and Main Street. The gathering hearkened back to another era, when after learning of the signing of the armistice on November 11, 1918, ending World War I, citizens recognized the war's end by informally gathering on the streets.

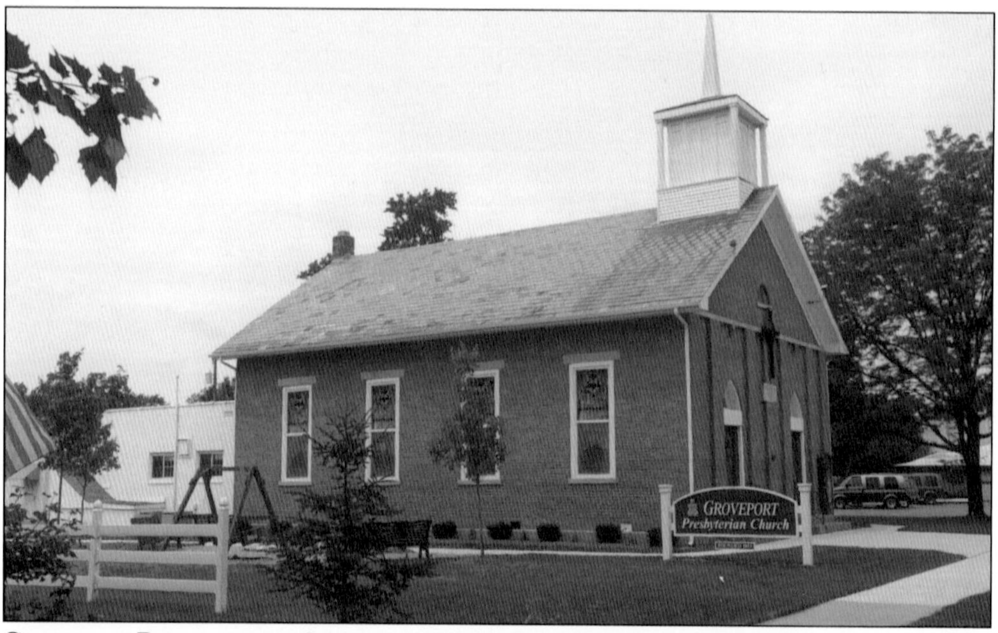

GROVEPORT PRESBYTERIAN CHURCH. Completed on October 5, 1853, and located on College Street at Shoemaker Alley, this is the oldest church building in continuous use in Groveport. In 1949, a kitchen, office, and classroom space was added to the rear of the structure. The Presbyterian congregation was organized in the home of Samuel and Elizabeth Sharpe with 11 members in 1853.

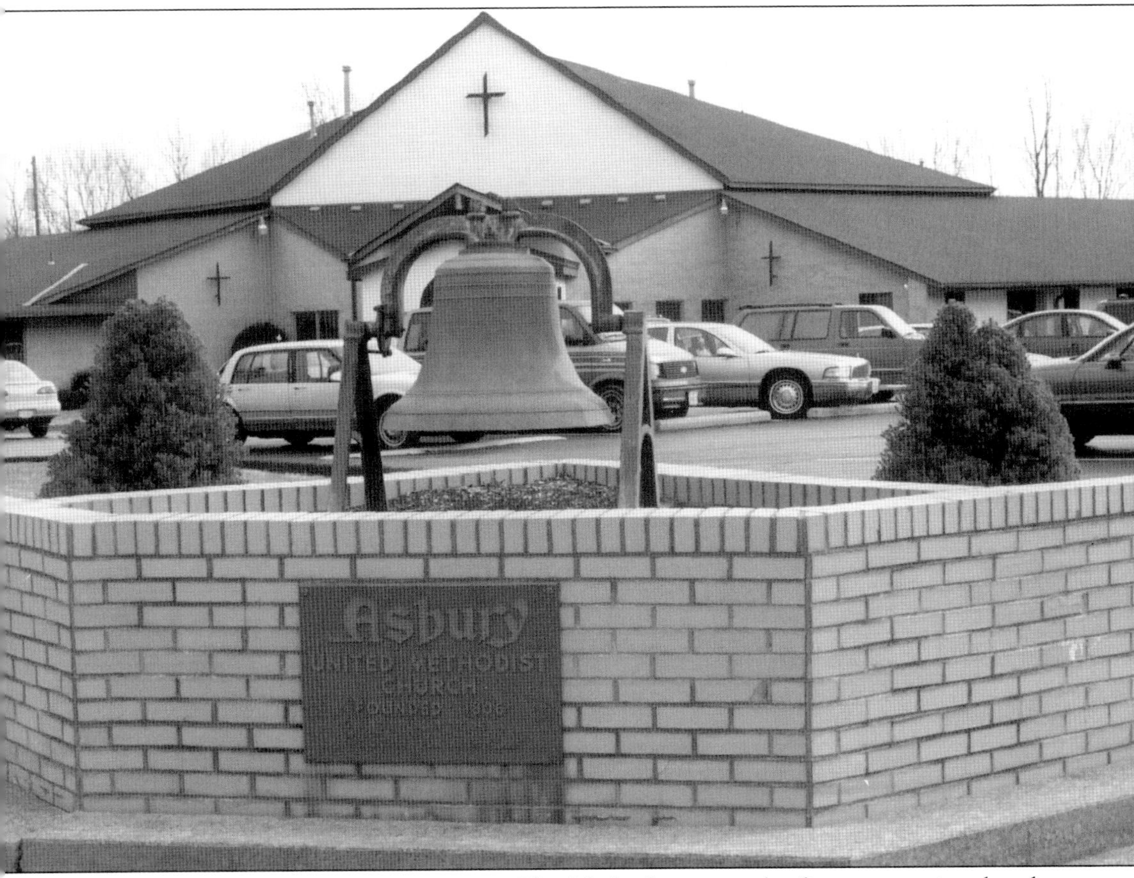

ASBURY UNITED METHODIST CHURCH. The Methodists were the first to organize churches in Madison Township. In the southern portion of the township, Hopewell Church formed in 1804 in the home of Ezekiel Groom with a church eventually being built on London-Lancaster Road near Little Walnut Creek. To the north, Asbury Church formed in 1806 in the home of John Stevenson. By 1820, Asbury Methodists were meeting in a log structure on Stevenson's property near Blacklick Creek along Shannon Road. The congregation split in 1840, and the Asbury congregation built its first chapel at Noe-Bixby Road and Winchester Pike. A brick church was later built on the northeast corner of the two roads in 1872 at a cost of $7,000. The church pictured here was built in 1966 to replace the old brick structure. The bell from the old church can be seen in this photo above the church sign.

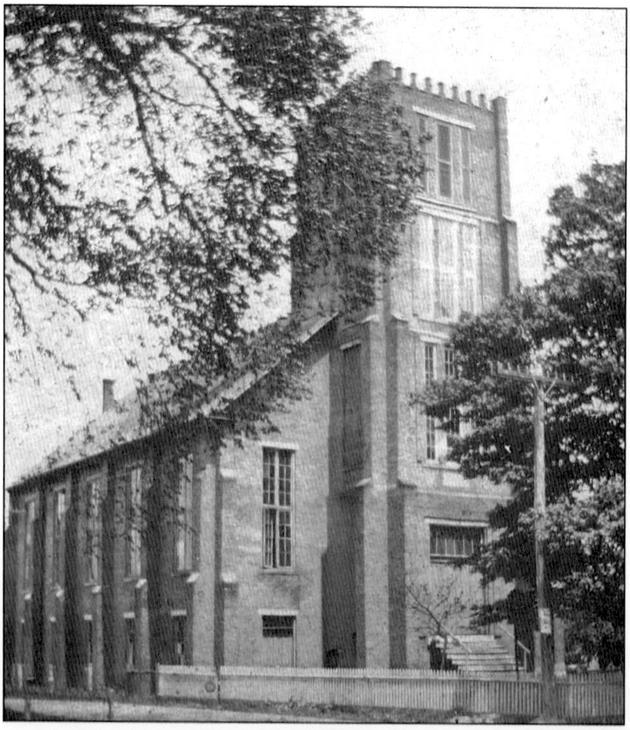

GROVEPORT UNITED METHODIST CHURCH, C. 1900. This church, built in 1851 at College and Main Streets on land donated by William Rarey, replaced the original church constructed there in 1836. The main sanctuary of this church was on the second floor with Sunday school classrooms situated on the first floor. The church bell, cast in England, was donated by John S. Rarey. The Groveport Methodist Church formed in 1836 under its official name of Wesley Chapel.

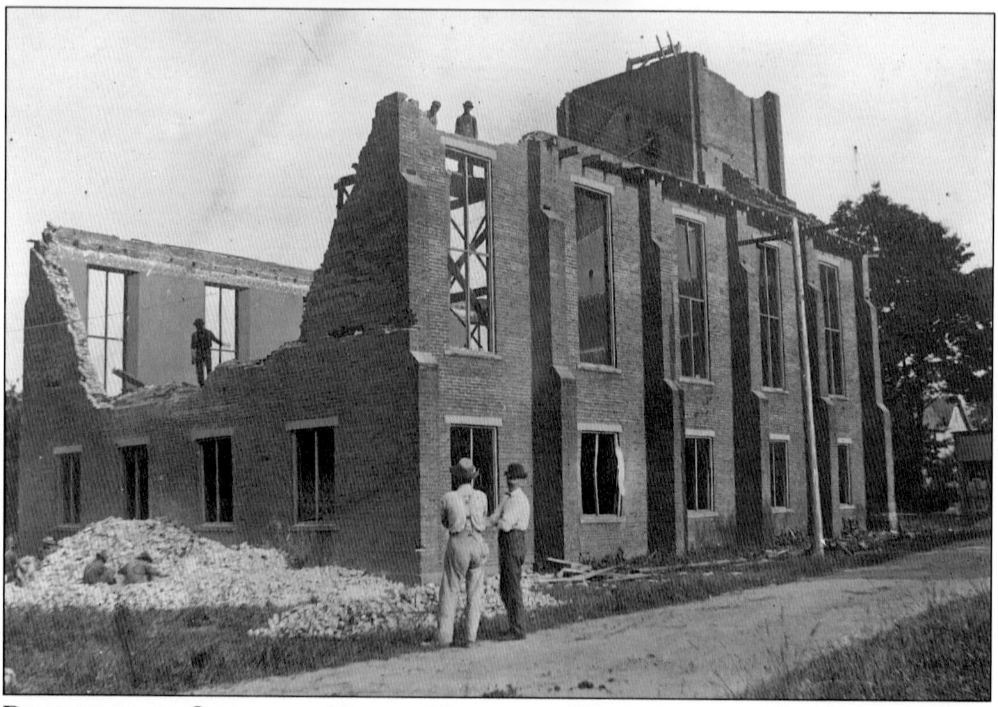

DEMOLITION OF GROVEPORT UNITED METHODIST CHURCH, 1907. The church was torn down to make way for the construction of a new, larger church that could meet the demands of the growing Groveport Methodist congregation. The dirt path in the foreground is College Street. Workers saved the bell for its installation in the new building.

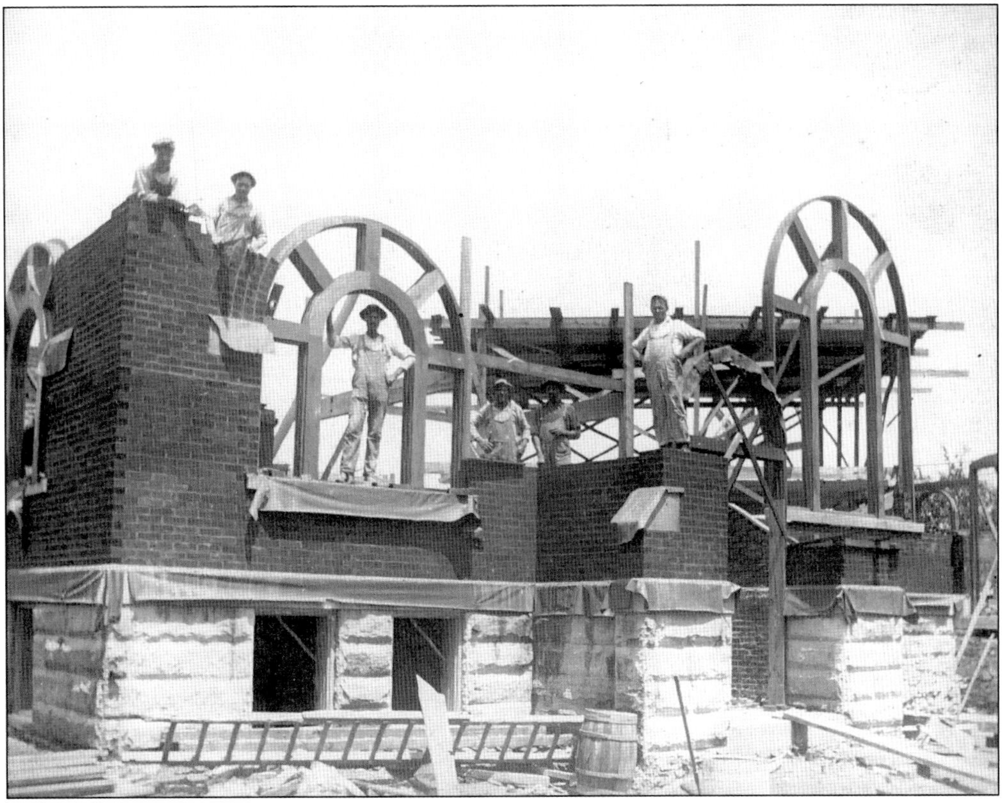

CONSTRUCTION OF GROVEPORT UNITED METHODIST CHURCH, 1908. This photo shows the church's signature arched windows being put in place as the building rises. Charles "Scout" Rarey submitted the $25,000 bid to build the new church. Rarey resigned his job as Franklin County Juvenile Court clerk to devote all his efforts to constructing the church.

GROVEPORT UNITED METHODIST CHURCH, C. 1950. Completed in 1908, this church remains the home of the Groveport Methodist congregation. The building is noted for its arched, fanned stained glass windows and fine stonework. It is made of cranberry red brick produced at the former brick yard that operated along the Ohio and Erie Canal in town.

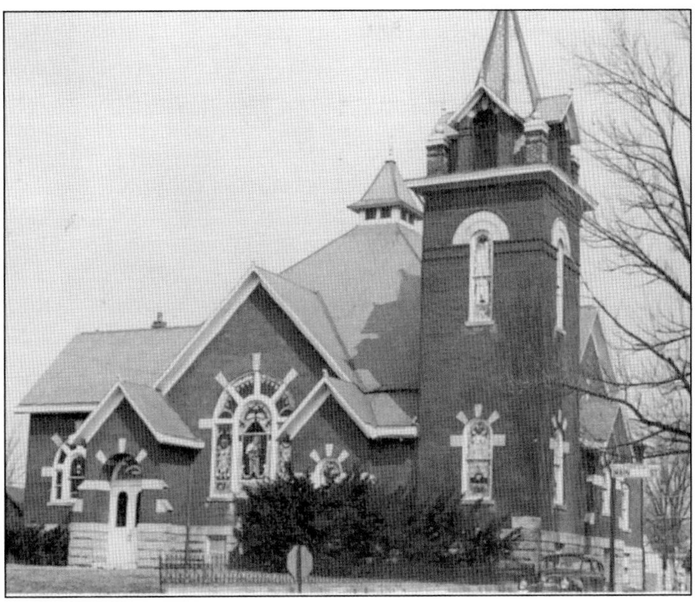

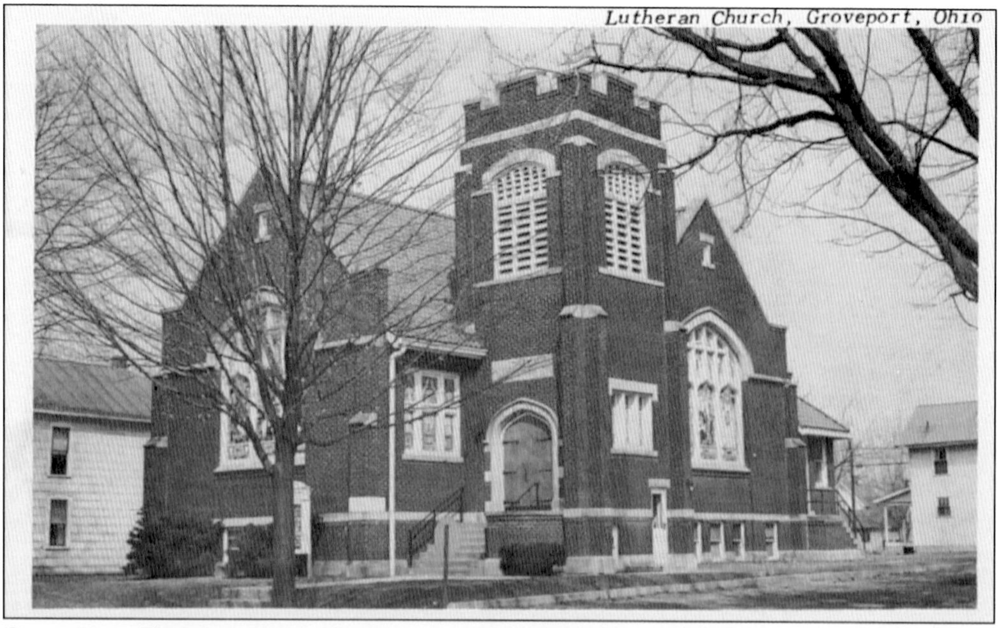

GROVEPORT ZION LUTHERAN CHURCH, C. 1919. The Lutheran Church formed in Groveport in 1911, and held its first meetings at Groveport Town Hall. This brick structure was built in 1918 on the northwest corner of Center and Main streets. The Lutherans met there until 1968, when a new structure was built on west Main Street, east of Hendron Road.

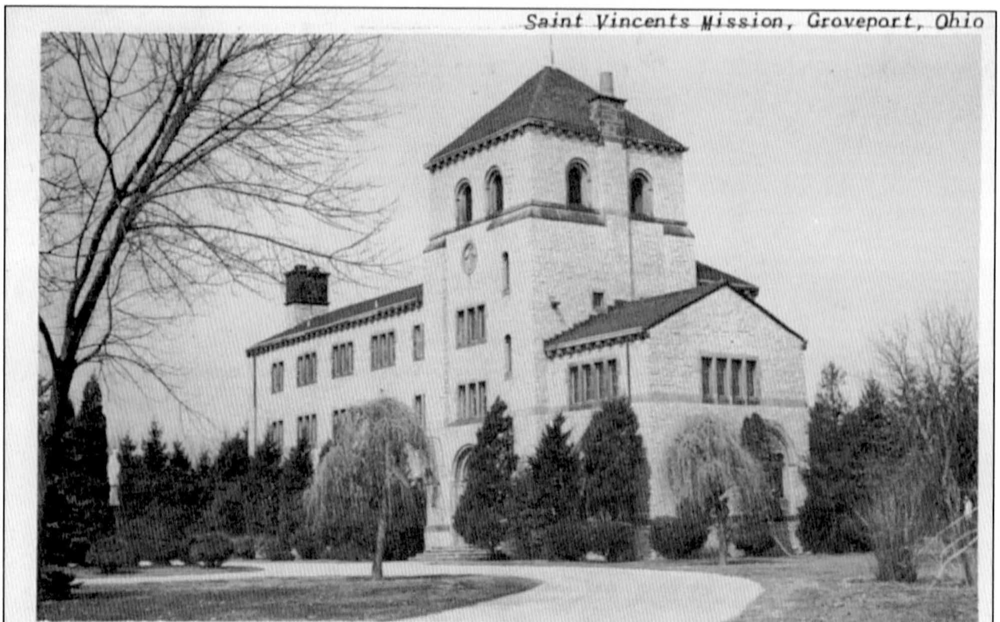

ST. VINCENT'S MISSION HOME. Opened in 1933 at the western end of Naomi Court in Groveport, the Mission served St. Mary's Catholic Parish as well as providing a place for Catholic missionaries to the Midwest to use as a headquarters and place of rest. This building is now the corporate headquarters for United McGill. The original St. Mary's Catholic Church in Groveport was built at Front and Blacklick streets in 1871.

Five

GROVEPORT STREET SCENES

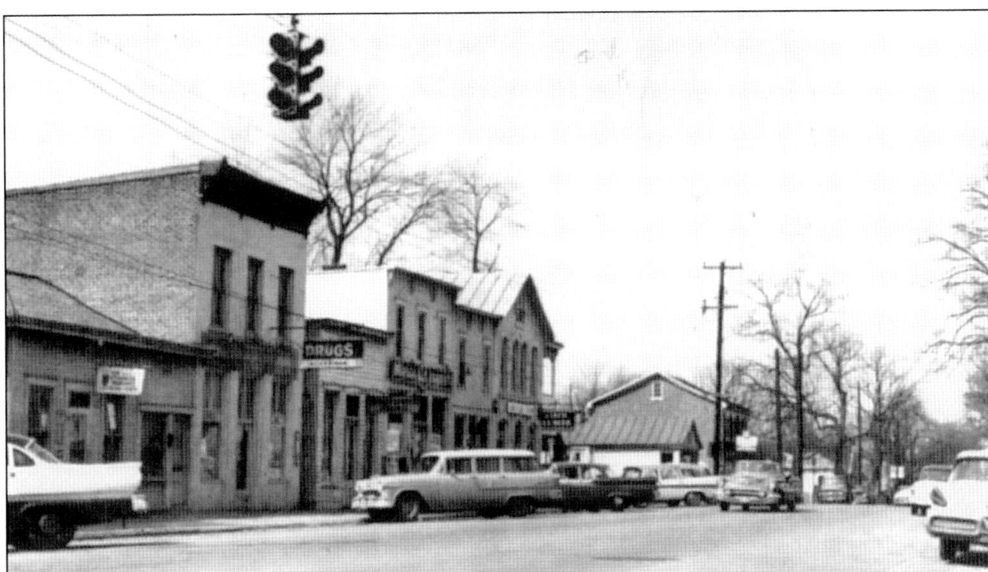

MAIN STREET, C. 1960. This is a view of Main Street looking west from Front Street. Ackerman Drugs is the two story building at the left. The two-story building at the right of the row of commercial structures is the Birch Tavern. This tavern, built in 1872, burned down in 1988, and the site is now a small village green featuring the town Christmas tree. The Birch Tavern moved next door and is still in operation.

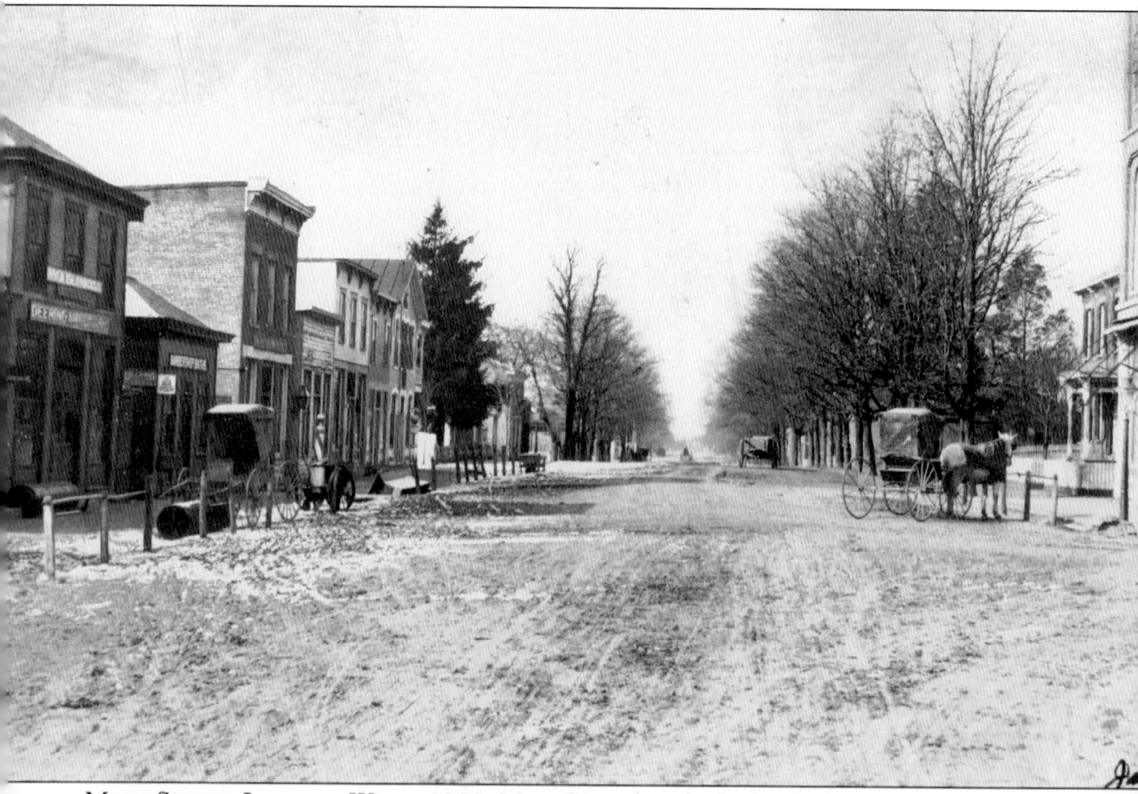

MAIN STREET LOOKING WEST, 1908. Main Street has the look of a frontier western town in this view from Front Street looking west. Town Hall is on the far right. The commercial row on the left includes a farm equipment store, a barbershop, pharmacy, shoe store, and tavern. Note the hitching posts along the street. The village paved Main Street with bricks in 1911. Until then residents contended with a dirt road that became a muddy quagmire in wet periods and a dust bowl during dry times. Besides the mud and dust, pedestrians also had to keep a watchful eye out for horse droppings. People often dealt with the mud by spreading ashes from their wood stoves on the street near their home and at crosswalks. Sprinkling wagons were used to keep the dust down in dry periods. The village spread gravel along the side of the street for use as a sidewalk.

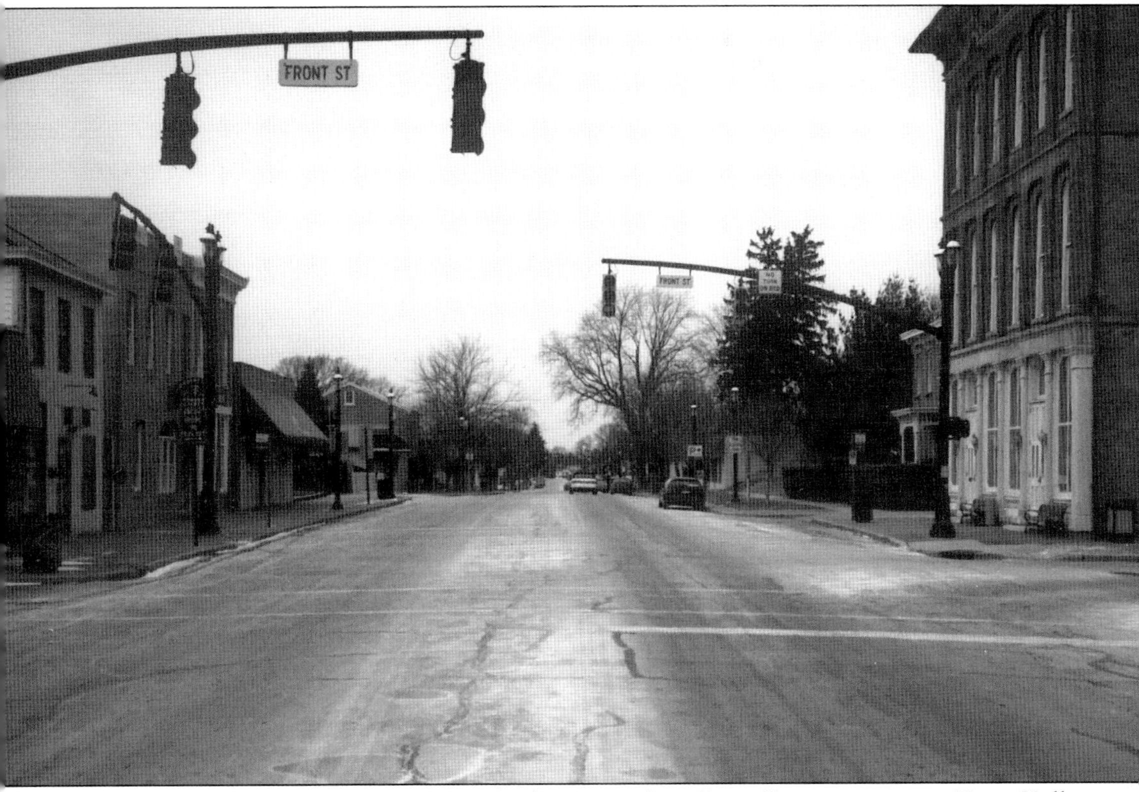

Main Street Looking West, 1997. Looking west from Front Street we can see Town Hall to the right and the commercial row of buildings still to the left, which have undergone a facelift over the years. Gone are the hitching posts, mud, and animal droppings. The Birch Tavern occupies the building with the awning at the end of the commercial row. The former pharmacy is now occupied by Dr. Thomas Webb, dentist, and the Groveport-Canal Animal Clinic. In the 1990s, the length of Main Street from Front Street west to State Route 317 underwent renovation and reconstruction. The street was widened and repaved, new sidewalks and streetlights were installed, and new utility lines put in. A casualty of this reconstruction was the canopy over the street once formed by large shade trees. New trees were planted to replace those lost.

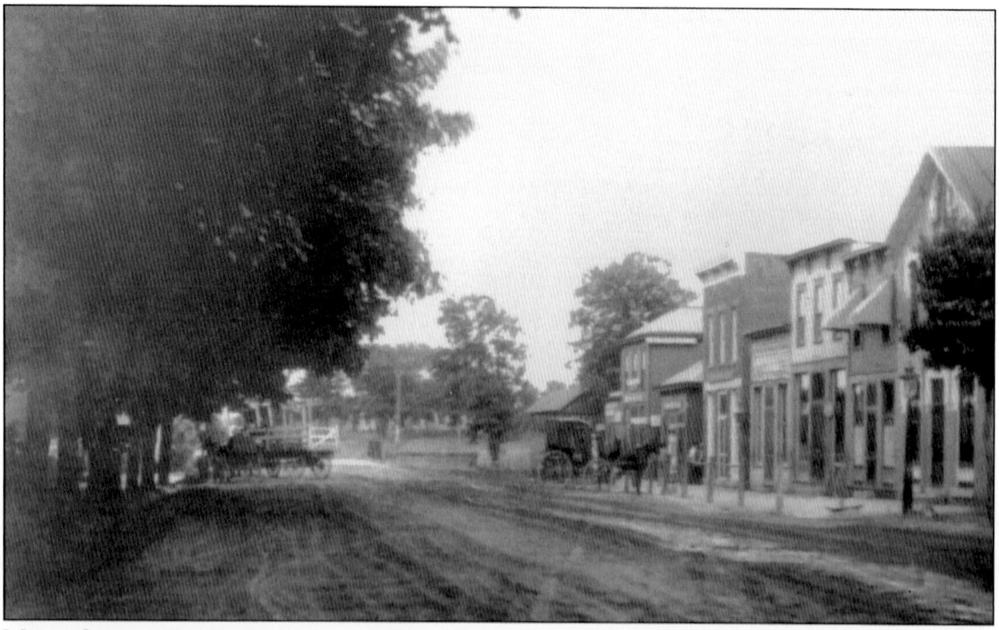

MAIN STREET LOOKING EAST, 1908. This is a view of Main Street, looking east from approximately Crooked Alley. The trees of the Elmont Hotel can be seen in the background. The guard rail of the iron turn bridge over the canal can be seen in the center left background. The commercial row of buildings can be seen on the right.

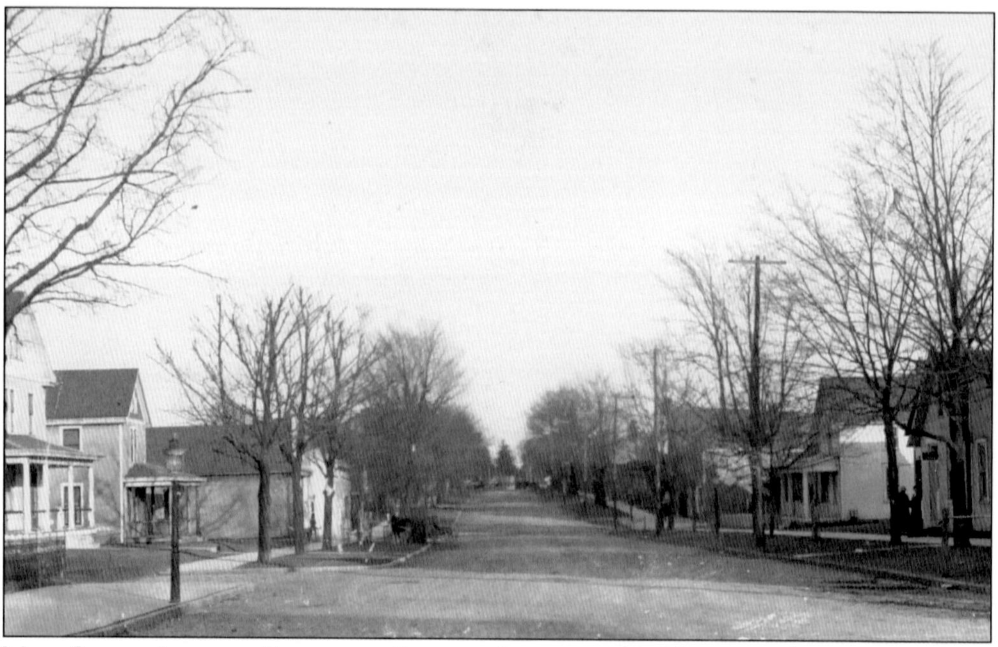

MAIN STREET LOOKING EAST FROM COLLEGE STREET, 1908. This view of Main Street shows a mixture of commercial and residential structures. The second, third, and fourth buildings on the left—including the Dildine home, Clinger Grocery, and Barnhart home—were lost in a devastating fire in 1932. Fire trucks from as far away as Columbus' Thurman Avenue station were called in to help the Groveport volunteer firefighters battle the blaze.

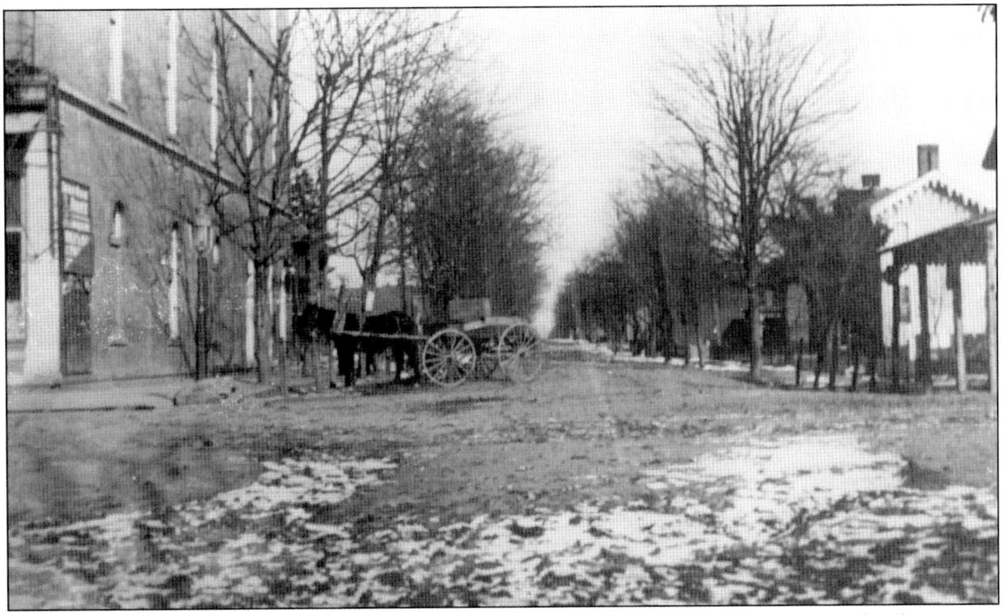

FRONT STREET LOOKING NORTH FROM MAIN STREET, 1908. Front Street was the first street paved in Groveport in 1909. One of the main traffic arteries laid out when the village was platted, the street features some of the town's oldest homes along its still brick paved right of way. The Ohio and Erie Canal coursed just to the east of the street and during canal days property owners' homes faced Front Street, while some had businesses that lined the canal bank at the rear of their lots.

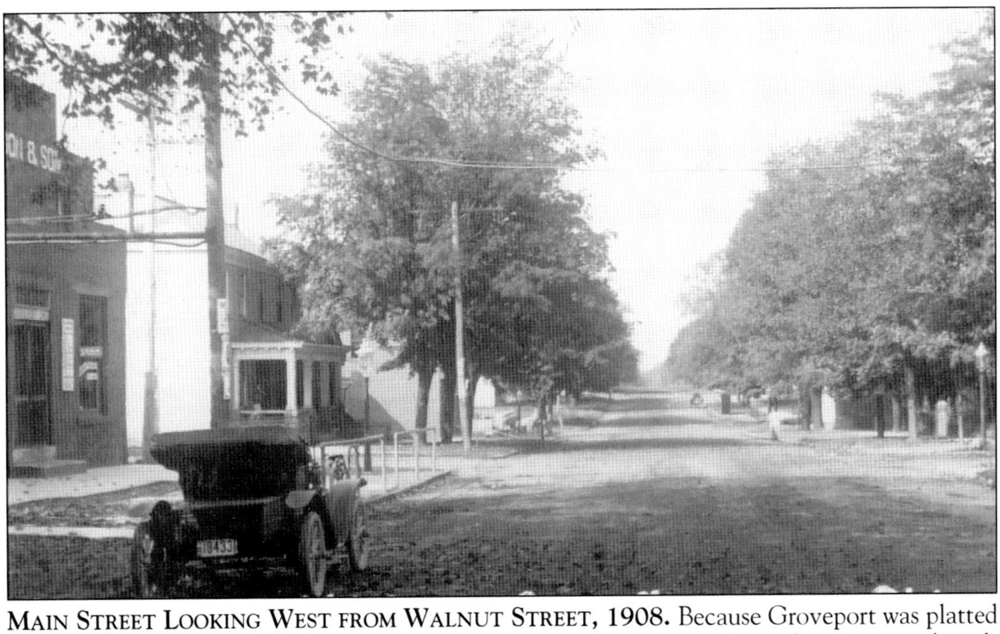

MAIN STREET LOOKING WEST FROM WALNUT STREET, 1908. Because Groveport was platted originally as two towns, it has no defined downtown or town square. In reality its entire length of Main Street is the village's "downtown," featuring a mixture of homes and businesses along its course. Here we see a sign of the future wave of transportation in the form of the car parked along the dusty street.

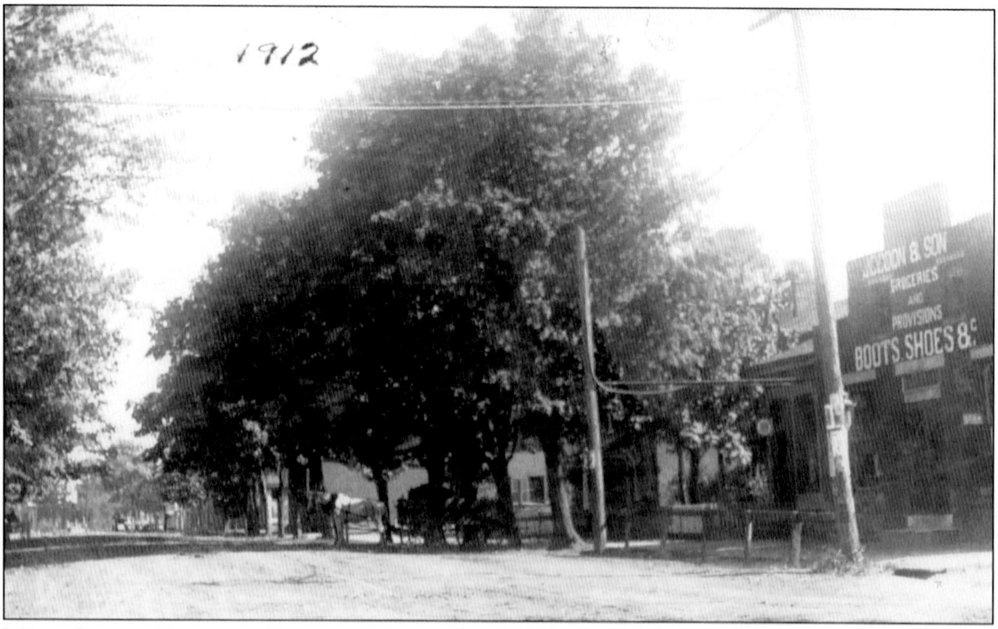

MAIN STREET LOOKING EAST FROM J.C. COON GENERAL STORE, 1908. J.C. Coon and Son general store can be seen at the right of this photo. The sign above the store reads, "J.C. Coon & Son, groceries and provisions, boots, shoes..." Also visible are some of the large shade trees that once lined Main Street.

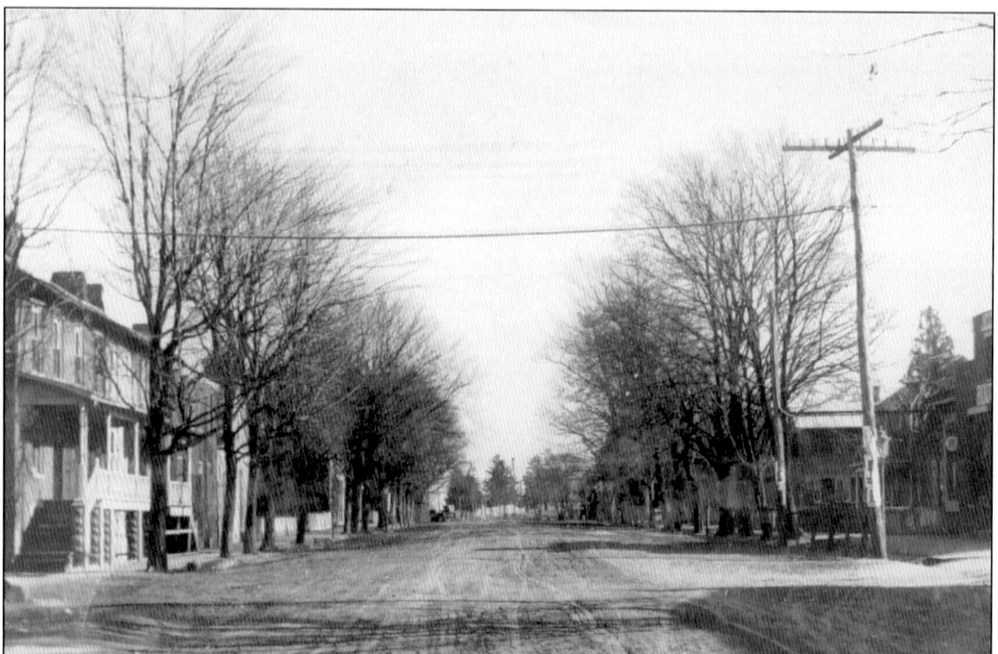

MAIN STREET LOOKING EAST FROM WALNUT STREET, 1908. The cedar trees planted by John S. Rarey at his former home Cedarlawn can be viewed in the center background of this photo. The long brick building on the left was built in 1830, and served as a tavern/inn and stagecoach stop for many years.

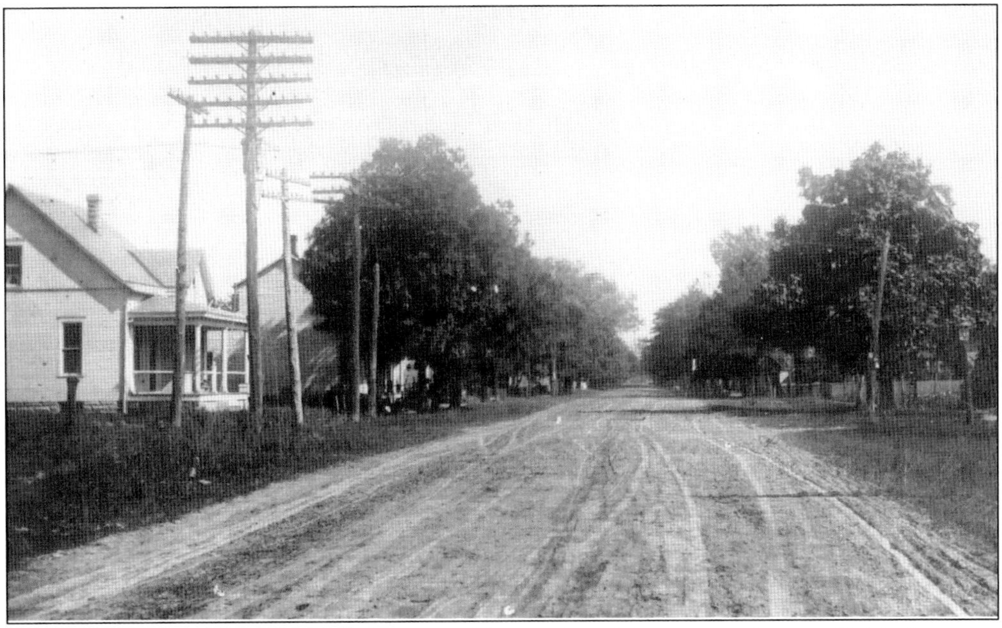

West Main Street, 1908. A few scattered homes lined the western limits of Main Street at this time. Note the high grass along the dirt street giving the area a rural feel. This area also lacked the gravel sidewalks present in the more densely populated and commercially active eastern section of the street.

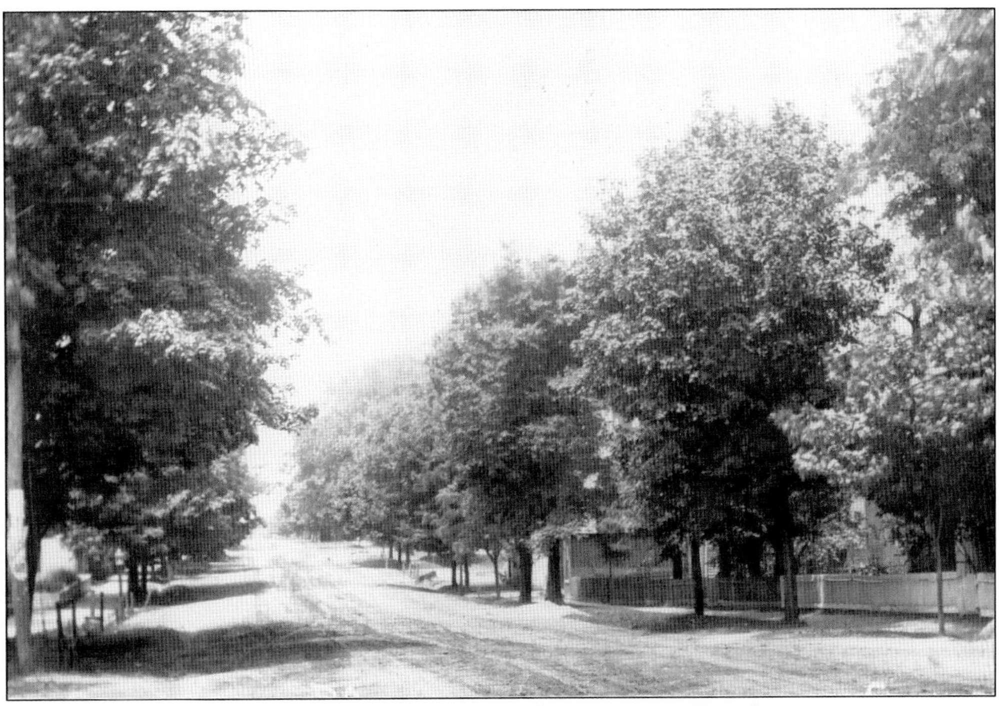

Main Street Looking West from old Post Office, 1911. Seen here is a center section of Main Street looking west just prior to the street being paved. Because Groveport formed as two towns it has no traditional defined downtown.

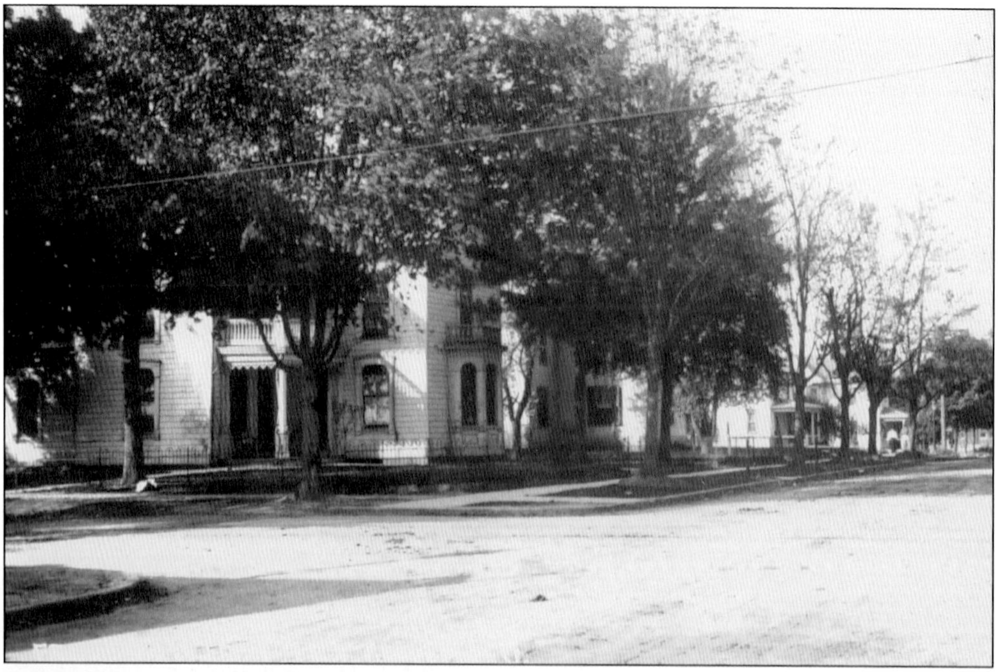

Front Street Looking North from Blacklick Street, 1908. The electric Scioto Valley Traction Line tracks can be barely seen in the dust crossing from left to right. The prominent large white frame house in the photo has long since gone and been replaced by a brick home.

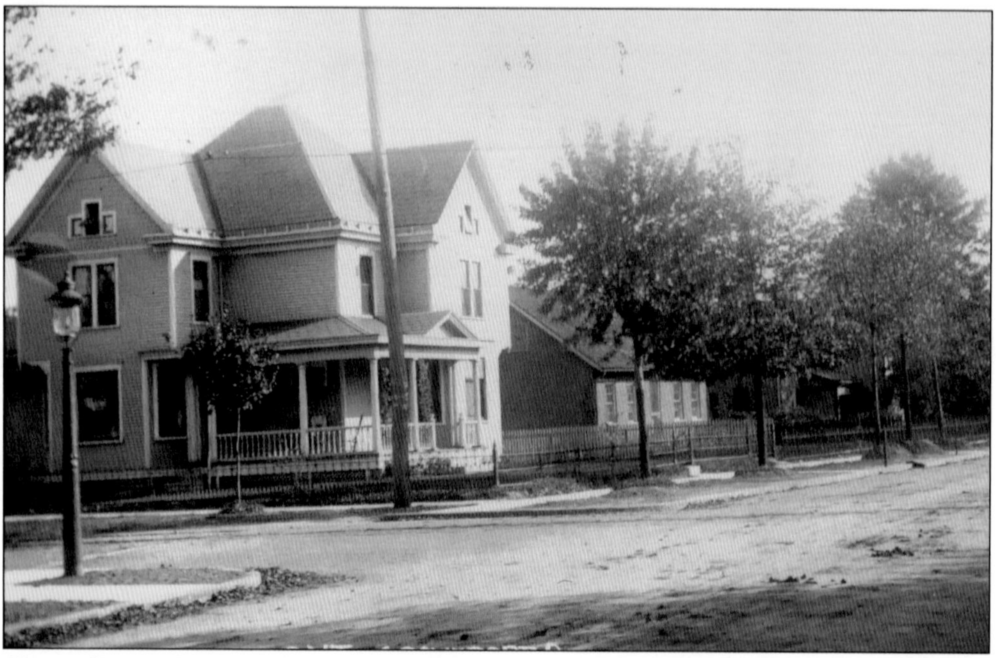

Front Street Looking South from Blacklick Street, 1908. The home featured in this photo still stands in Groveport, though its wrought-iron fence is no longer present. The house to its immediate right also remains and is considered one of the oldest homes in town. Note the gas streetlight on the corner to the left and the horse droppings visible in the dusty street.

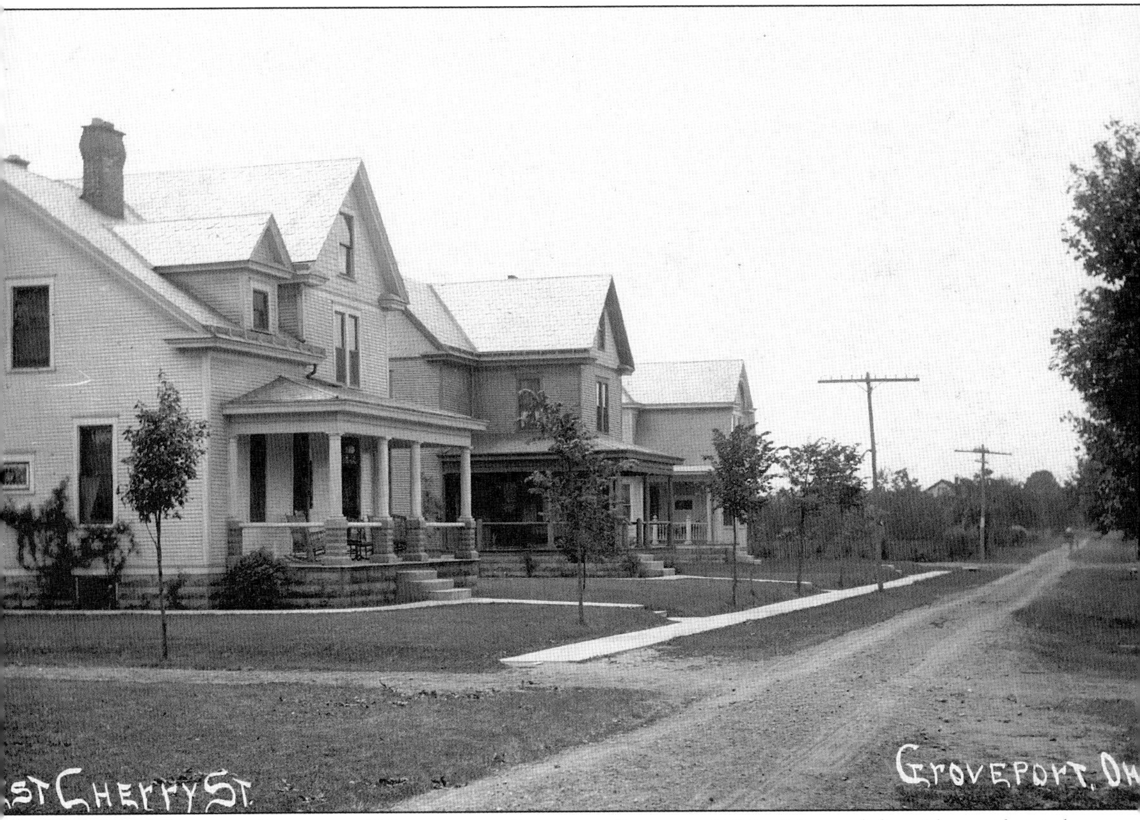

CHERRY STREET LOOKING WEST FROM COLLEGE STREET, 1908. Most of the side residential streets in town were mere dirt paths for many years. Here we see Cherry Street just as it is beginning to be developed with three new homes and a concrete sidewalk. The dirt path crossing the street is Raver Alley. Groveport paved, in brick, its three major streets first—Front Street in 1909, Main Street in 1911, and College Street in 1915. Blacklick Street was brick paved in 1923, followed by Naomi Court in 1931, and Walnut, Elm, and Cherry streets in 1939. The newly paved streets soon would become the domain of the automobile. The first known automobile in Groveport was believed to be owned by Charles Arnold in the early twentieth century and it is said to have looked like a surrey with big wooden wheels and a hand cranked engine under the seat.

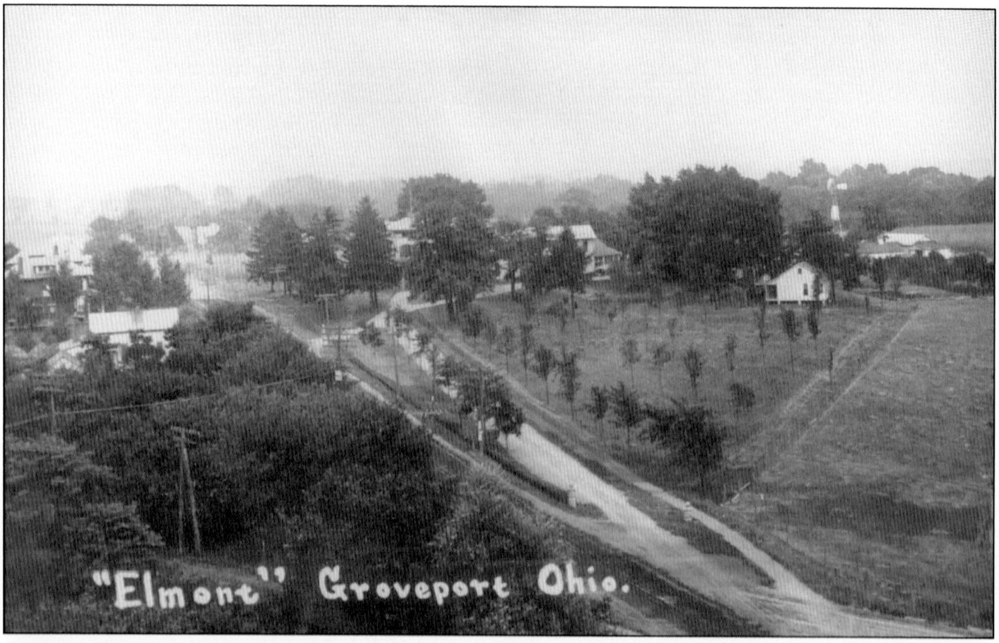

Aerial View of Main Street from Town Hall, 1908. This photo was taken from atop Town Hall. The dirt road cutting diagonally through the picture is Main Street. The Elmont Hotel is nestled in the center background within the ring of cedar trees originally planted by John S. Rarey. One of the hotel guest cottages can be seen in the right background.

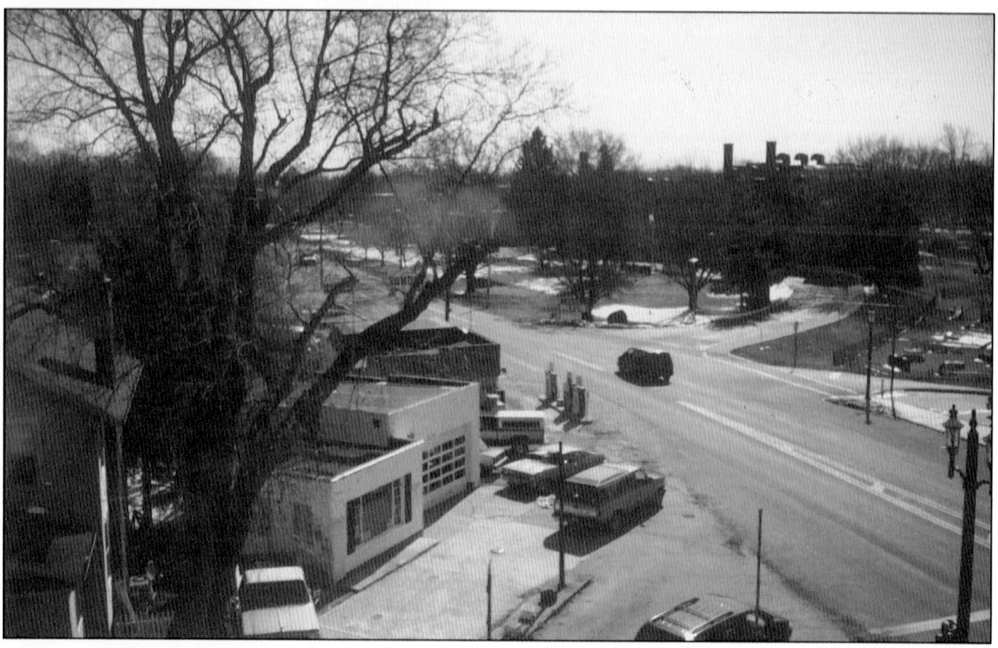

Aerial View of Main Street, 2000. This is a modern view taken from the third floor of Town Hall looking east. Groveport Elementary is the large building in the background and service stations now sit along Main Street. Wirt Road, coming in from the right, follows the old right-of-way of the Ohio and Erie Canal.

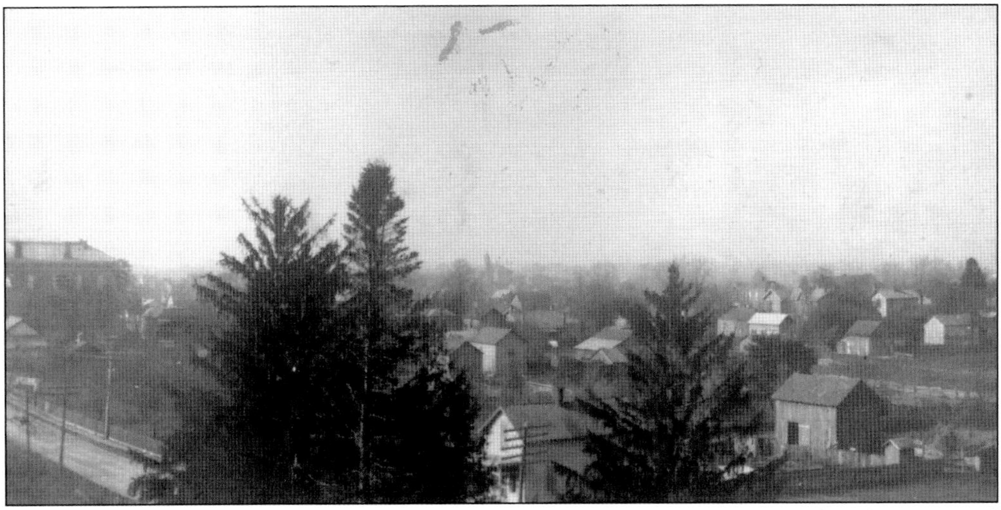

AERIAL VIEW OF GROVEPORT FROM ELMONT HOTEL, 1908. The roof of the Elmont Hotel provides this vantage point, looking west, for a view of Groveport. The Town Hall is at the left and Rarey's cedar trees dominate the foreground. Main Street can be viewed cutting in at the left. This perspective shows the village as a collection of homes and outbuildings.

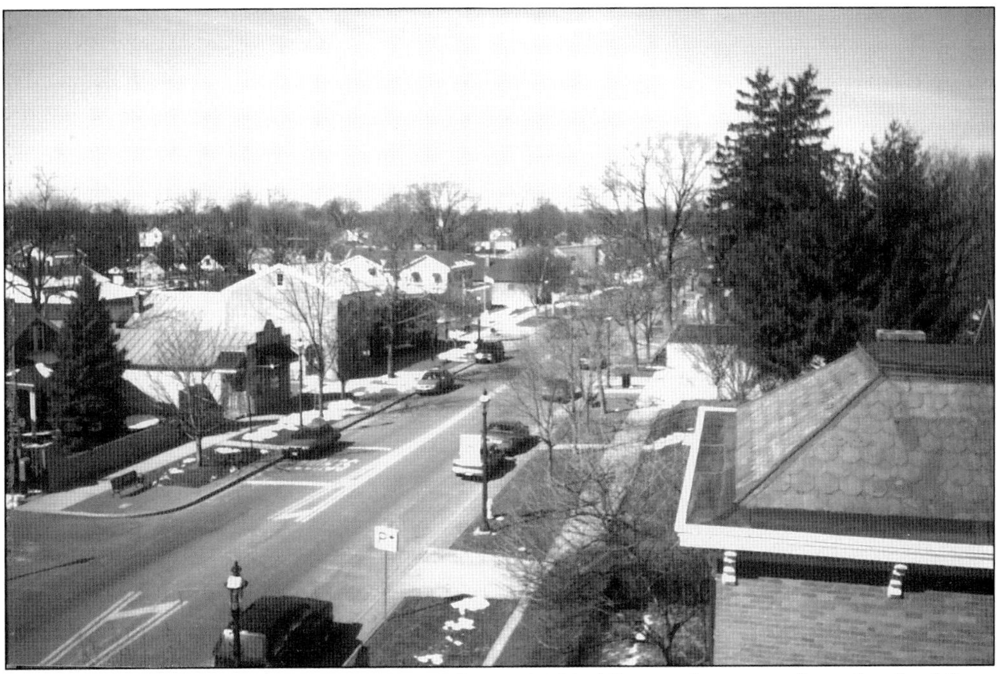

AERIAL VIEW OF MAIN STREET LOOKING EAST, 2000. This modern view from the third floor of Town Hall shows the reconstructed Main Street with its new electric streetlights (modeled after the old gaslights) and brick lined curbs. Note how the street is a mixture of both residences and commercial enterprises.

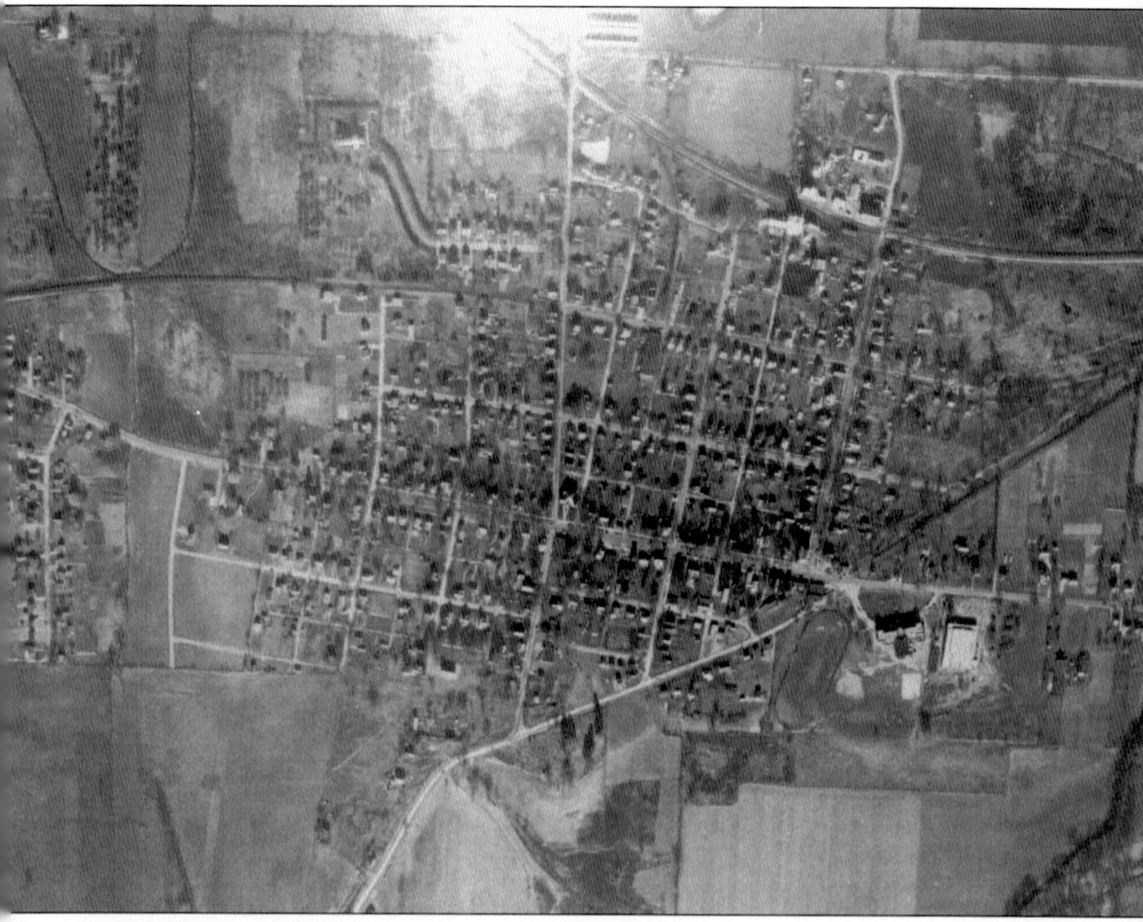

AERIAL VIEW OF GROVEPORT, 1952. The remnants of the Ohio and Erie Canal can be seen as a dark line cutting diagonally through town from the upper right. Also, the traction line right of way can be viewed coming in at center left and into Blacklick Street. The railroad curves in from the top of the photo. College Street forms a straight line from the top through the middle of the picture. Groveport School is visible in the lower right along Main Street, which cuts a swath through the middle of the photo from left to right. The new gymnasium sits beside the school. At the far left a new housing development, Kessler Addition, can be seen forming around Madison and Kessler streets. A curving driveway at approximately the top center of the photo leads to the Catholic Mission. At the very top of the photo along College Street one can see rows of grain silos, which were once situated on the north side of Corbett Road.

Six

BUSINESS

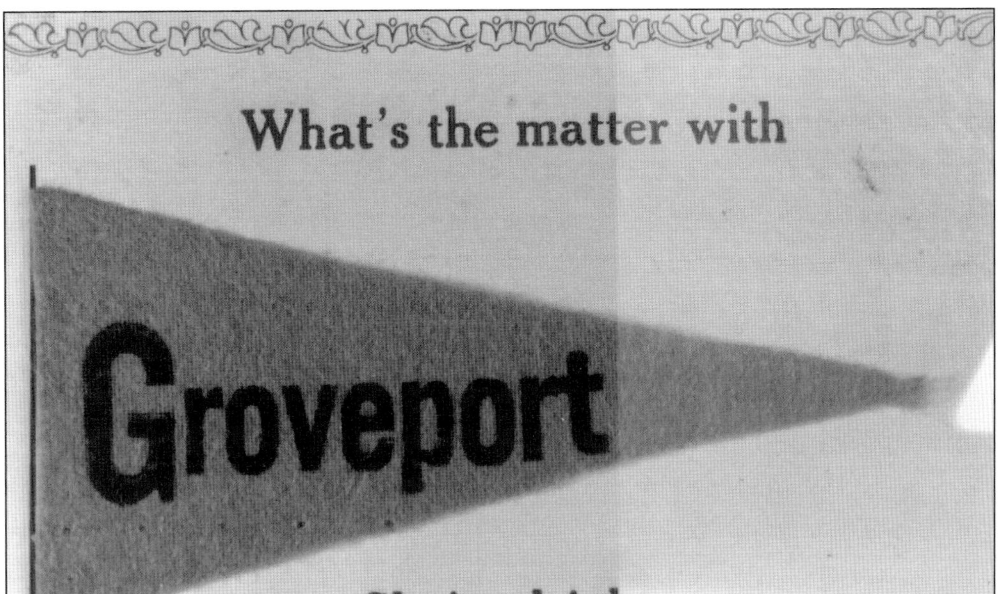

GROVEPORT GREETING. This early twentieth century postcard was used as a way of promoting the village. Booster efforts to attract businesses and residents are ongoing in just about every municipality from the time a town is platted to the present day.

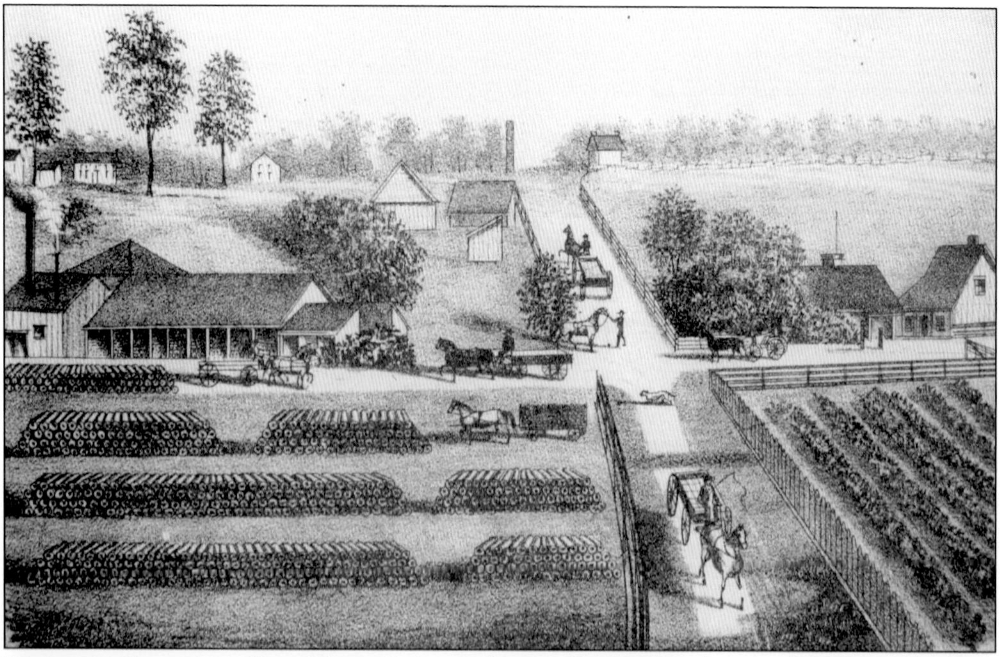

MADISON TOWNSHIP TILE WORKS. Located near Canal Winchester, the tile works took advantage of the vast supply of good clay and strata of Bedford shale on hand in Madison Township for the making of brick and tile. It opened in 1872 and closed in 1920.

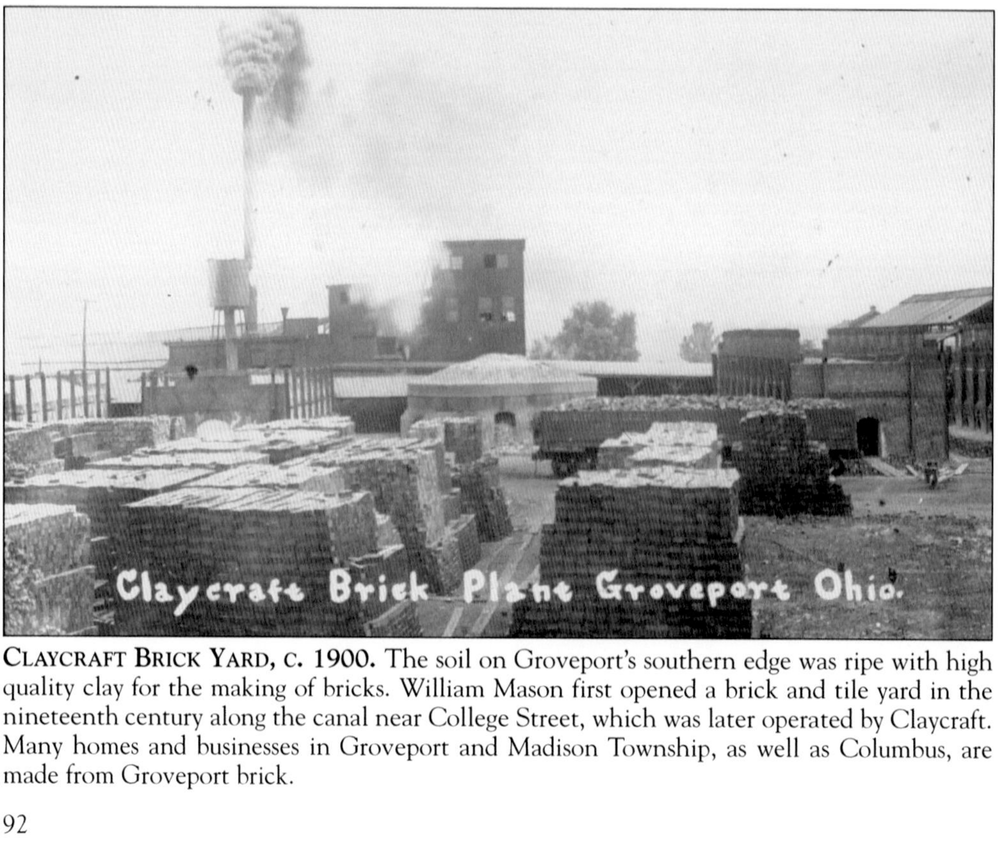

CLAYCRAFT BRICK YARD, C. 1900. The soil on Groveport's southern edge was ripe with high quality clay for the making of bricks. William Mason first opened a brick and tile yard in the nineteenth century along the canal near College Street, which was later operated by Claycraft. Many homes and businesses in Groveport and Madison Township, as well as Columbus, are made from Groveport brick.

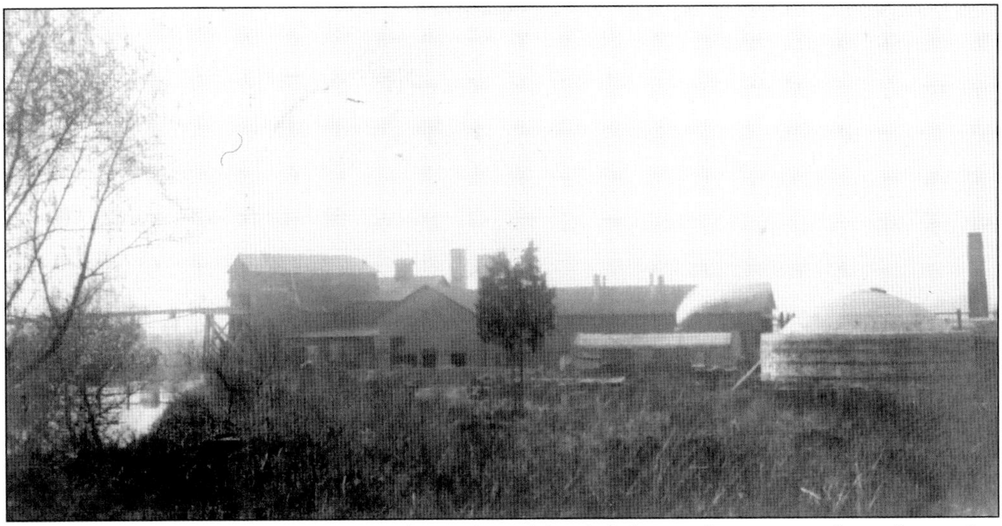

CLAYCRAFT BRICK YARD, 1907. A large domed brick kiln can be seen to the right in this photo. The Ohio and Erie Canal is on the left and the raised tressel over the canal and Canada can be seen to the rear. Claycraft suffered a major fire in 1911, but rebuilt and continued in operation until the 1920s, when the plant closed.

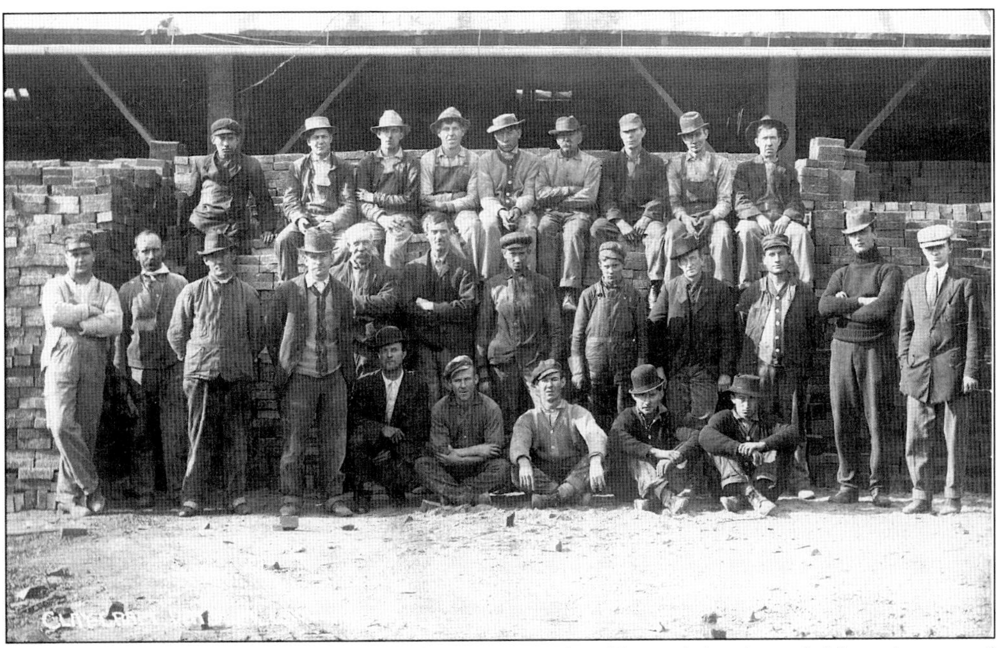

CLAYCRAFT DAY SHIFT, C. 1900. Workers pose at the Claycraft brick yard. Note the rugged clothing worn by the employees. Unfortunately the names of these workers are not available. Debate remains on why the brick yard closed. One explanation was that the supply of clay was depleted. Another speculation is that talk of the workers unionizing led to a management decision to close down.

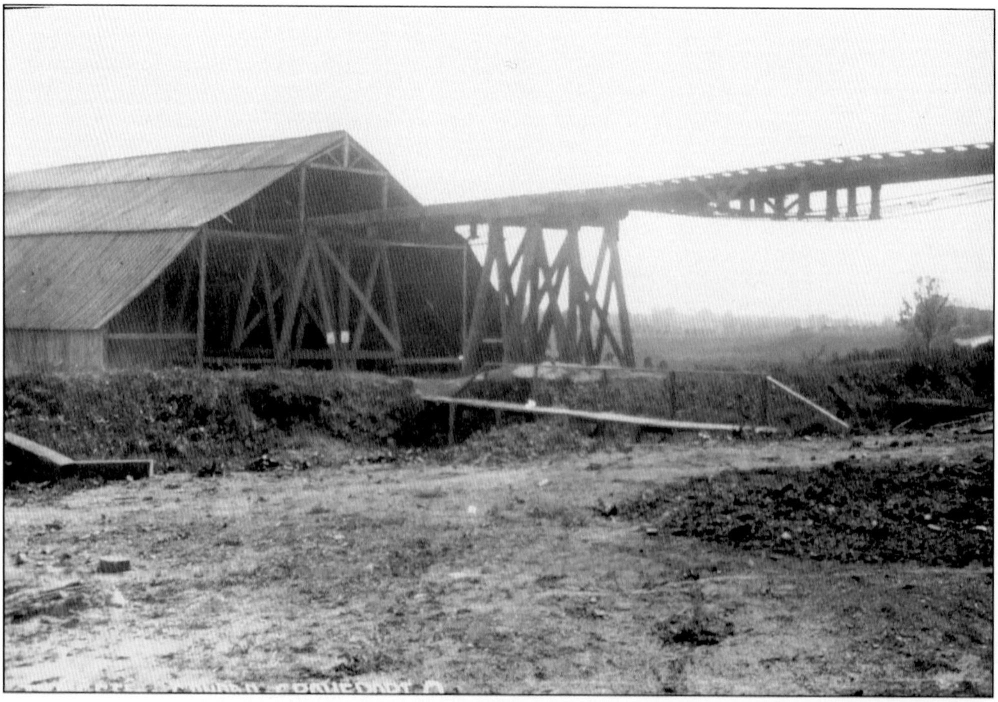

CLAYCRAFT TRESSEL AND CANADA OVER CANAL. This tressel enabled workers to move product over the Ohio and Erie Canal, which is the ditch visible in the foreground in the photo showing the tressel raised (above). The raised tressel allowed canal boats to pass underneath. The photo below shows the tressel in the lowered position. The plant's location along the canal enabled the company to ship its products with relative ease.

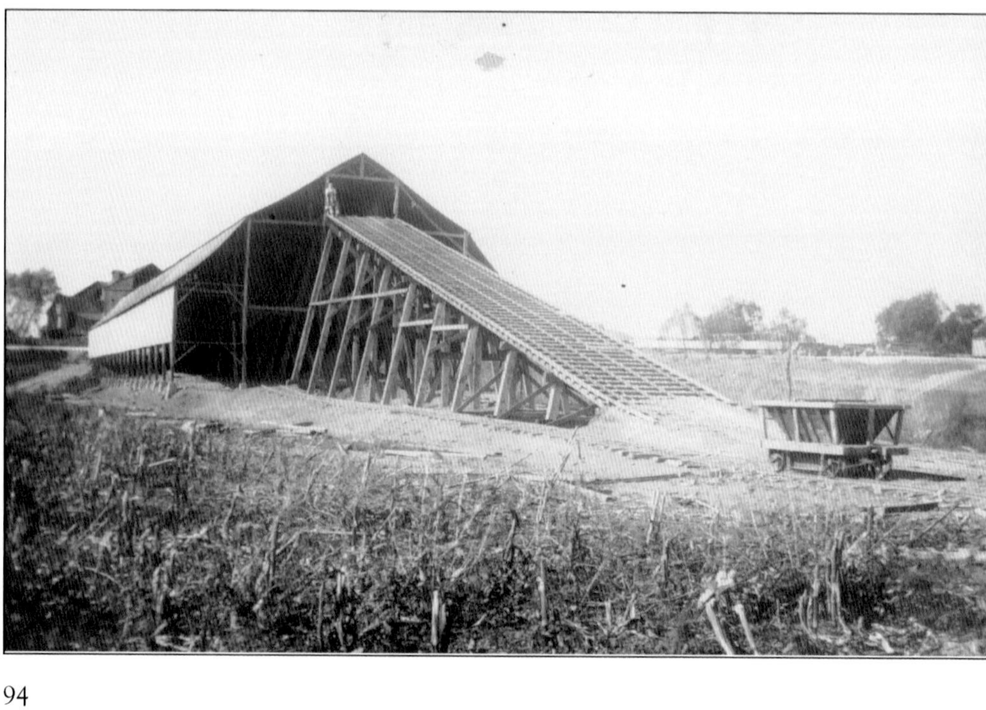

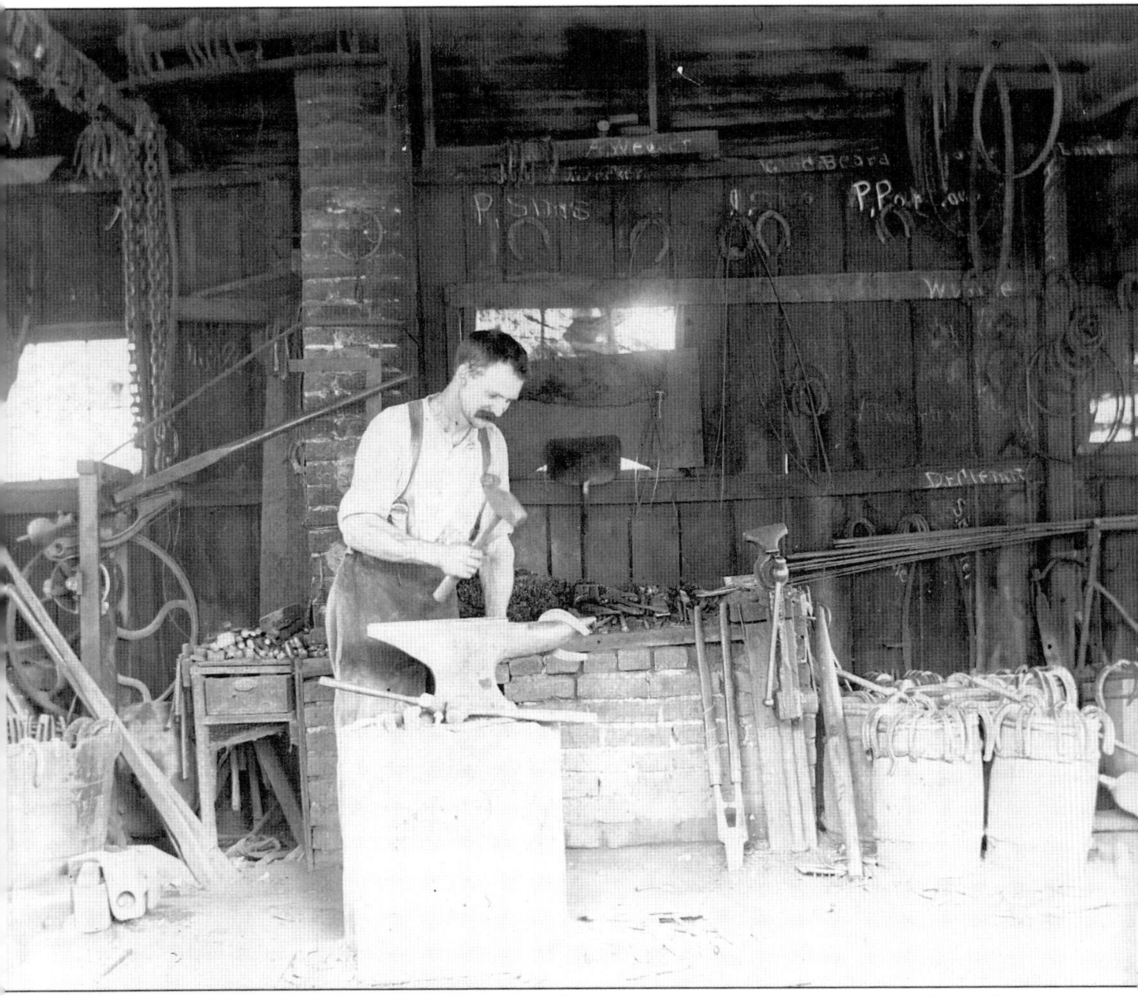

FRANK WILLIAMS, BLACKSMITH. Frank Williams, shown here hammering a horseshoe on his anvil, worked as a blacksmith in the early twentieth century in a shop in what is now the parking lot behind the commercial buildings on Groveport's east Main Street at Wirt Road. Horseshoes abound in this shop. Barrels of horseshoes can be seen to the lower right, hanging on the walls and rafters, and in a barrel at lower left. Williams' forge wheel is at the lower left. His tools are stacked beside him along the bricks. Blacksmiths played a vital role in early America in keeping horses shod to protect the animals' feet. Horses and mules were the life blood of the agricultural economy performing much of the work now done by machines. Besides the work, horses also served as the main form of transportation for most people. Because of their role, the proper care and protection of horses was of the utmost importance.

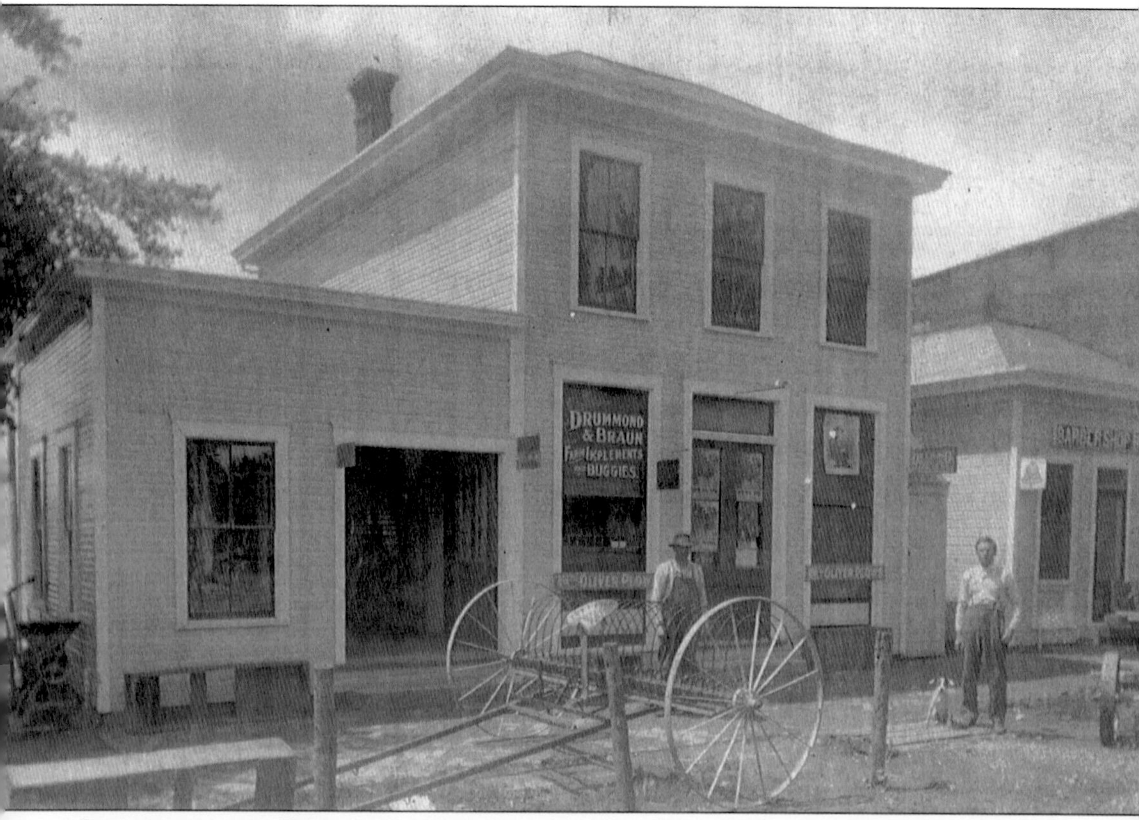

DRUMMOND AND BRAUN, C. 1900. Most businesses in nineteenth and twentieth century Groveport served the agricultural Madison Township community. Drummond and Braun Farm Implements and Buggies, located on Main Street opposite from the Town Hall, was one such business. Pictured here is an unidentified man at left and at right, Carl Braun along with his dog. The town featured enterprises such as grain dealers, grocers, physicians, sawmills, wagon makers, livestock dealers, and a host of other similar businesses aimed at helping Madison Township farmers, while also making a profit. Note the hitching post and still unpaved street. Groveport was primarily an agrarian community until the 1970s, when urban growth from Columbus and in the surrounding area began to replace the township's farms.

Bigelow Hardware, c. 1900. Hardware stores also supplied area farmers. This store was one of several hardware stores to have operated in the village over the years. It is located on the southeast corner of Main Street and Brook Alley. The building is still in use today and is now operated as Hanson House.

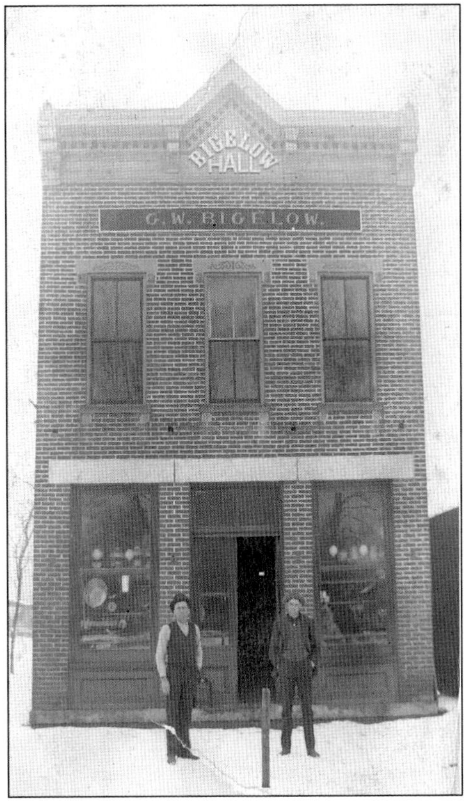

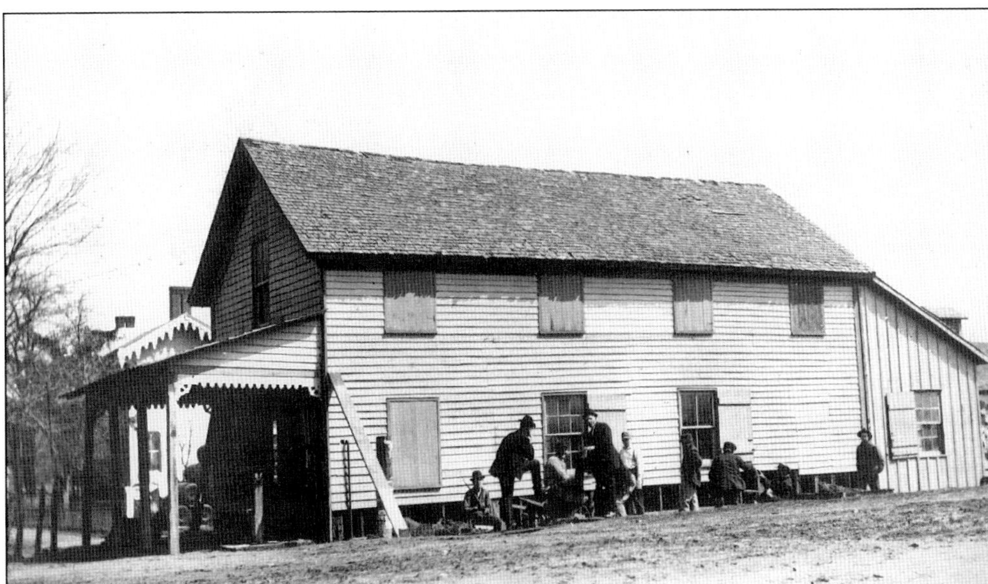

Saloon, 1908. Canal towns were known for their saloons and Groveport was no exception. This is one of several saloons that existed in the village during its canal heyday. It was located on the northeast corner of Main and Front streets. The canal passed behind this saloon on the right. Though the canal towpath was on the opposite bank, planks were available along the shore near the saloon to allow canalers to walk from their boat to the saloon.

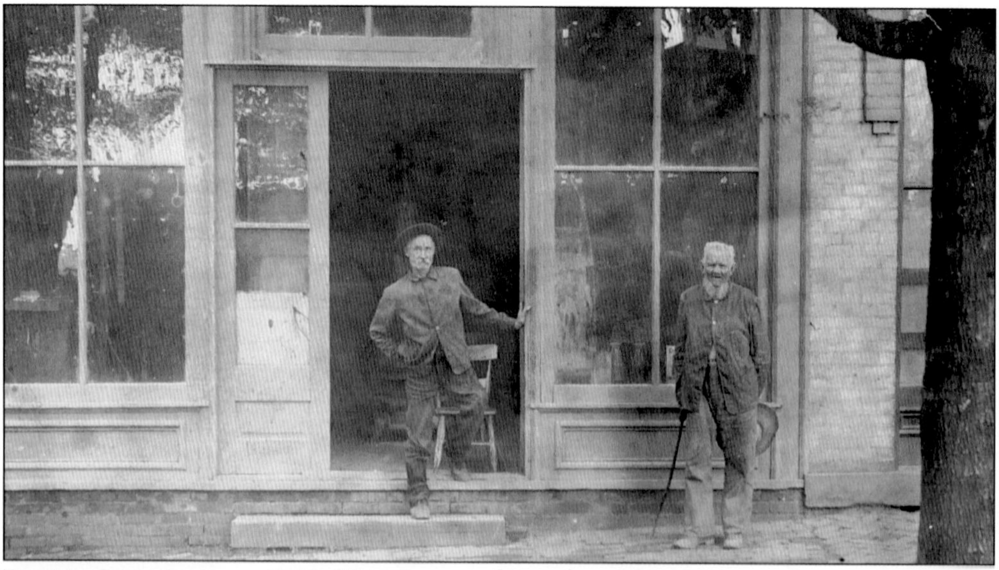

Boring Shoe Shop, c. 1900. This shop was located on Main Street in the commercial row of buildings across from Town Hall. The brick structure to the right is a tavern. Unfortunately the identities of the two gentlemen pictured here are unknown.

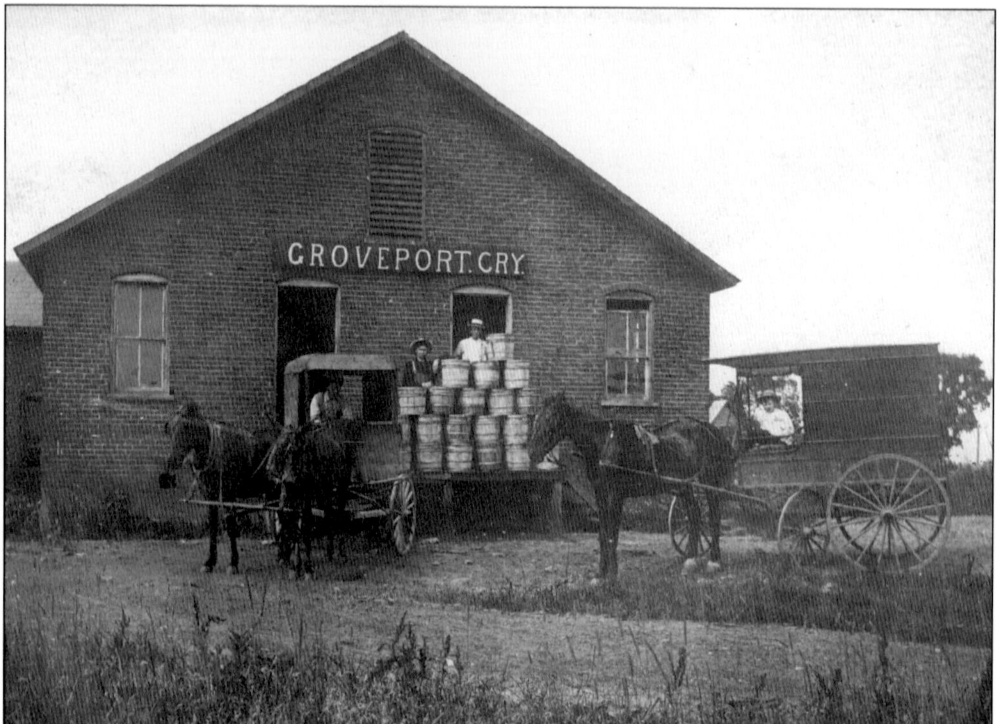

Butter Tubs at Groveport Creamery, c. 1907. A stack of butter tubs awaits delivery on the loading dock of the creamery, which was located on Blacklick Street at Church Street. G. William Woerlein owned and operated the creamery. Milk was purchased from Madison Township farmers for resale and to be made into butter.

GROVEPORT CREAMERY ORDER ENVELOPE. An order and payment envelope for the Groveport Creamery. Customers wrote down the amount of milk, butter, etc. they wanted and placed the payment inside. The envelopes also featured advertising from other area businesses, such as John Schleppi & Son Farm Implements.

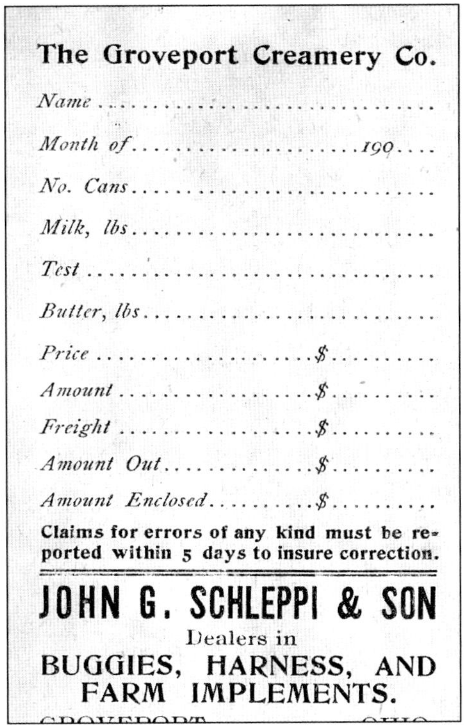

The Groveport Creamery Co.

Name ....

Month of .... *190*....

No. Cans ....

Milk, lbs ....

Test ....

Butter, lbs ....

Price ....$..........

Amount ....$..........

Freight ....$..........

Amount Out ....$..........

Amount Enclosed ....$..........

Claims for errors of any kind must be reported within 5 days to insure correction.

JOHN G. SCHLEPPI & SON

Dealers in

BUGGIES, HARNESS, AND FARM IMPLEMENTS.

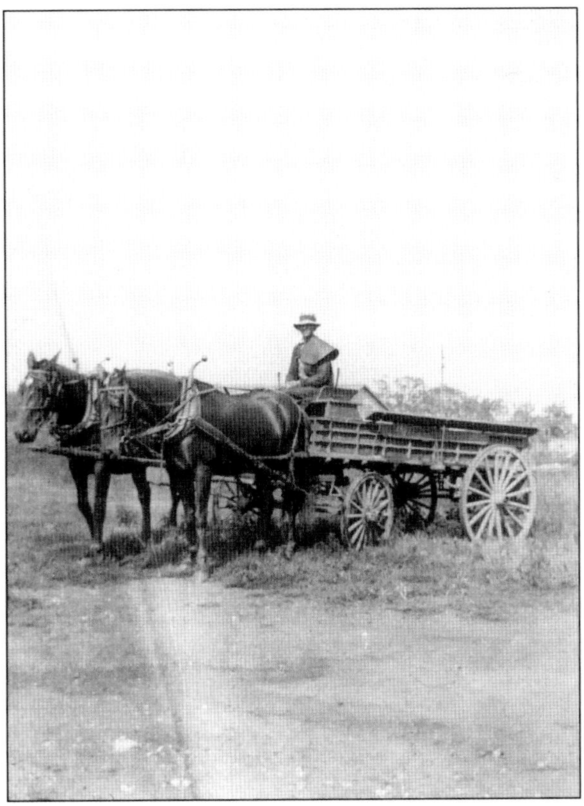

BILL PAINTER ON ICE WAGON. Groveport homes used ice boxes to refrigerate their food. Ice was delivered to homes once a week. Customers placed order cards on their doors or windows stating how many pounds of ice they needed. The ice man would then cut the necessary amount from a 300-pound block of ice. The ice plant was located at the rear of the Groveport Creamery on Blacklick Street.

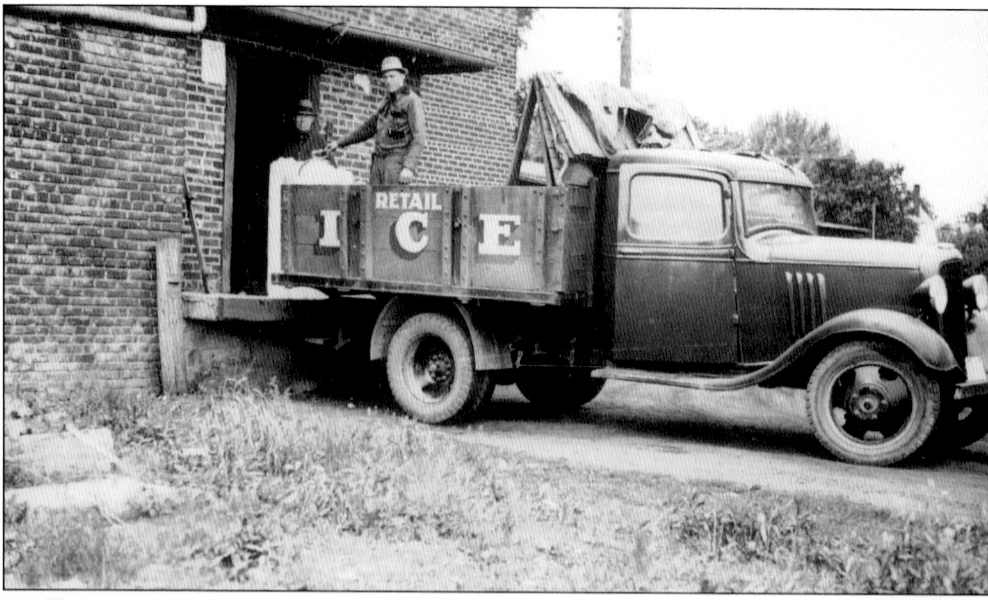

ICE TRUCK, 1936. During the Great Depression of the 1930s, as the story goes, Groveport kids would distract the ice delivery man and while others broke off pieces of ice from the back of his truck. The kids would then sell the small chunks of ice to street laborers or other workers in the village for a penny a piece on hot summer days.

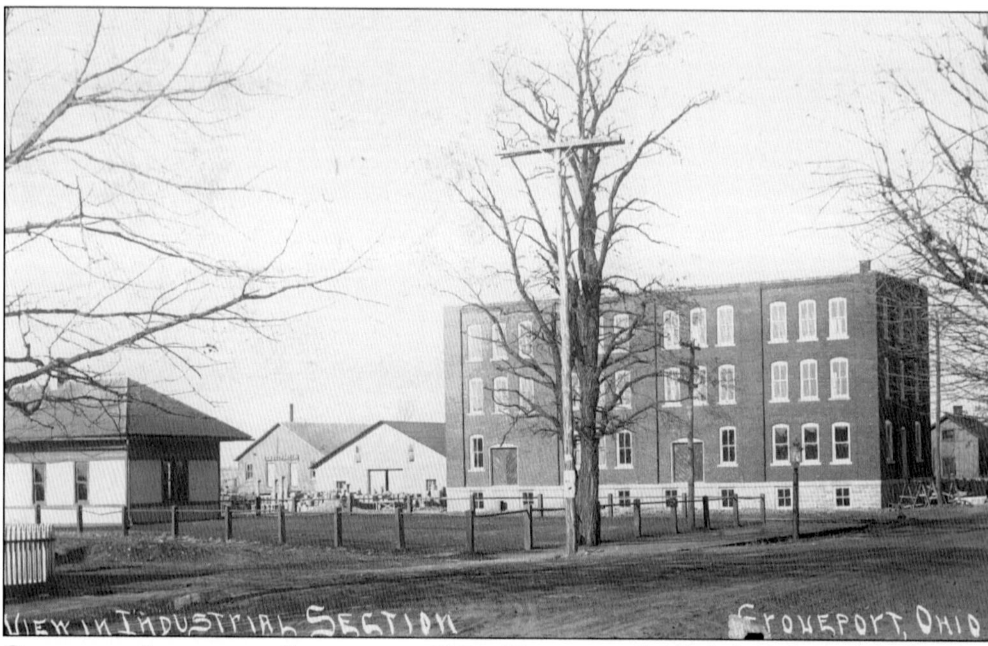

GROVEPORT INDUSTRIAL SECTION, C. 1908. This postcard, labeled "Industrial Section," is a view of the Groveport rail yard looking north from Front Street. The large brick railroad warehouse in the photo still stands today. At left is the Groveport railroad depot. When the Ohio and Erie Canal fell into disuse in the late nineteenth and early twentieth centuries, the rail yard became the hub of business activity for shipping and receiving.

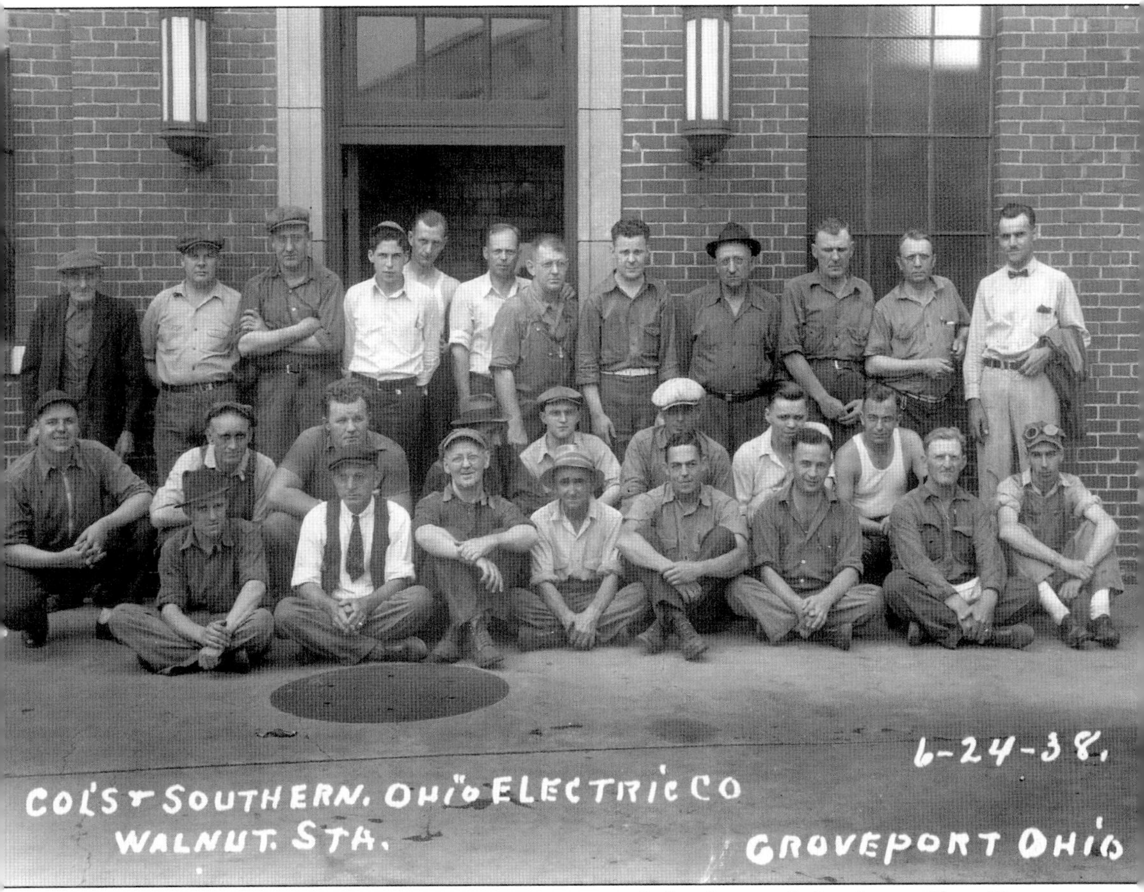

BIG WALNUT POWER PLANT WORKERS, 1938. Columbus and Southern Ohio Electric Company's Big Walnut Power Plant in Madison Township provided much needed, steady work, for area men during the Great Depression of the 1930s. The plant paid 40 cents per hour for a five hour shift over a five day work week. The plant generated electricity for Groveport and the township. Pictured here, from left to right, are the following: (front row) Oats Hardman, Ernest Early, Peachy Carruthers, Carl Bittler, John Nelson, Grover Leonard, Rex Powell, and Leo Ray; (middle row) Jack Nelson, Ed Johnson, Hollis Aldridge, Bill Kinsel, (unidentified), Floyd Foster, Fred Waters, and Carl Crist; (back row) Chet Helber, Pat Meloy, Dan Jewit, Ben Knipe, Herman Petty, Frank Meyers, Merle Solt, George Addington, Lowell Solt, Hi Root, Dick Morgan, and Lew Snyder.

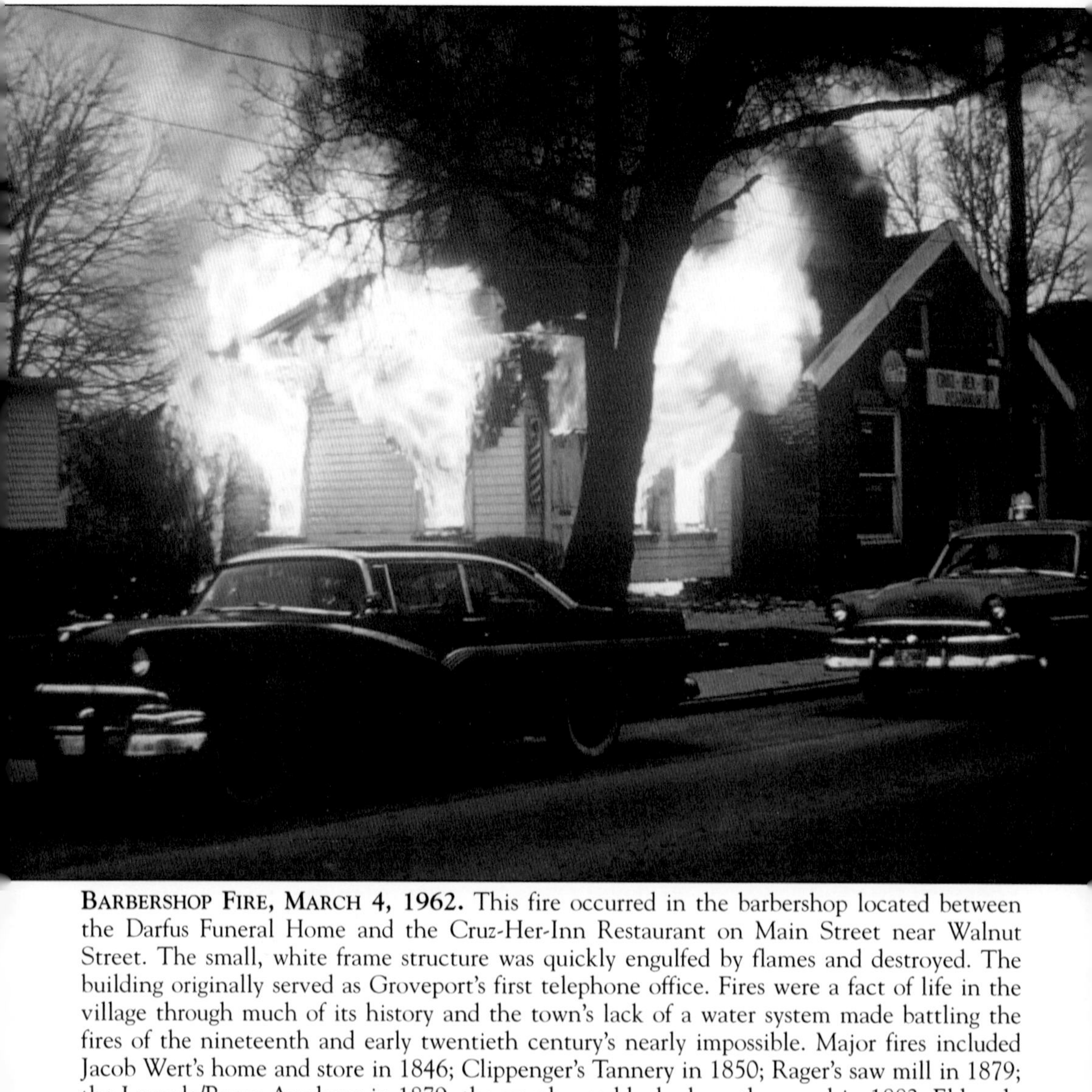

Barbershop Fire, March 4, 1962. This fire occurred in the barbershop located between the Darfus Funeral Home and the Cruz-Her-Inn Restaurant on Main Street near Walnut Street. The small, white frame structure was quickly engulfed by flames and destroyed. The building originally served as Groveport's first telephone office. Fires were a fact of life in the village through much of its history and the town's lack of a water system made battling the fires of the nineteenth and early twentieth century's nearly impossible. Major fires included Jacob Wert's home and store in 1846; Clippenger's Tannery in 1850; Rager's saw mill in 1879; the Laypole/Rarey Academy in 1879; the warehouse block along the canal in 1882; Eldorado Mills, 1884; and Dr. Saylor's barn in 1897. But a large fire on Main Street near Brook Alley, in December,1932, that destroyed two homes and a grocery led to the construction of a town water works and waterlines in 1936.

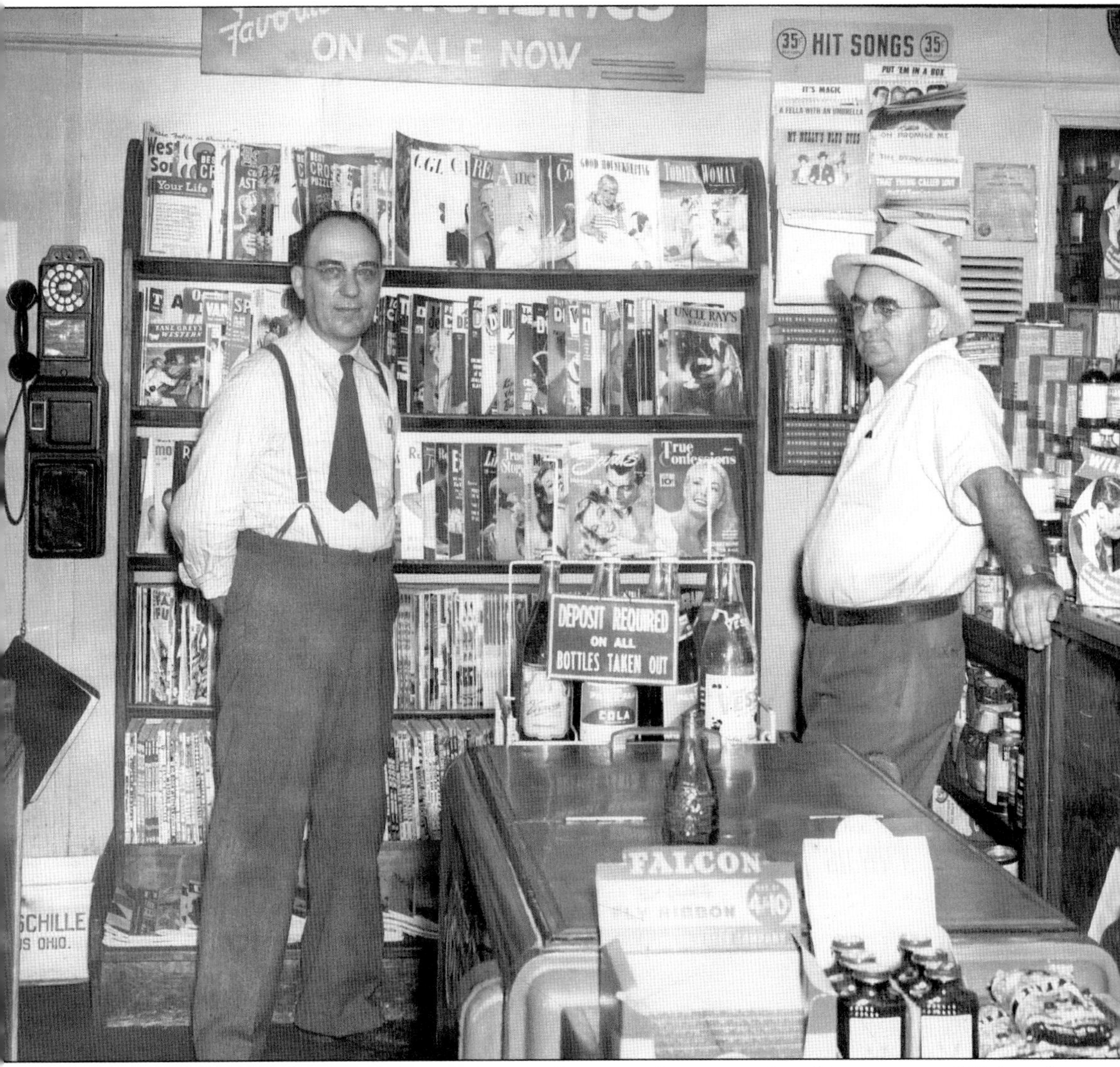

KENNETH "DOC" ACKERMAN, C. 1950S. A pharmacy first opened in Groveport in 1876, and then was moved to a site on Main Street opposite Town Hall in 1882 by John and Frank Rarey. They were followed in ownership by Lew Eyman, W. R. Smith, Bob Terry, J. R. Moore, and Charles Henninger. In 1937, Kenneth "Doc" Ackerman took over, and along with his son Lyle, operated the pharmacy until 1967, when it was sold to John Hougland. Ackerman compounded his own medicines, ointments, and powders making them up from a handwritten book of formulas he kept and continuously updated. To serve the agricultural community, Ackerman carried and made up veterinary medicines for farmers' livestock and people's pets. He also carried patent medicines such as "Wahoo Bitters." He was known to keep his store open long hours to accommodate his customers and would also open up after hours in customers' times of need when illnesses struck. Ackerman is pictured here at left with an unidentified customer.

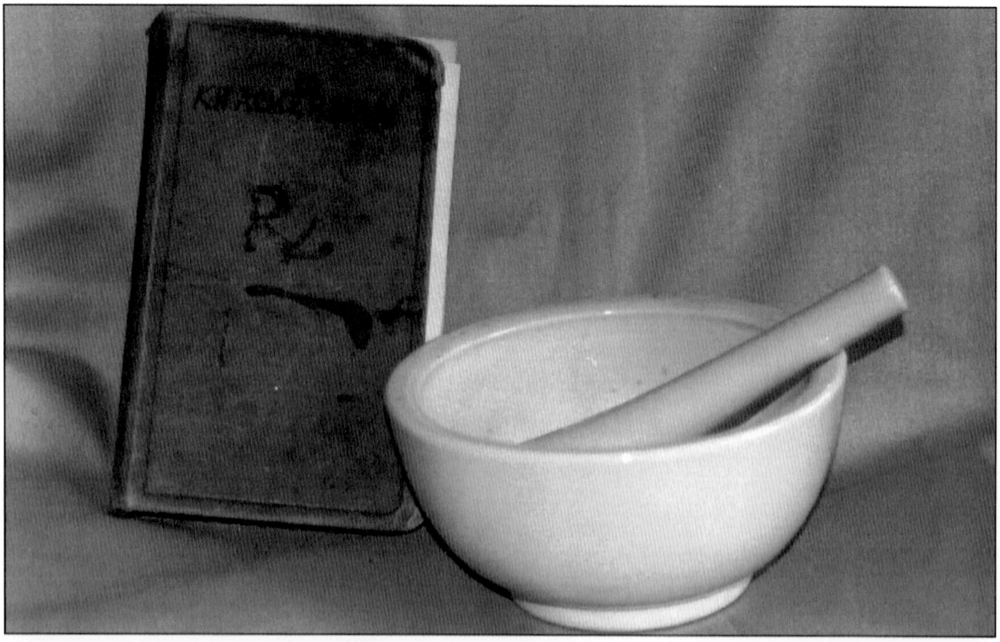

ACKERMAN'S FORMULA BOOK/MORTAR AND PESTLE. Pictured here is Doc Ackerman's personal handwritten formula book as well as one of his sets of mortar and pestles he used to mix and make medicines. He owned several sets of mortars and pestles of various sizes to accommodate the amounts of medicines he had to make.

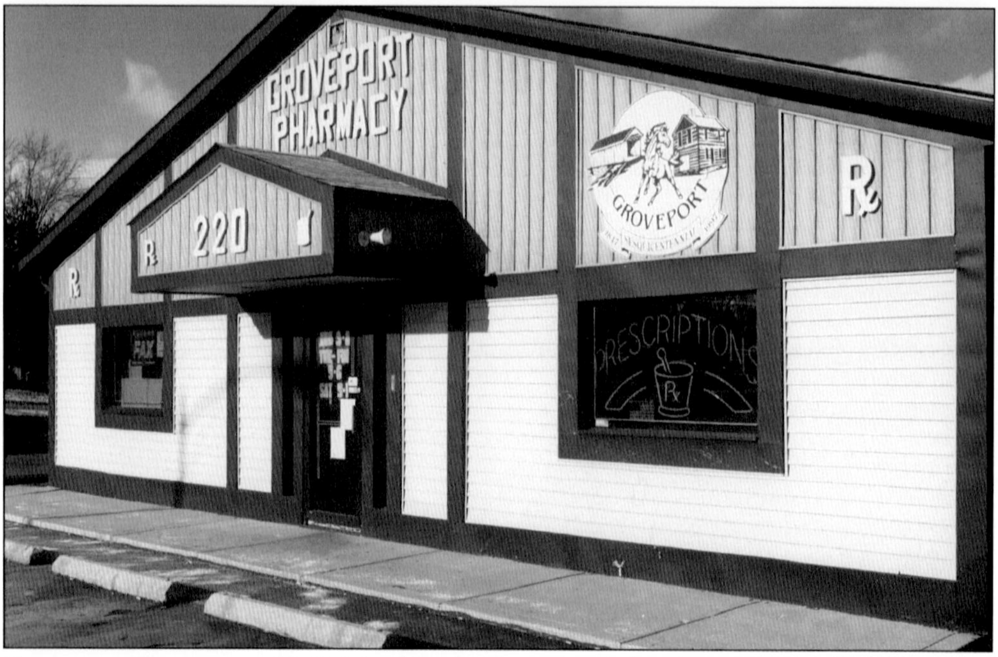

GROVEPORT PHARMACY, 2002. John Hougland purchased the pharmacy in 1967 and operated it at its original location until 1978, when he moved to a larger, modern building on west Main Street north of Madison Street. Hougland retired in 2002, closing the pharmacy, thus ending a rich 126 years of independent pharmacy operations in the village.

Seven

RURAL VIEWS

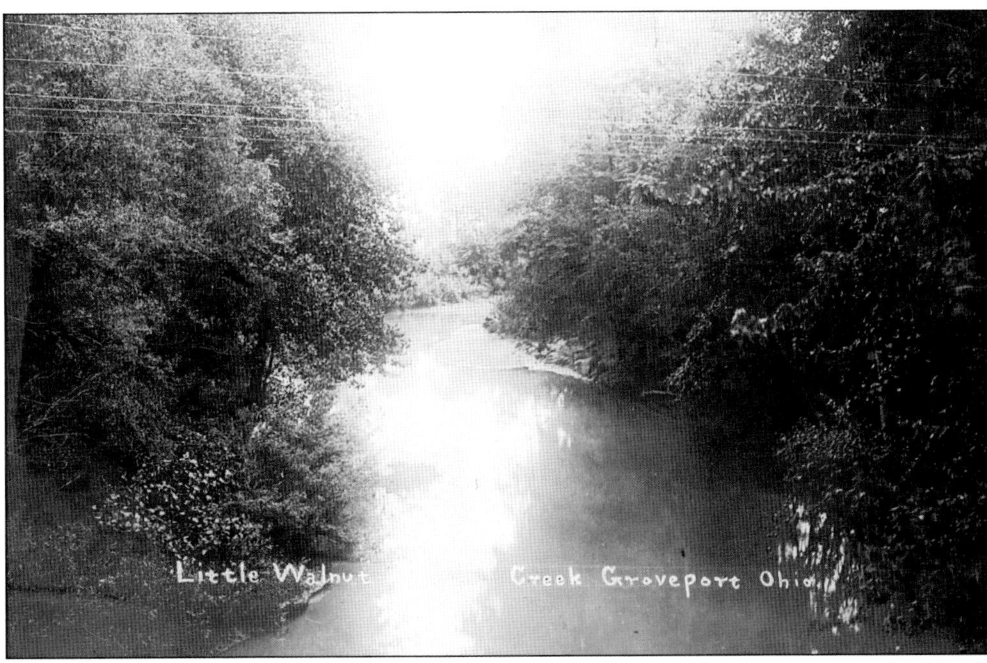

LITTLE WALNUT CREEK. Over the centuries, winter thaws and spring rains pushed Little Walnut Creek over its banks into the surrounding forest lowlands, enriching the soil. By the early nineteenth century, this fertile land and fresh water beckoned settlers to Madison Township from Virginia, Pennsylvania, and other eastern states. Little Walnut Creek would later feed the Ohio and Erie Canal in the area, its waters serving as the life blood of the community.

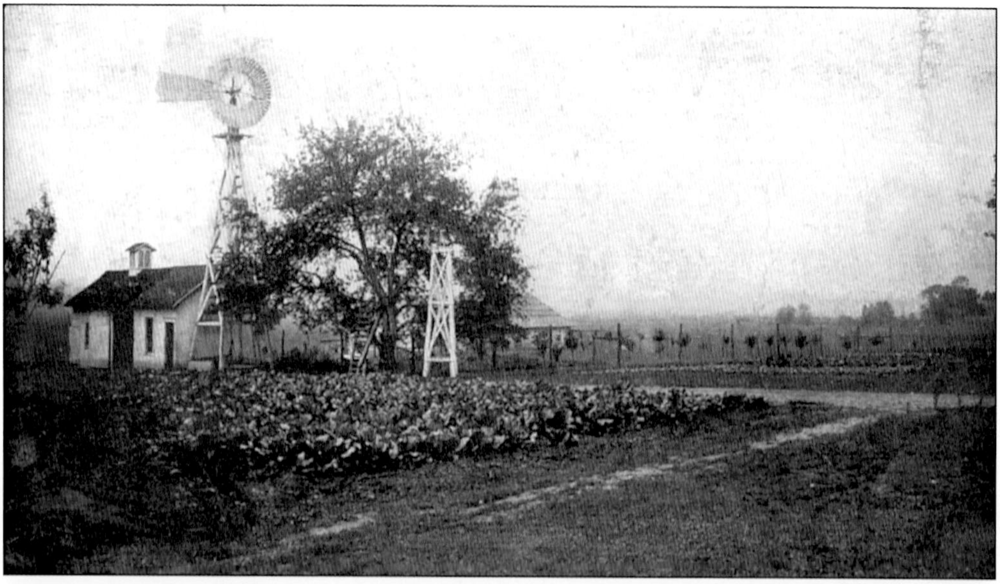

ELMONT GARDEN, 1908. A view of the Elmont Hotel's garden, located south of the hotel, looking east. The garden featured 14 acres of potatoes and another 40 acres with tomatoes, cabbage, beets, onions, peas, beans, asparagus, melons, apples, plums, cherries, and strawberries. Livestock was also as plentiful as hotel guests with cows, pigs, horses, turkeys, ducks and eight hundred chickens raised on the premises.

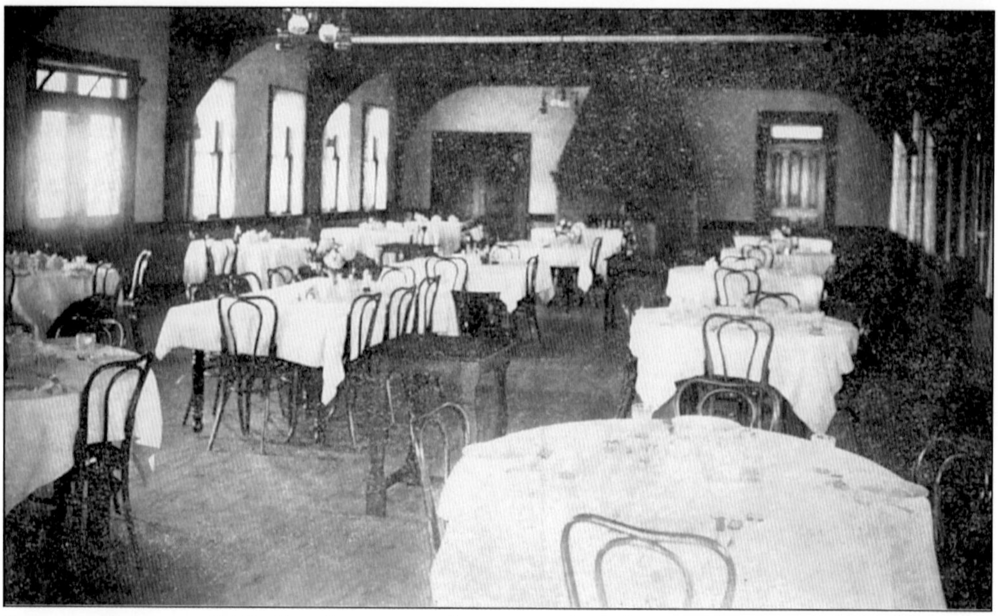

ELMONT DINING, 1908. Hotel guests or those attending functions at the hotel were treated to fine dining in an elegantly appointed dining hall. The Elmont was nearly self-sufficient in feeding its guests as the dining hall served food grown or raised from the hotel's own garden and livestock.

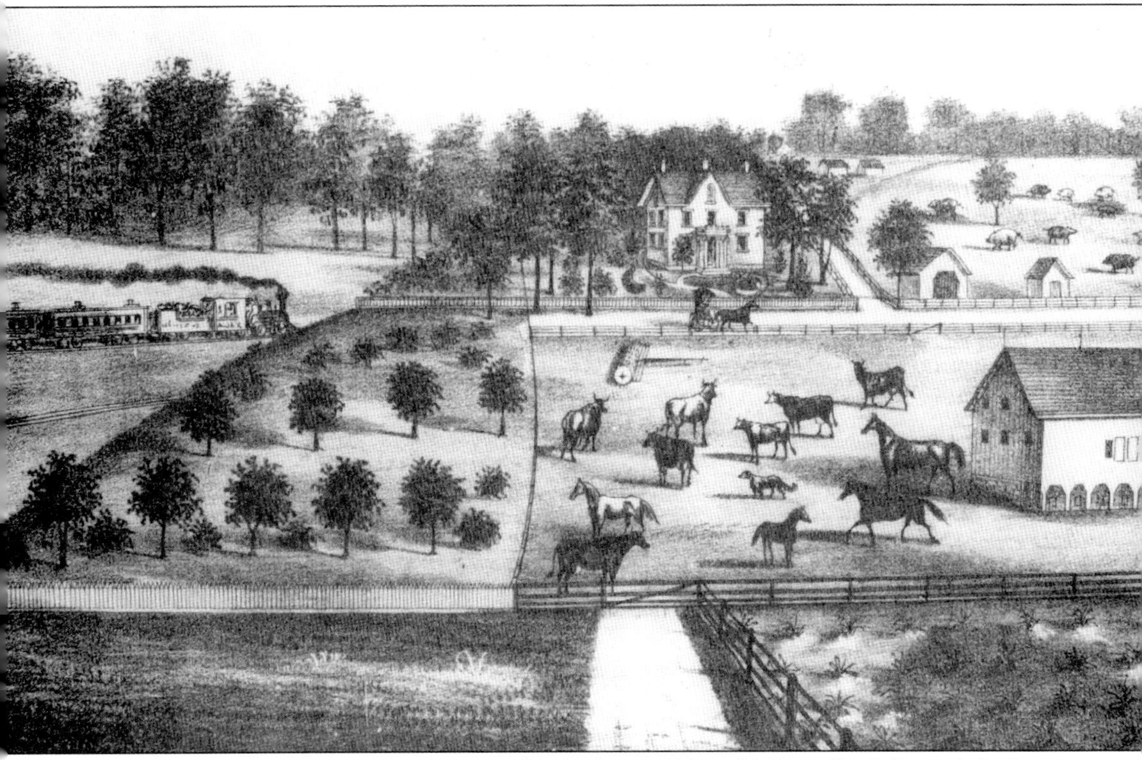

WEST BANK FARM, 1872. This lithograph of John G. Edwards' West Bank Farm (which was once located near Edwards Station, southeast of the intersection of Williams Road and Alum Creek Drive in Madison Township) comes from the *Atlas of Franklin County, 1872*. Early Franklin County histories refer to Madison Township as being the garden spot of the county because of its rich, fertile soil. This representation of Edwards' property provides a glimpse of a nineteenth century Central Ohio farm that featured livestock, orchards, grain fields, outbuildings, an ample barn, and homestead. To the left in the picture is the Hocking Valley Railroad, which ran from Columbus through Groveport and Canal Winchester to points in Southeastern Ohio. The railroad became the primary form of shipping for area farmers following the Civil War. For much of the twentieth century until the early 1970s, this farm was worked by the Woods and Page families. Interstate 270 now slices to the east and south of where this farm once stood and the farm site itself is now occupied by the Madison Mills subdivision.

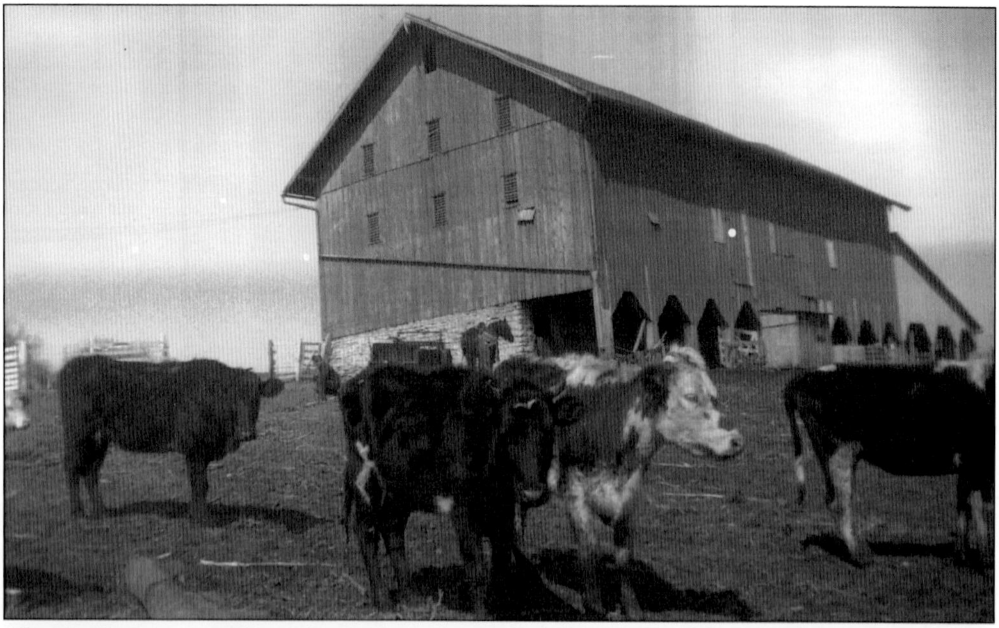

WOODS BARN, C. 1950S. This is the original barn from John Edwards' West Bank Farm as it looked in the mid-twentieth century when the farm was operated by the Woods family. The barn was built into an embankment with livestock stalls and milking areas accessible in the lower arched openings. Hay and grain storage areas could be reached on the opposite higher side.

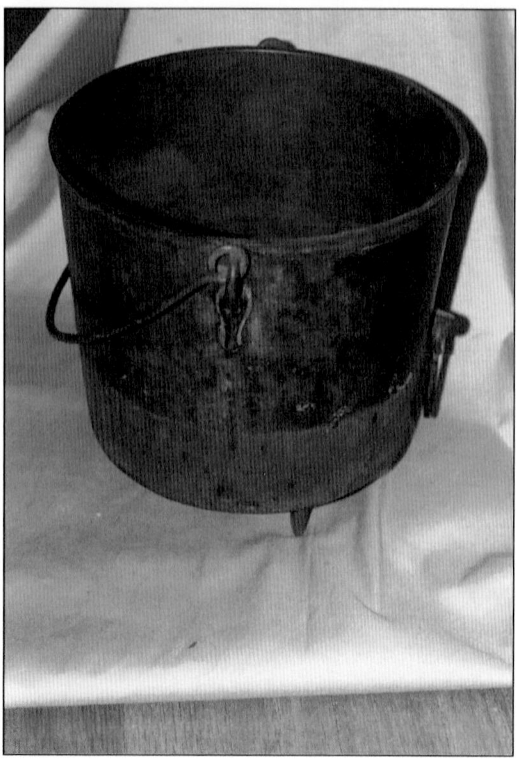

BEAN POT. The Woods family used this bean pot for cooking beans, and other vegetables, all grown on their Madison Township farm for their own use. The farm was almost completely self-sufficient in supplying its own food for Harry and Mae Woods and their 12 offspring. In addition to growing vegetables and grains, the family raised hogs, cattle, horses, turkeys, chickens, and even kept peacocks.

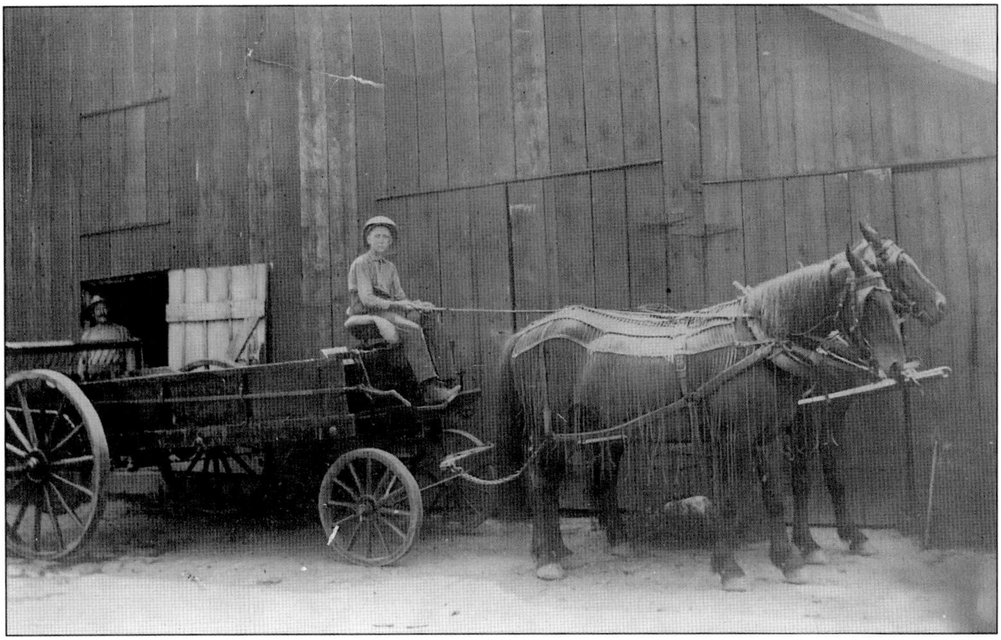

FARM WAGON, 1907. Walter Koebel sits on the wagon and his father stands in the barn doorway on their Madison Township farm west of Groveport. Horses did the bulk of the muscle work on the farms well into the twentieth century, as mechanization did not become common until mid-century.

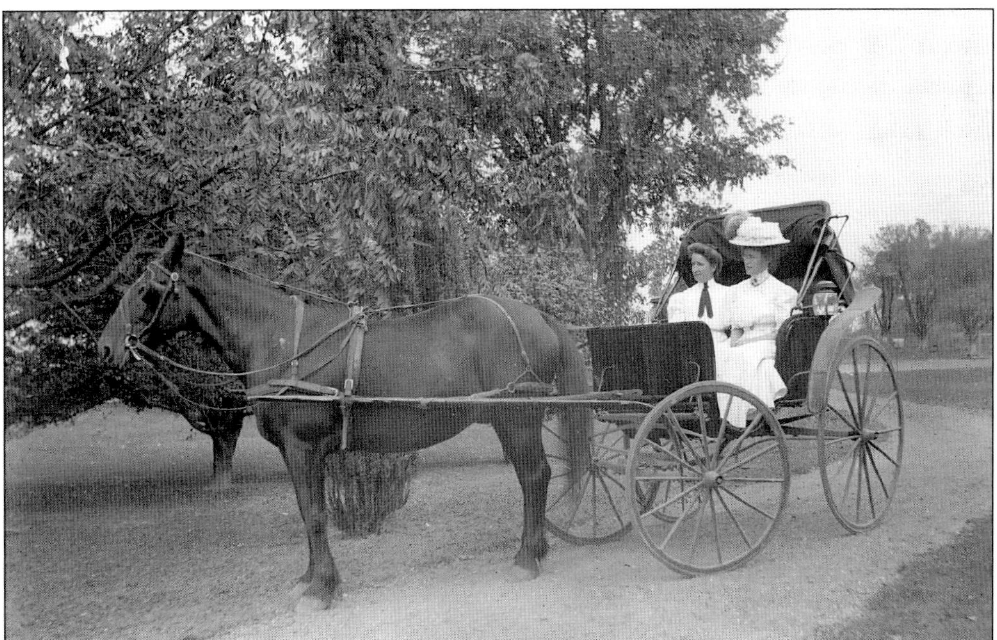

LEIGH SISTERS, 1908. The Leigh sisters, Elizabeth and Nettie, lived in rural Madison Township southeast of Groveport. Here they are dressed in fine clothes perhaps to attend church or some other social function. At the right of the carriage just above the rear wheel one can see a lamp used to light the way when traveling at dark.

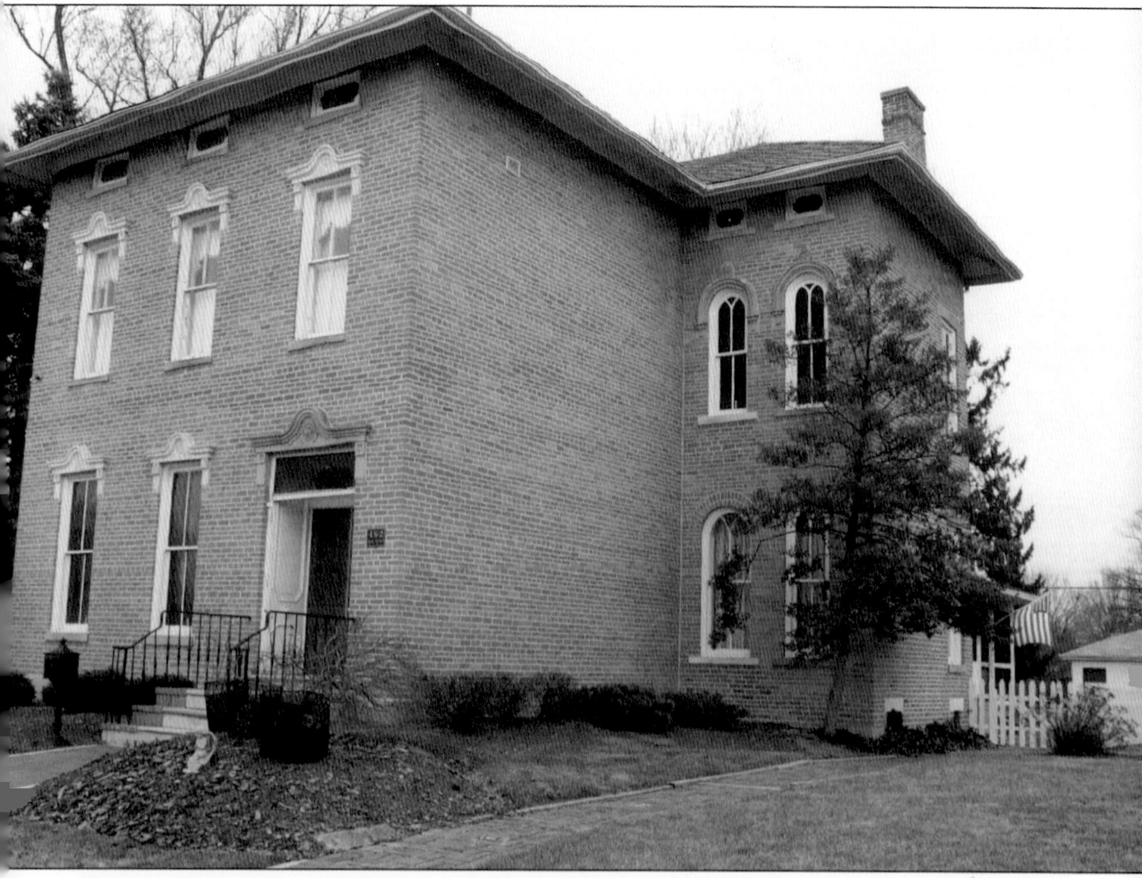

Saylor House. Dr. John Saylor built this brick home, which also contained his physician's office, on Groveport's Main Street in 1870. Though residing in a village, most everyone living in Groveport was a farmer in their own way. Residents maintained vegetable gardens in their yards for their own use and sometimes sale. Residential lots in the older sections of Groveport were purposely laid out in large sections to allow for big gardens and the keeping of small amounts of livestock as many people raised chickens and tended hogs in town. Most also stabled their own horses. Many of the former small barns, stables, and chicken coops are still standing in town and are used as garages or storage buildings. A 1920 Franklin County livestock audit revealed 16 cows, 4 sheep, 32 hogs, dozens of horses, and 1,543 chickens, ducks, and geese being kept within the Groveport village limits. Saylor's fine house also had an agrarian aspect as the doctor was known to store wheat in the unfinished front room of his stately home. This home is now the private residence of the Gale family.

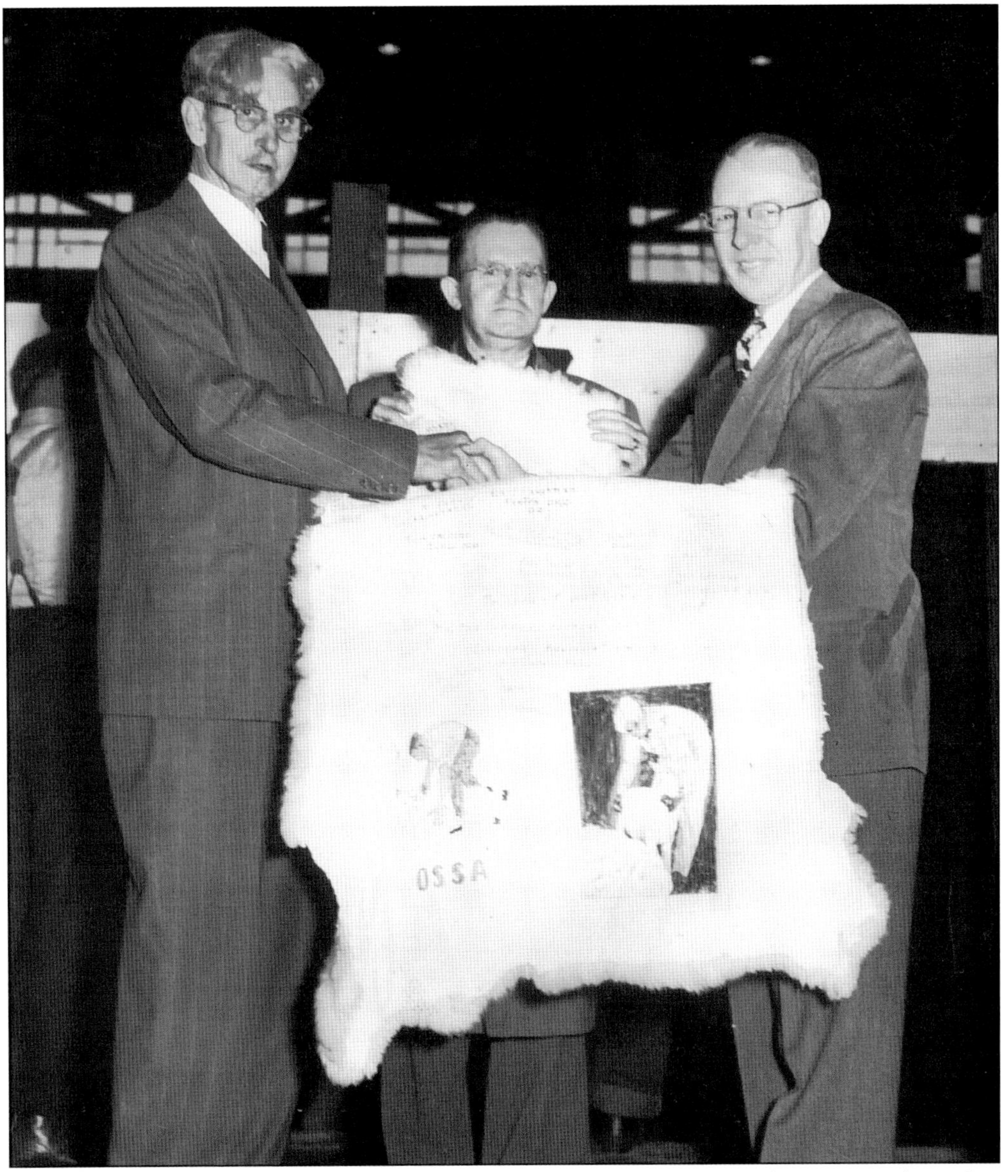

GRANT WATKINS. Grant Watkins (at left), born April 24, 1883, in his parents' log cabin on London-Lancaster Road in Madison Township, was renowned for his skills as a cowboy and champion sheep shearer. He left home at the age of 16 to head west where he worked for several years riding herd on cattle in California and busting broncos. He also traveled the length of Death Valley by horseback. While in Nevada in 1903, he developed an interest in sheep shearing which led to a life long career that took him to 11 states, Australia, New Zealand, and parts of Asia. He once sheared 307 sheep in one day. In 1928, he sheared a total of 10,049 sheep. Throughout his lifetime, Watkins is said to have sheared more than 600,000 sheep. His skills brought him in contact with many people, most notably White Bull, the son of the great Native American Chief Sitting Bull. Watkins later was inducted as a blood brother into the Sioux Nation. Though a world traveler, Watkins maintained a home on Elm Street in Groveport as well as a farm on London-Lancaster Road. He lived to be nearly 81 years old, passing away in 1964.

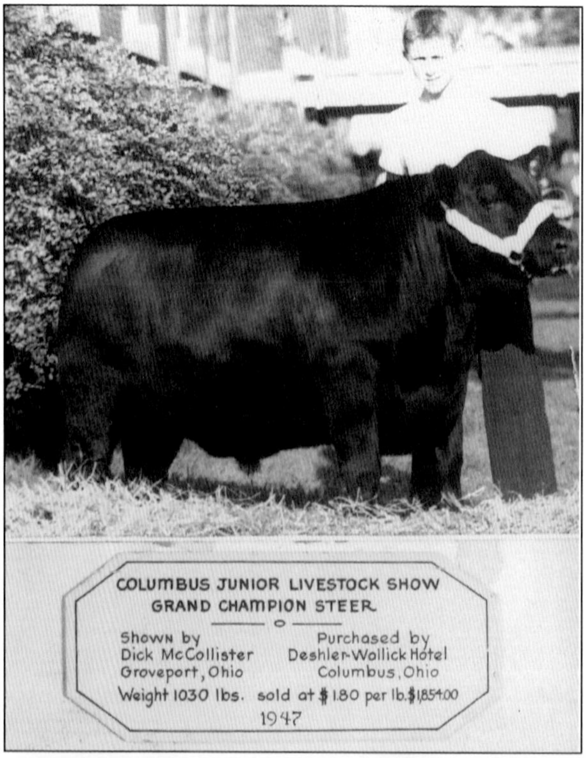

DICK MCCOLLISTER'S GRAND CHAMPION STEER. The agricultural community of Groveport and Madison Township has produced numerous livestock and produce prize winners at the Franklin County Fair, Ohio State Fair, and other events over the years. McCollister's steer was the grand champion of the Columbus Junior Livestock show in 1947. The steer weighed 1,030 pounds and sold to the Deshler-Wallick Hotel of Columbus for $1,854.

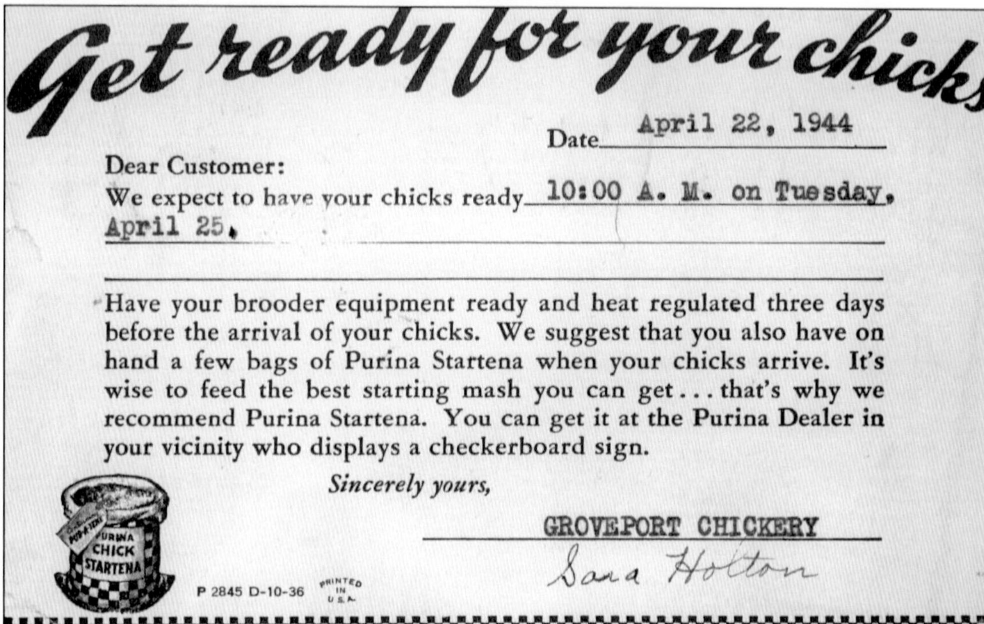

Get ready for your chicks

Date April 22, 1944

Dear Customer:

We expect to have your chicks ready 10:00 A. M. on Tuesday, April 25.

Have your brooder equipment ready and heat regulated three days before the arrival of your chicks. We suggest that you also have on hand a few bags of Purina Startena when your chicks arrive. It's wise to feed the best starting mash you can get . . . that's why we recommend Purina Startena. You can get it at the Purina Dealer in your vicinity who displays a checkerboard sign.

Sincerely yours,

GROVEPORT CHICKERY

Sara Holton

PURINA CHICK STARTENA

P 2845 D-10-36 PRINTED IN U.S.A.

GROVEPORT CHICKERY, 1944. The Groveport Chickery operated in Groveport in a small brick building just off Main Street west of West Street. The business supplied Madison Township farmers (and Groveport residents who kept chickens) with young chicks, chick food, and equipment for maintaining chickens. This card is a notice to Bertha Leyndecker that her order of chicks is ready for delivery.

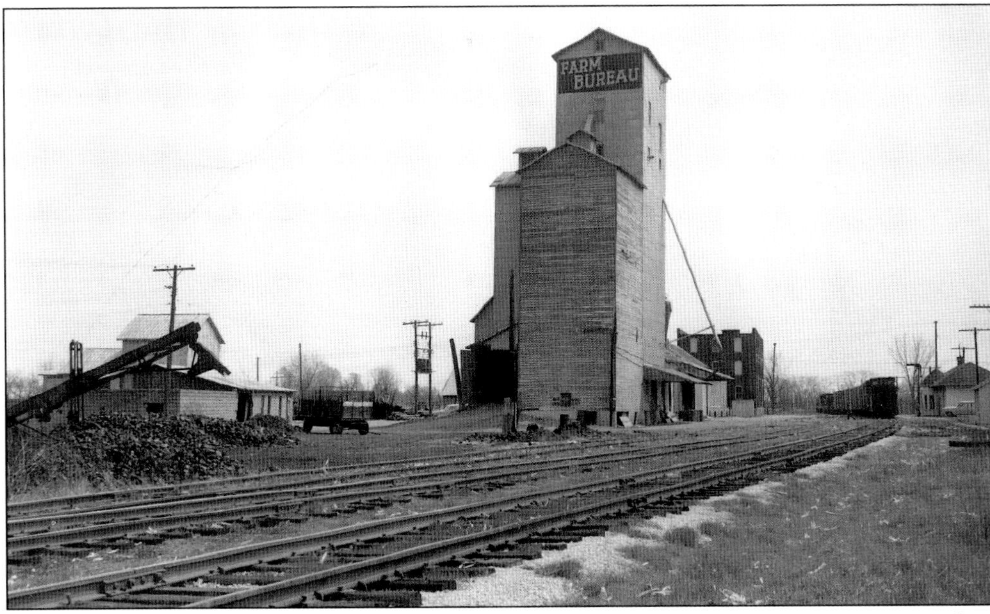

FARM BUREAU ELEVATOR, GROVEPORT, 1958. Two grain elevators once operated in Groveport to assist Madison Township farmers—North Grain and the Farm Bureau. This is a view of the Farm Bureau looking east. The depot can be seen in the background at the right. Note the three sets of tracks, indicative of the amount of rail traffic in the area at the time.

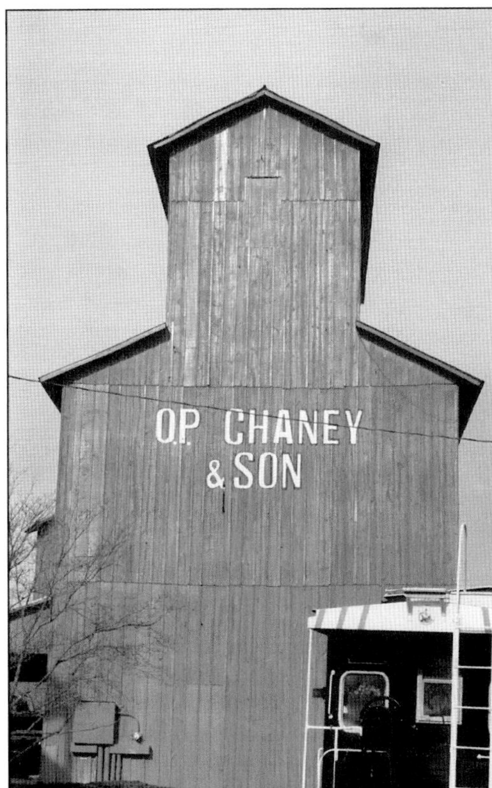

O.P. CHANEY GRAIN ELEVATOR. The Village of Canal Winchester and the Canal Winchester Area Historical Society (CWAHS) are restoring the former O.P. Chaney grain elevator at Oak and North High streets in Canal Winchester. The elevator was built by O.P. Chaney in 1887, and served Madison Township farmers under various owners until 1978. The CWAHS plans to use the restored elevator as an agricultural museum as well as meeting and office space for the society.

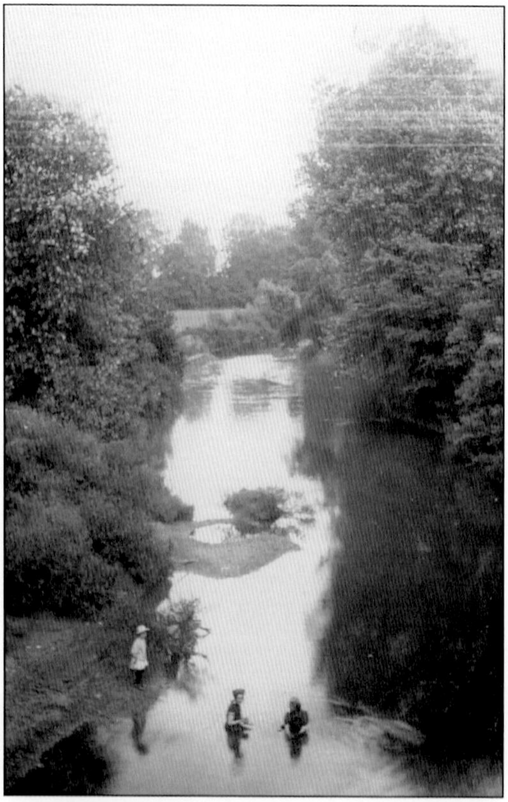

SWIMMING IN LITTLE WALNUT CREEK, C. 1908. Before public swimming pools were common, the best way to cool off on a hot summer's day was to take a dip in the cool, refreshing waters of one of Madison Township's many creeks. Here two swimmers wade in while a young child looks on from the bank of Little Walnut Creek, just southeast of Groveport.

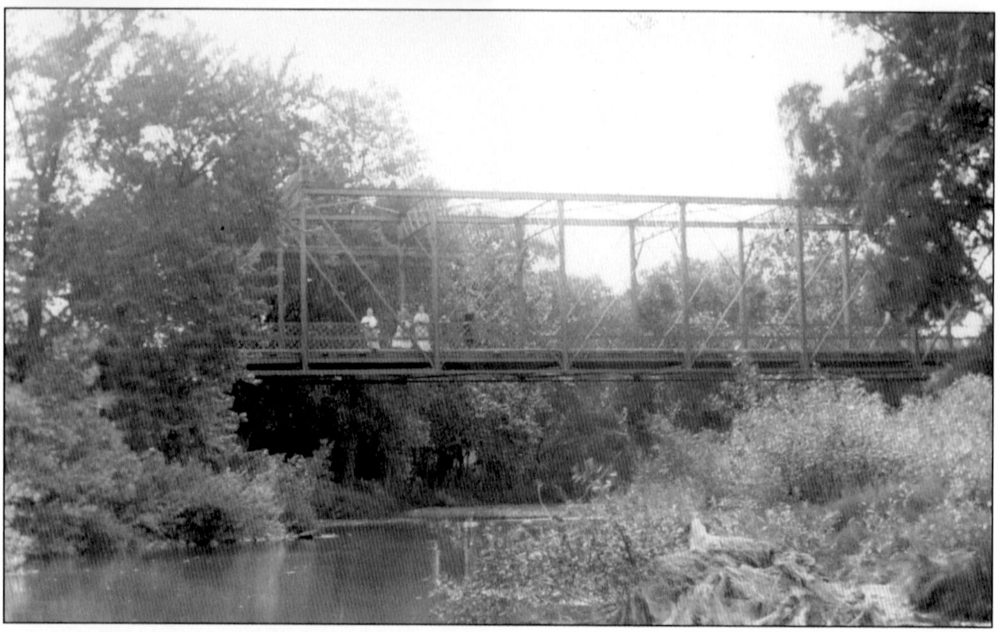

DECKER BRIDGE, C. 1908. The Decker Bridge, spanning Little Walnut Creek southeast of Groveport on Richardson Road, was an iron/steel bridge of a design common for its era. The bridge is named for the Decker family, one of the earliest settlers in central Madison Township, who owned land along the creek near what is now Richardson Road.

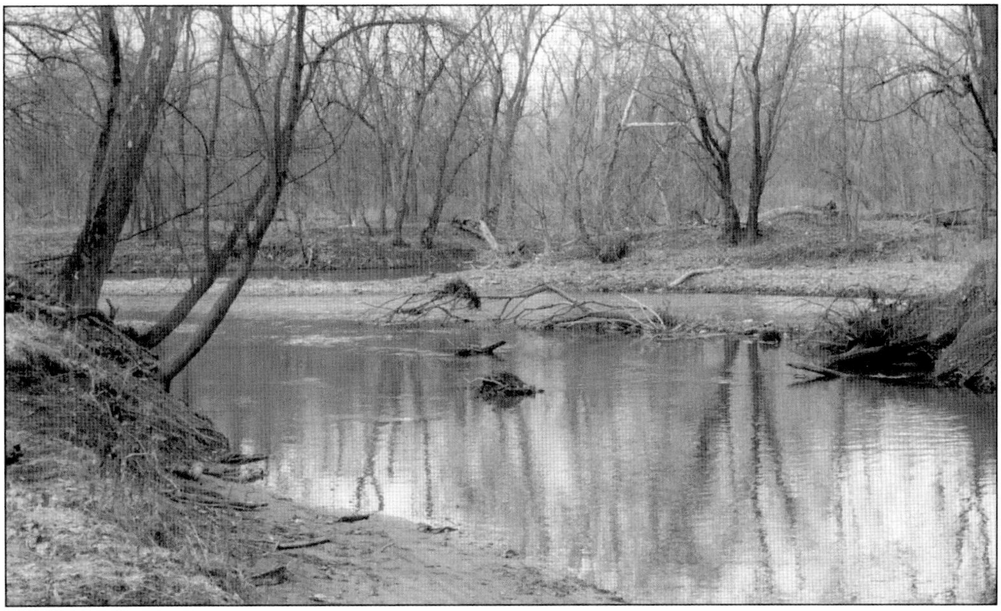

THREE CREEKS CONFLUENCE, 2002. A unique natural element is visible in Three Creeks Metro Park on Bixby Road in Madison Township. It is here that three creeks—Blacklick, Big Walnut, and Alum—all merge into one (Big Walnut) and continue on their way to empty into the Scioto River downstream. Here Blacklick is in the foreground, Big Walnut comes in from the right center, and Alum can be viewed flowing in the background.

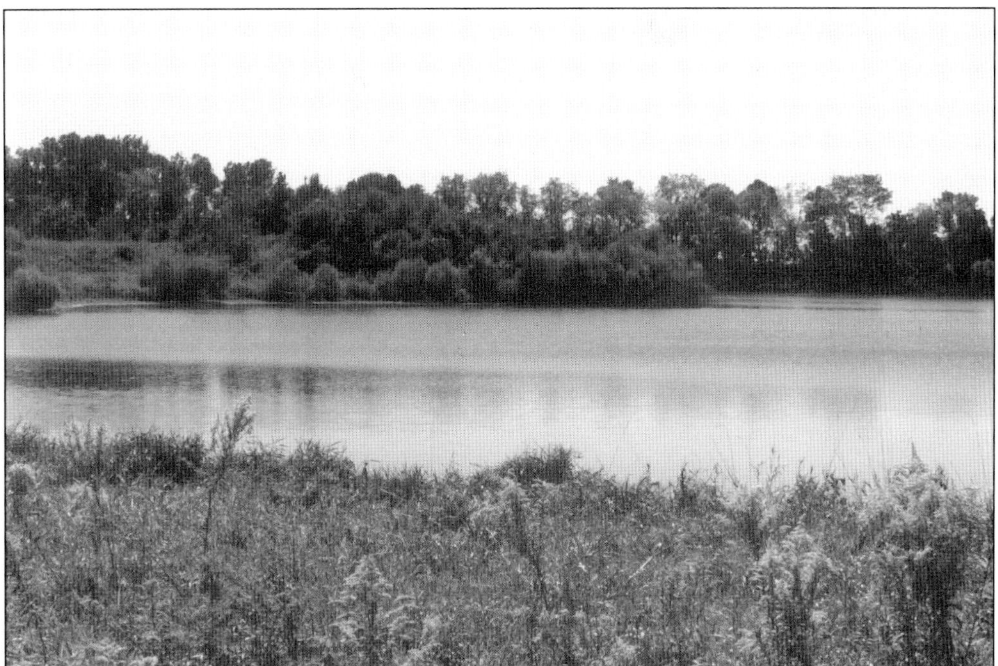

PICKERINGTON PONDS. Pickerington Ponds are glacial kettle ponds that formed on the eastern edge of Madison Township at the Fairfield County line. The Ponds are the home to a variety of wildlife and waterfowl and are now protected as a Metro Park.

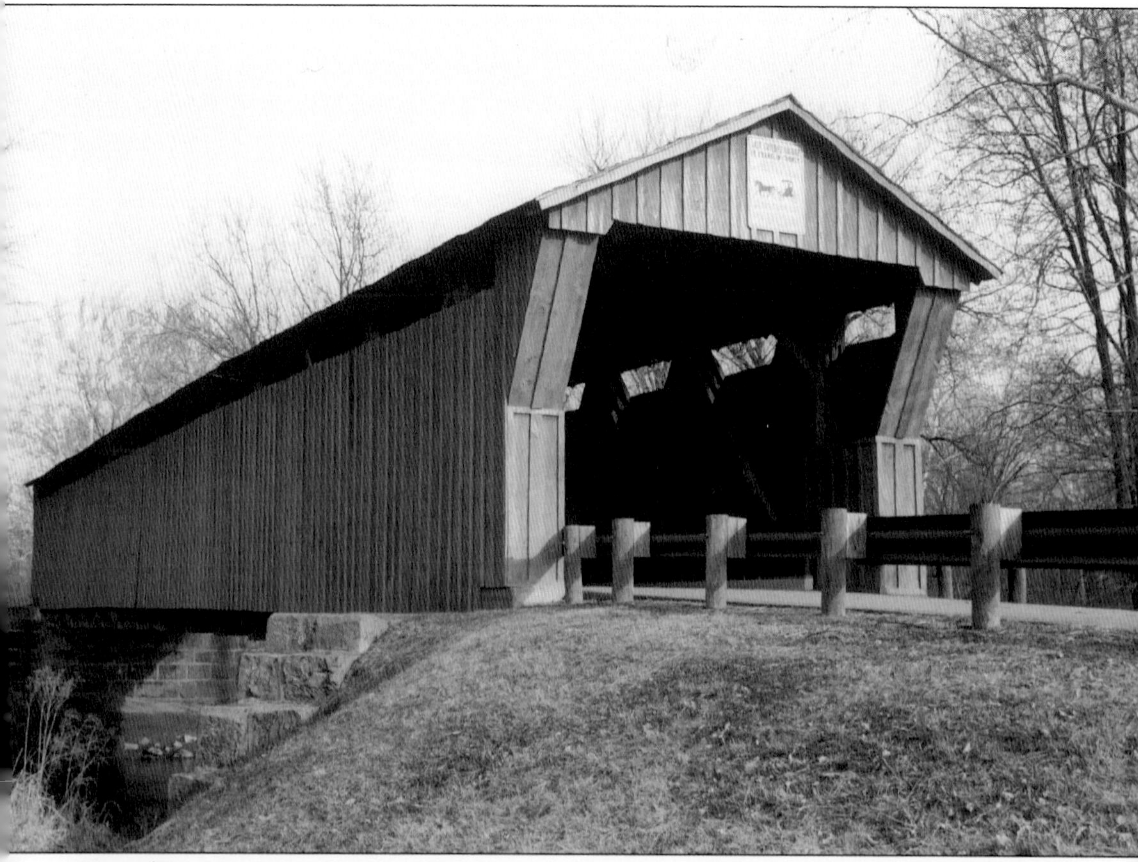

DIETZ/BERGSTRESSER COVERED BRIDGE. This bridge, located on Ashbrook Road in Canal Winchester/Madison Township, is the last existing covered bridge in Franklin County. It was built in 1887 in response to requests by township farmers for a way to transport produce over Little Walnut Creek to the canal and railroad for shipping. The Columbus Bridge Company constructed the bridge at a cost of $2,690 and Groveport's Michael Corbett built the bridge's abutments. The bridge is made up of double and triple truss members of pine and oak. By the 1950s, a road was built to bypass the bridge. The bridge was restored in the early 1990s by the W.J. Steidensticker Company using both original and new materials. The structure is now owned and maintained by Canal Winchester. (Information obtained from the Ohio Historical Society marker at the bridge site.)

Eight

MODERN COMMUNITY

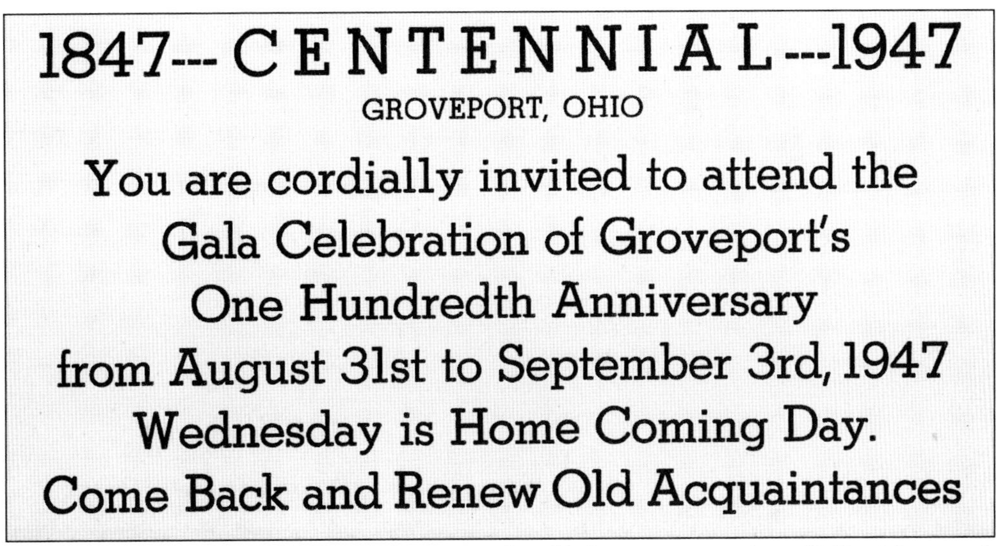
1847---CENTENNIAL---1947

GROVEPORT, OHIO

You are cordially invited to attend the
Gala Celebration of Groveport's
One Hundredth Anniversary
from August 31st to September 3rd, 1947
Wednesday is Home Coming Day.
Come Back and Renew Old Acquaintances

GROVEPORT CENTENNIAL, 1947. Groveport heralded its centennial in 1947 with a week long celebration from August 30 to September 3. A centennial committee, led by Charles Coon and Warren Rarey, compiled a special centennial historical booklet and organized a carnival, concerts, athletic contests, speeches, dances, parades, and fireworks to note the town's incorporation in 1847.

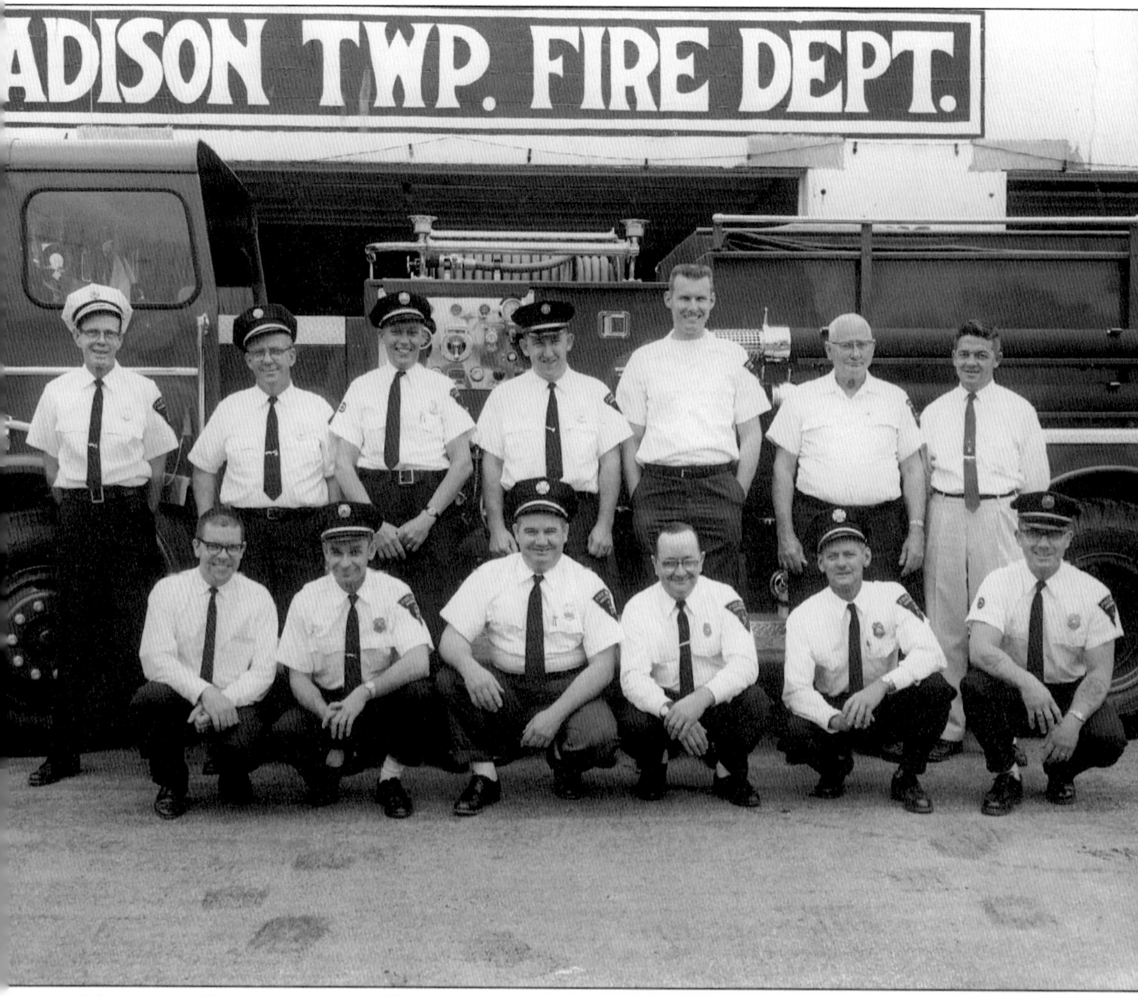

MADISON TOWNSHIP FIRE DEPARTMENT, 1963. The Groveport and Madison Township Volunteer Fire Department organized in the 1930s. In 1947, the name was shortened to the Madison Township Fire Department and a fire engine house was built on the southeast corner of College and Canal streets in Groveport. This station served the community until a new station was built in 1985, on South Hamilton Road. An emergency squad formed in 1948, when the volunteers rebuilt an old soft drink delivery truck. Full time firefighters replaced the volunteer system in the 1970s. The department now maintains two stations—the one on South Hamilton Road and the other on Gender Road. These volunteers, posing here with their brand new 1963 Seagraves fire engine, served during the mid-1960s. They are, from left to right, as follows: (front row) Dick Jameson (chaplain), Jim Luellen, Charlie Clark, Tom Wolfe, Del Norris, and Dick McCollister; (back row) Kenneth Shoemaker, Dan Mershon, Mac Carruthers, George Thompson, Paul "Shotgun" Glendening, Worley Rager, and Bob Williams.

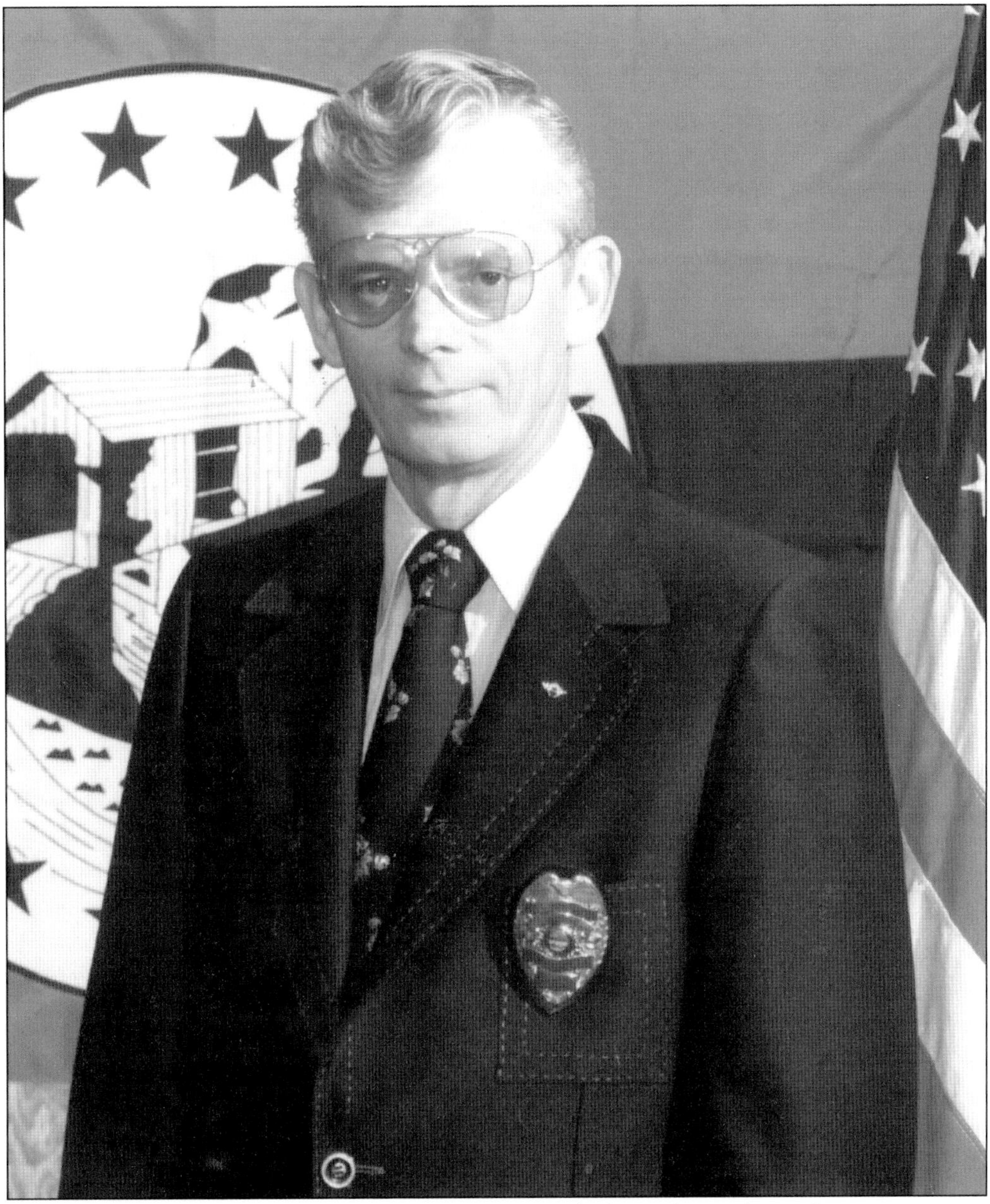

Al Whipple. For much of its history, Groveport relied on the traditional part-time town marshal system (where in the nineteenth century the marshal's pay sometimes was that he could keep any stray hog or other animal he found roaming about the village) for its policing. That era ended in 1966, when the village hired its first full time police chief, Al Whipple. Whipple first served alone, but in a few years he and the village government built his department into a fully manned staff. Whipple was known for his straight forward demeanor, fairness, and his ability to read situations. He is said to have brought in the early principles of community policing into the force where officers interact positively with citizens on a regular basis. Whipple served as chief until 1980, when he retired after suffering a back injury while making an arrest. He passed away in 2001 at the age of 68.

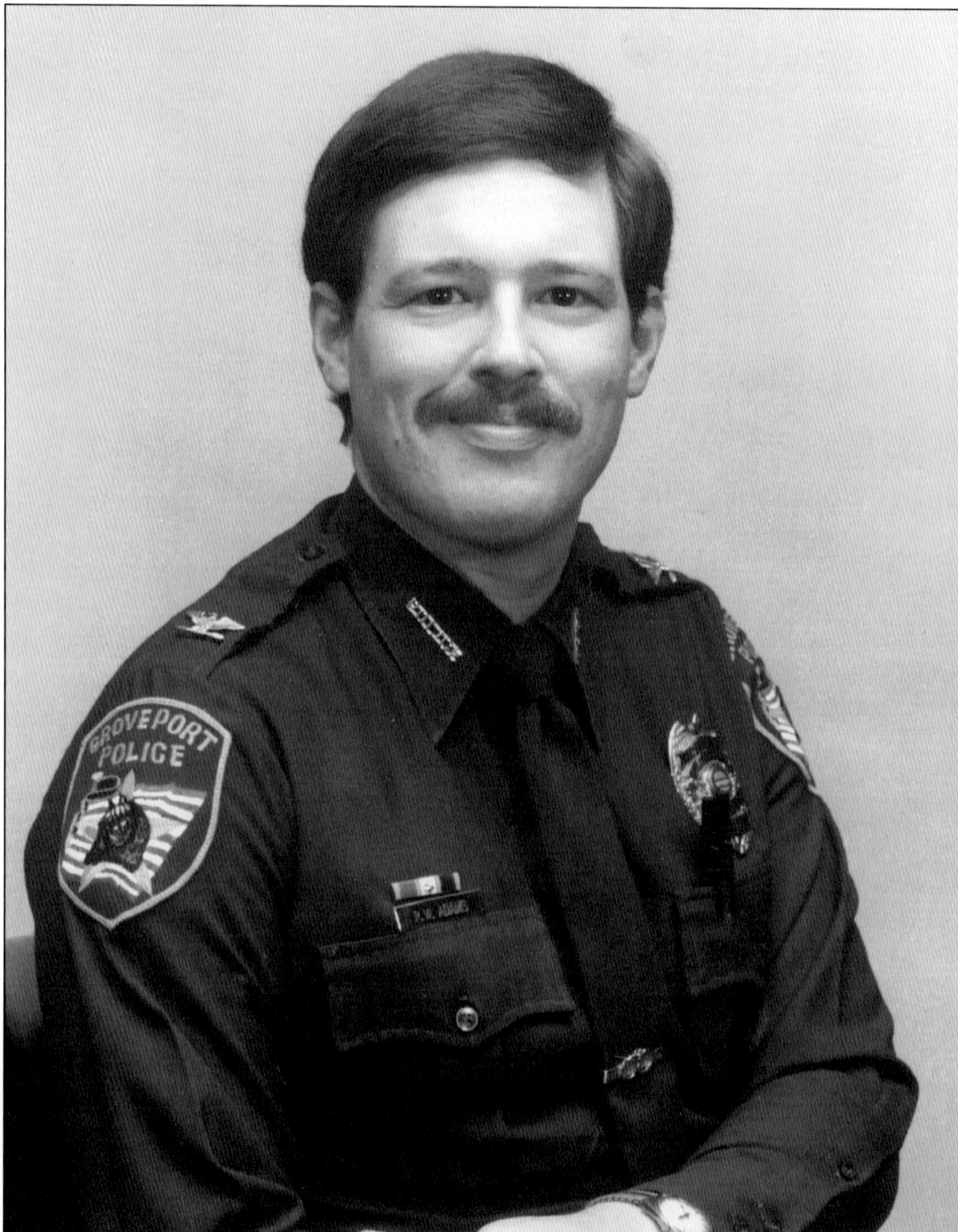

ROGER ADAMS. Lifelong Groveport resident Roger Adams became Groveport's second police chief in 1981, replacing Al Whipple. Adams, a 1967 graduate of Groveport Madison High School, worked as a dispatcher for the fire and police departments while still in school. He joined the Groveport police force as a reserve under Whipple in 1969, becoming a full fledged officer in 1974, and a sergeant by 1979. The department grew under Adams' leadership from six full-time officers in 1981 to 12 by the time the chief retired in 2001, after 32 years of service. It is notable that in his years as chief, not a single officer was severely hurt or killed while under Adams' command. The growth of the police force coincided with the rapid growth of the village in the latter years of the twentieth and early years of the twenty-first centuries.

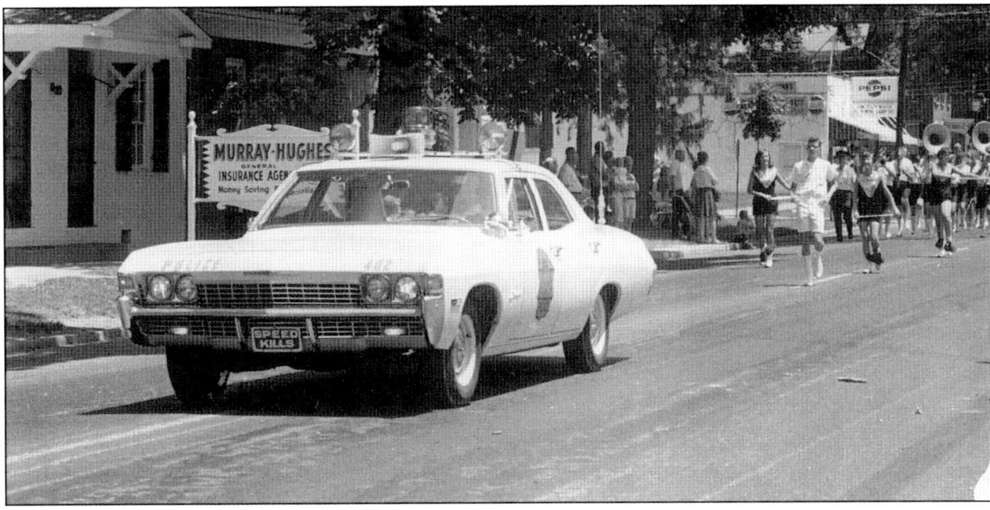

GROVEPORT POLICE CRUISER ON PARADE, 1972. The Groveport Police Department grew in both manpower and equipment under Chief Al Whipple's leadership. Here a new Groveport patrol car, followed by the Groveport Madison High School Marching Band, leads an Independence Day parade down Groveport's Main Street.

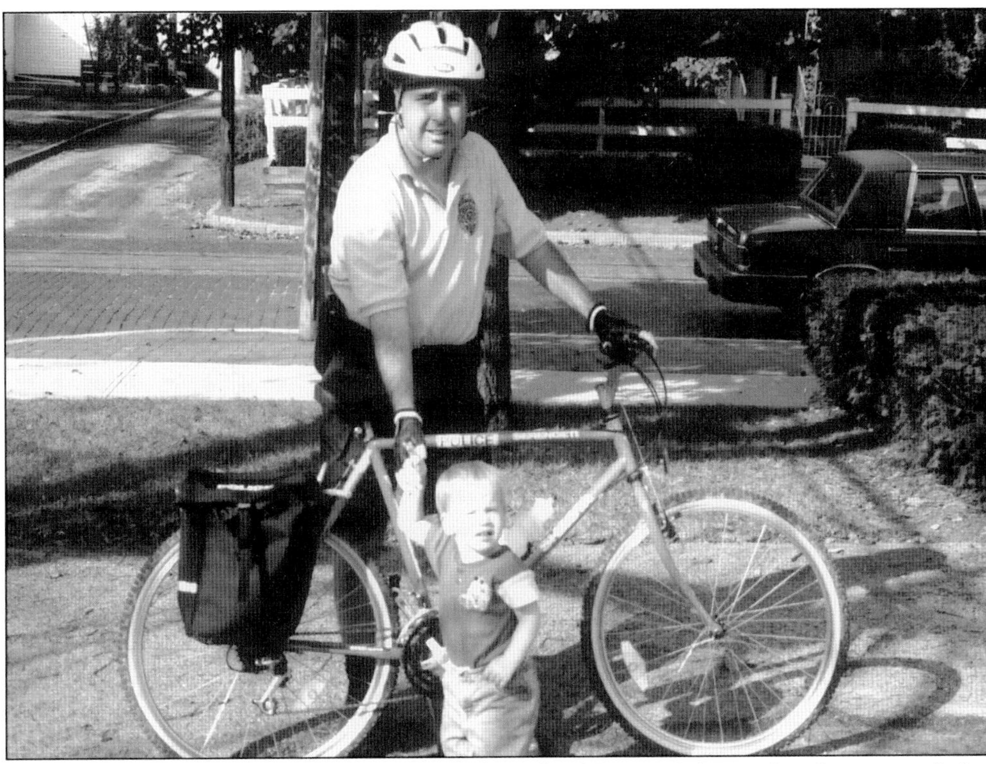

GROVEPORT BICYCLE PATROL, 2000. Under Chief Roger Adams, the Groveport Police Department expanded its philosophy of community policing by adding bicycle patrols throughout the village. The bike patrols gave officers quick access to areas not easily reached by cruiser, and also removed officers from their cars so they could be more in touch with the citizenry. Here Sgt. Shawn Cleary greets a friendly citizen.

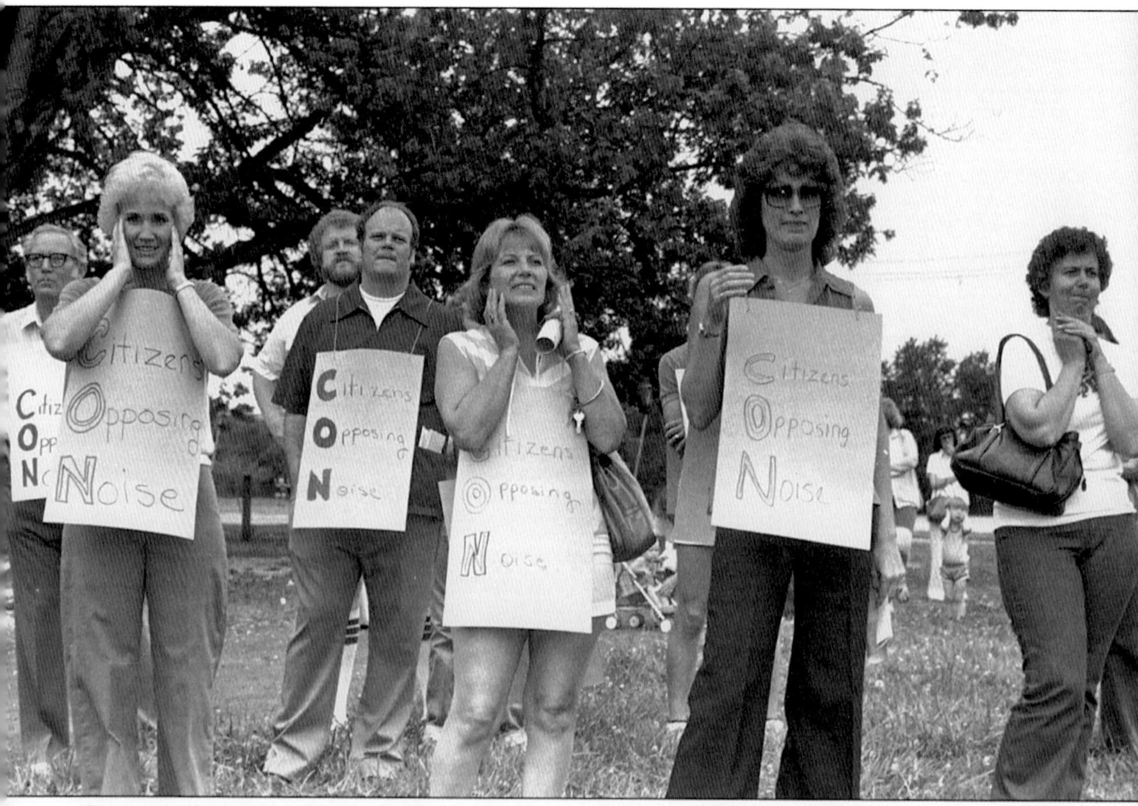

CITIZENS OPPOSING NOISE (CON) PROTEST, 1981. By 1951 air traffic at Lockbourne Air Force Base (which later would be renamed Rickenbacker Air Force Base and then Rickenbacker Port Authority), located southwest of Groveport, grew significantly when the base expanded and became home to units of the Strategic Air Command. Groveport Village Council complained to Air Force officials about the frequency of low flying, loud planes over the village in 1952. In 1954, council requested the Air Force delay training flights over Groveport during funerals and the village cemetery. Problems with aircraft noise continued with the expansion of air cargo freight service at the Rickenbacker Port Authority in the 1980s. During the 1980s, the increased aircraft noise over schools and homes led Groveport residents to take action to reduce the noise levels of jet aircraft flying directly over the town. The citizens' efforts resulted in a noise agreement among the village, military officials, and Port Authority representatives for soundproofing Groveport Elementary and the Groveport Freshman School and the establishment of air noise corridors. By 2002, however, new concerns arose over ever increasing aircraft traffic as the Port Authority continued to grow.

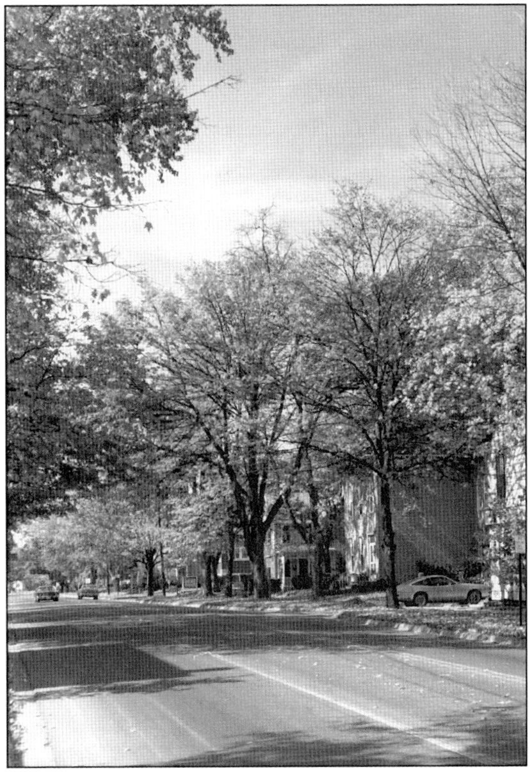

GROVEPORT'S MAIN STREET, 1980S. This view of Main Street, looking west from College Street, shows the large shade trees that once lined both sides of the street along the length of the street's right of way through town. Most of the mature trees were removed when the reconstruction and renovation of Main Street was completed in the mid-1990s. New younger trees were planted in their place.

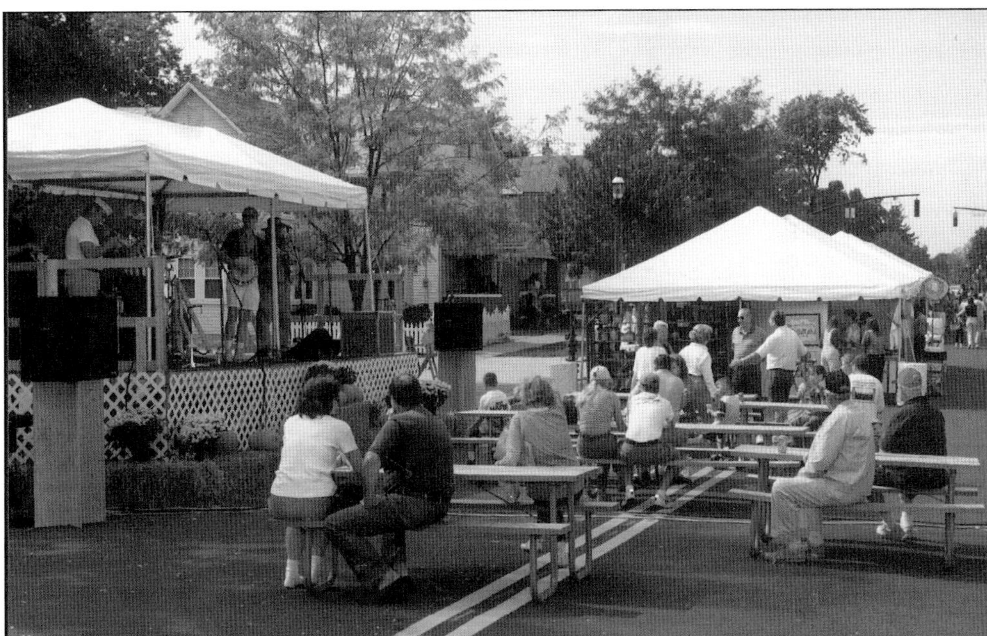

GROVEPORT FESTIVAL OF THE ARTS. In 1991, Groveport began an annual arts festival held in September on Main Street, from Walnut Street to College Street. The festival featured local and regional artists as well as musical entertainment. The village discontinued the festival in 1998 because of low attendance.

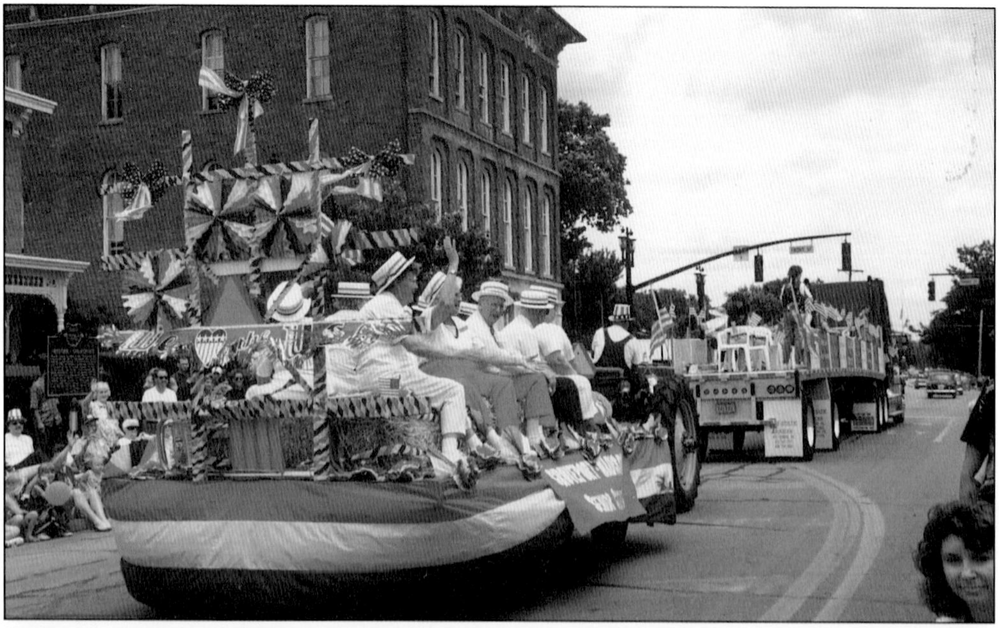

SESQUICENTENNIAL, 1997. Groveport celebrated its 150th birthday with year long events throughout 1997, including historical speakers, a reenactment of the first village council meeting, and a four day Independence Day celebration. Also incorporated into the festivities were Apple Butter Day, the arts festival, and a special Christmas cotillion at Town Hall. Pictured here is the sesquicentennial Fourth of July parade on Main Street.

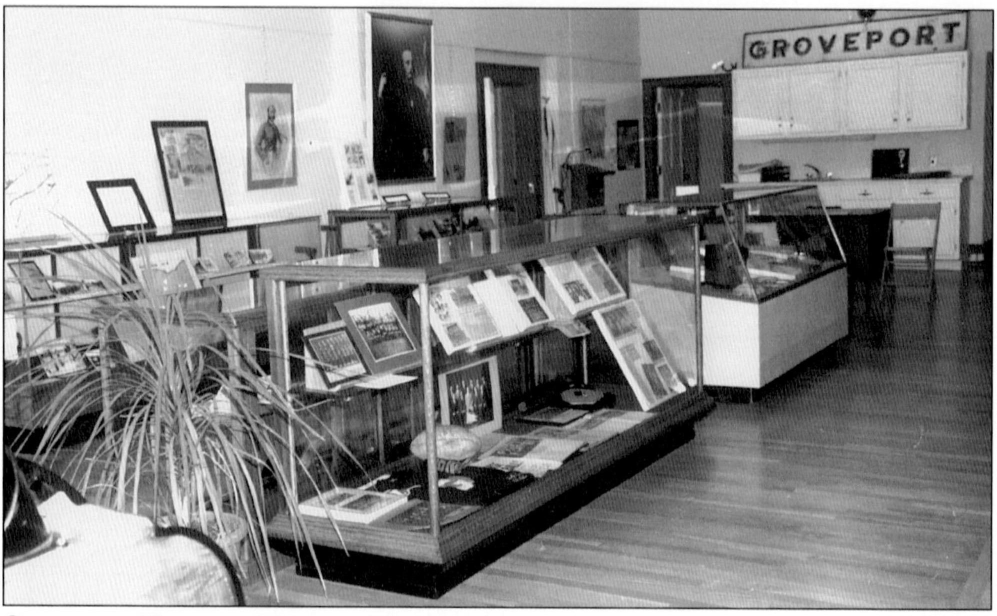

GROVEPORT HERITAGE MUSEUM. The Groveport Heritage and Preservation Society opened its Groveport Heritage Museum in 1995 in a small building on the southwest corner of Oak and Cherry streets. In 1997, the museum took up residence in the first floor east room of Groveport Town Hall. The museum serves as caretaker of Groveport's history by preserving the past through its collection of photographs, newspapers, maps, and artifacts.

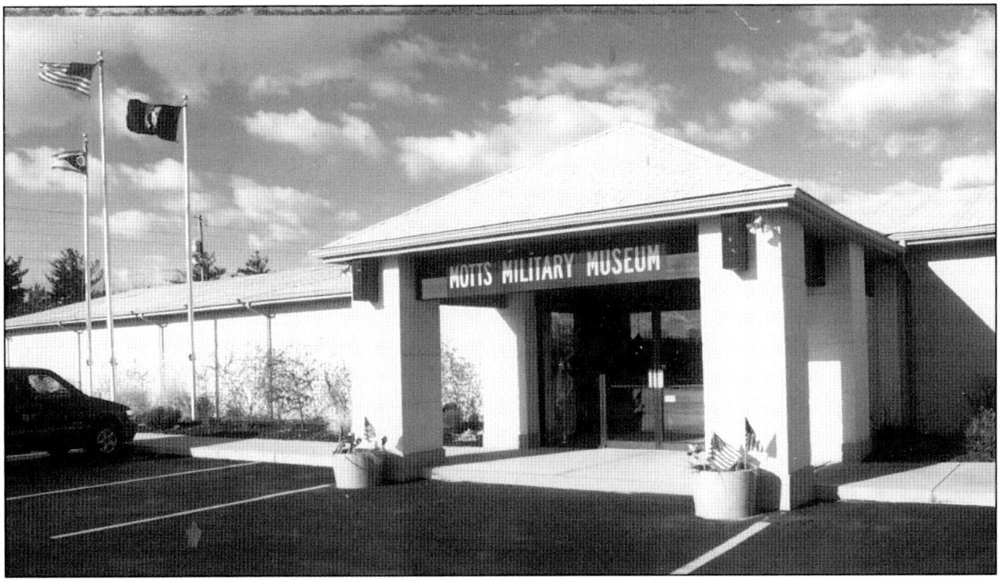

Motts Military Museum. Warren Motts established Motts Military Museum on South Hamilton Road in Groveport in 1999. The museum features a vast collection of military history and personal artifacts ranging from the Revolutionary War to the present day. The museum is notable for its ability to present the individual stories of pain and triumph of military service.

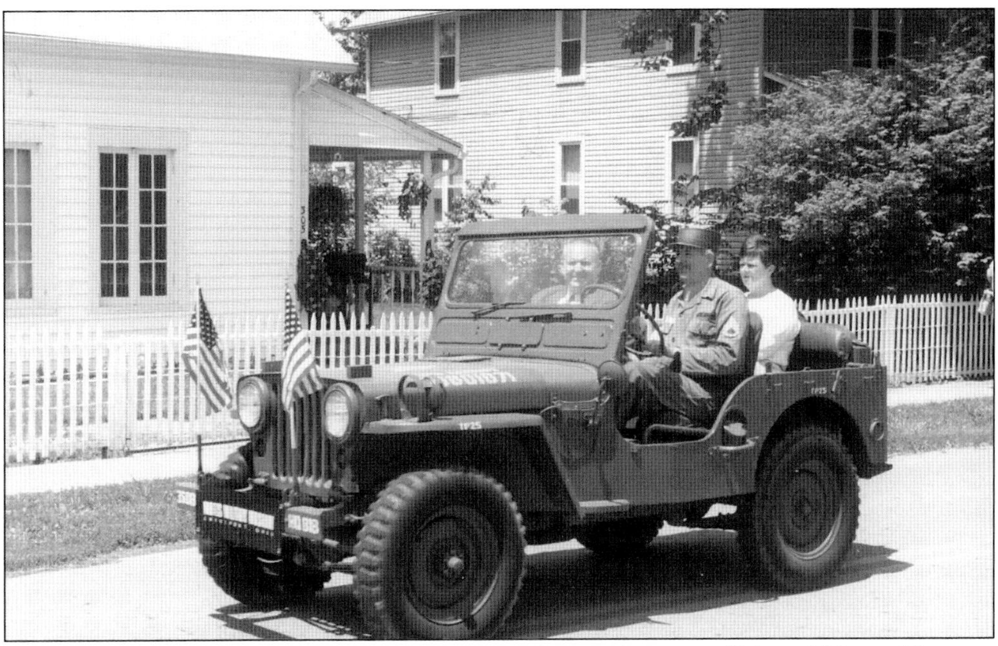

Warren Motts and Larry Flowers. Warren Motts, director of Motts Military Museum, drives a military jeep from the museum's collection in Groveport's 2001 Memorial Day parade. Seated with Motts is State Representative Larry Flowers, who served for many years as the Madison Township Fire Chief.

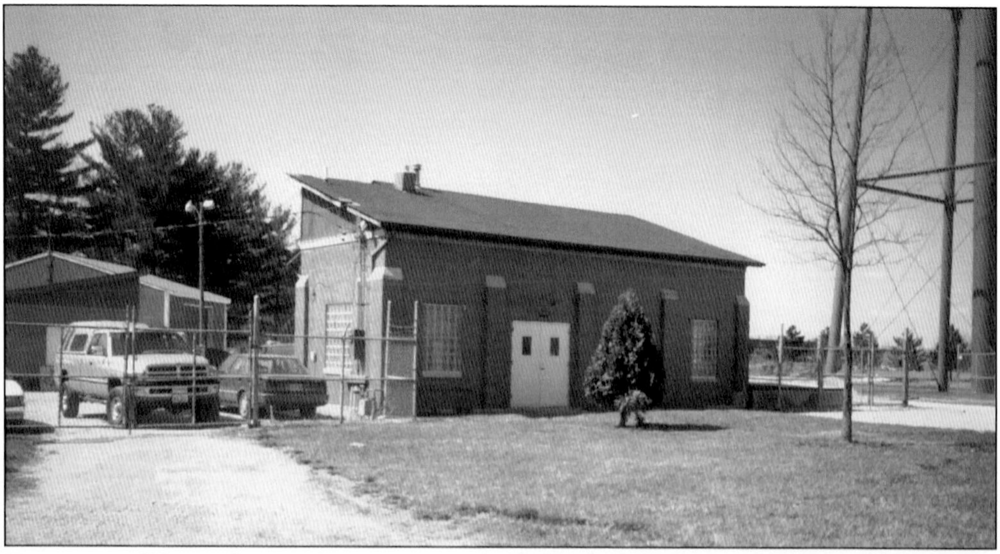

GROVEPORT WATER PLANT. In response to the lack of a water system to fight a major fire in 1932, Groveport built this water plant on South Hamilton Road in 1936. The workings of the plant were replaced in 1962, and the facility was expanded from 1965 to 68. From 1997 to 2002 the plant was completely refurbished and continues to supply water to village residents.

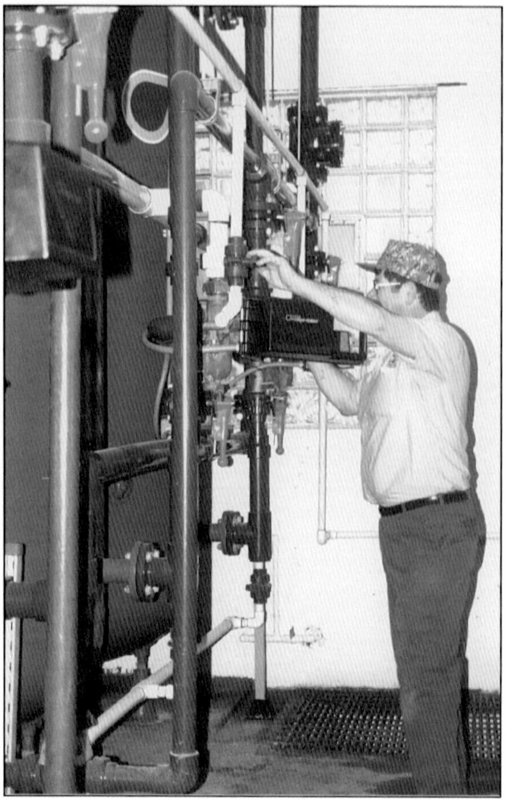

GROVEPORT WATER PLANT INTERIOR, 2001. Water plant employee Pat Wears checks over some of the new equipment in the refurbished Groveport water plant. The plant is monitored twenty four hours a day. Recently new wells were dug just north of the plant to supply it with another source of water.

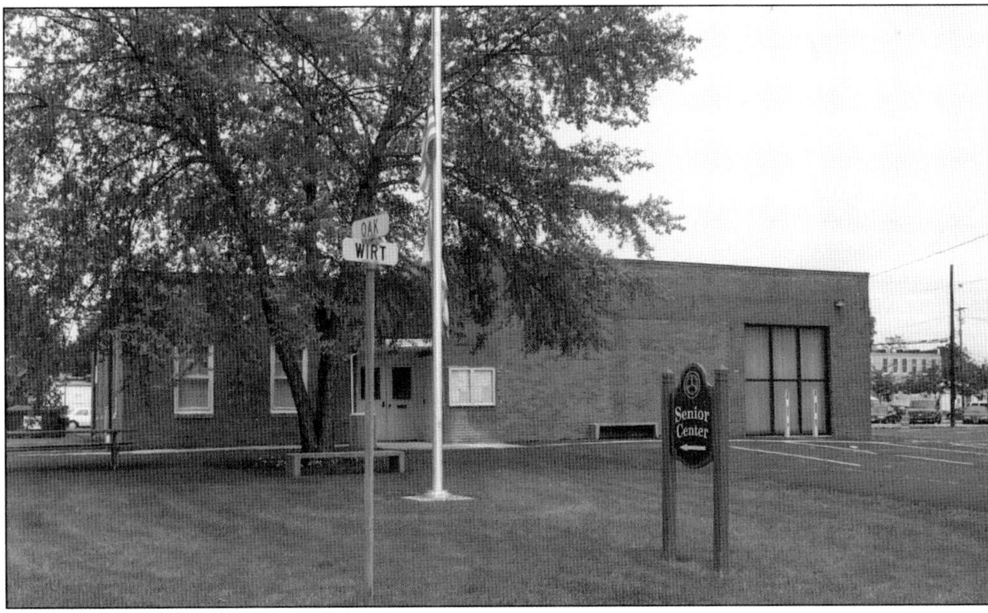

SENIOR CENTER. The Groveport Senior Center was established in the former Groveport Municipal Building on Cherry Street in 1997. Previously area seniors had shared facilities in Groveport Town Hall. The building features a dining hall, offices, and other rooms for recreational or meeting use. The center provides a recreational and communal outlet for local seniors to gather.

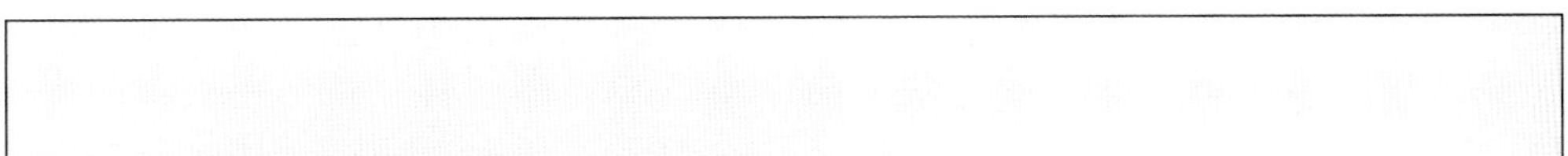

MADISON TOWNSHIP COMMUNITY CENTER. Dedicated in 1996 as part of a complex that includes the township police (which organized in 1972) and fire stations on South Hamilton Road across from Groveport Madison High School, this building houses the township offices as well as a large meeting space used for government business and by community members for social or other meetings.

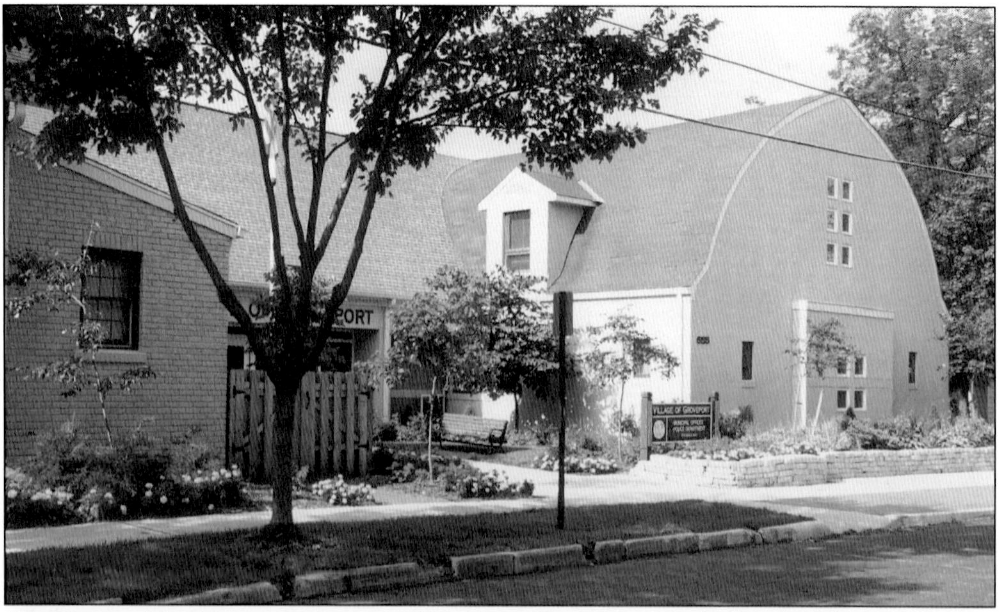

GROVEPORT MUNICIPAL BUILDING. The former St. Mary's Catholic Church on Blacklick Street was remodeled to become the home of the Groveport village government in 1995. The building contains the police department, a spacious council chamber, as well as the other government offices for the village.

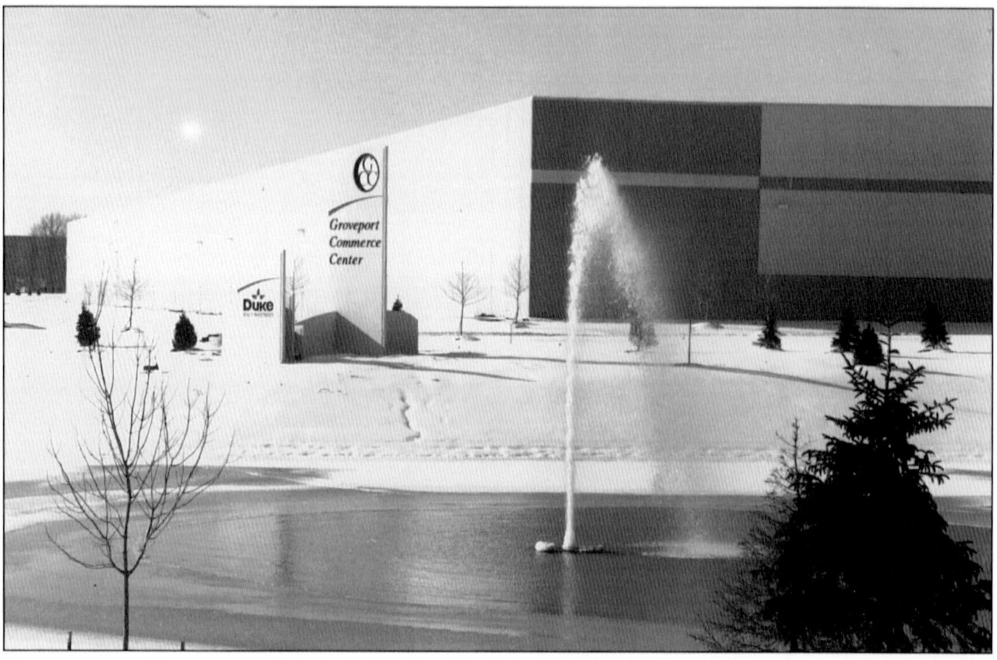

GROVEPORT COMMERCE PARK. In the twenty-first century, Groveport has come full circle. Where once it was a town bursting with warehouses and businesses supported by the canal and the railroad, warehouses are now being built in Groveport Commerce Park, a vast commercial development in western Groveport, spurred by the presence of the Rickenbacker air hub and nearby interstate highways.